COUNTING PEOPLE

COUNTING PEOPLE
The Census in History

HYMAN ALTERMAN

ILLUSTRATED WITH CHARTS AND GRAPHS

Harcourt, Brace & World, Inc., New York

The quotations from Professor Ping-ti Ho in the section on China in Part I, Chapter 5, are reprinted by permission of Harvard University Press from *Studies on the Population of China, 1368–1953* by Ping-ti Ho, Copyright, 1959, by the President and Fellows of Harvard College.

*This book is dedicated to
my mother and father, Anna and Abraham,
who would have wondered at it all.*

ACKNOWLEDGMENTS

In writing this book concerned with ancient and alien cultures, the author became indebted to many people: to early writers who kept alive the story of counting people, as well as to the many contemporaries from whom he sought answers to questions. Does a superstition about being measured have a parallel one about being counted in the same culture? When and by whom was the phrase "excepting Indians not taxed" first used? It is a mark of the community of scholars that there were no inquiries without a response.

In some cases, however, the assistance far exceeded the simple answer to a question. Dr. Karol J. Krótki, the controller of the Sudanese Pilot Census of 1953, now a professor in Canada, became a guide to the Sudan, its people and culture, and its first census. This is an expression of gratitude for the precious hours that Dr. Krótki gave me.

The staff of the Sudanese Mission to the United Nations was also very helpful. They opened their library to me and answered all questions cheerfully.

In response to a simple question, Dr. Denis Foster Johnston sent a warm reply and a book that was his doctoral thesis on the Navaho Indians. Again, a strange culture became more comprehensible with the guidance of a recognized authority. For the light that he shed, the author is grateful to Dr. Johnston.

Many hours can be spent in tracking down obscure volumes in writing a book such as this. Mrs. Gloria Weinrich, chief librarian of the Division of Research and Statistics of the New York State Department of Labor, made rare and out-of-print volumes materialize from faraway places. The author is indebted to her and her staff for having saved him innumerable hours of searching.

Anyone writing about the census must eventually seek help from the United States Bureau of the Census and its experts. The bureau's responses were not only prompt but also usually went beyond the simple answer to a question. The American people can be proud of this great organization.

Finally, the author is indebted to his family for bearing with him through trying days. I am grateful to my wife and three sons for their patience.

It goes without saying that any errors of fact or interpretation are the author's responsibility.

CONTENTS

Introduction

"What's one and one and one and one and one and one
and one and one and one and one?"
"I don't know," said Alice. "I lost count."
"She can't do Addition," the Red Queen interrupted."
                                    —*Through the Looking Glass*
                                              by Lewis Carroll

The story of the census is like a great historical pageant. Famous
and mighty persons—kings and their ministers and soldiers,
statesmen, scientists, and philosophers—parade across the stage.
A host of ordinary people from all times and places follow and do
their bidding. Passions are aroused and blood is shed. The name
of the Almighty is invoked, and a curse is cast, the effect of which
is felt for centuries. But, in one way or another, man persists in
seeking an answer to the question, "How many of us are there?"

The answer almost always eluded him, and not for lack of the
ability to do addition.

The idea of *number* is basic to human thought. It is believed by
anthropologists and archaeologists to extend so far back in time
that its origin is purely speculative. The concept of the difference
between *one* and *many* is believed to be one of man's earliest
generalizations, even when his knowledge of number did not include the ability to count the fingers of his hand. No primitive
tribe has ever been studied that did not show an awareness of this
difference.

11

It is widely believed that man learned to count long before he gave formal names to numbers. As society entered a stage of settled habitation and agriculture, the use of number became a necessity. Symbols began to be used to identify quantity. The fingers of his hand were man's earliest measure of "more than one." At later stages, pebbles, sticks, seashells, kernels of corn, scratches and notches, and other devices were used for this purpose.

Such methods of denoting quantity persist today among primitive tribes. One such method was observed on the island of Madagascar in the nineteenth century. A tribal chief, wanting to count his soldiers, had them march through a passage single file. As each soldier passed, a pebble was dropped to the ground. When ten pebbles had accumulated, one was set aside to represent the ten. When the number in the set-aside pile reached ten, one of these was separated to stand for one hundred. In a census of Africa's Gold Coast in 1891, grains of Indian corn and cowrie shells were used. At about the same time, in parts of India, bamboo sticks were used for the same purpose.

About five thousand years ago, the Sumerians of Mesopotamia are known to have employed a method of notation for numbers and numerals. By 3000 B.C. the Egyptians, having developed a complex economy, were able to write large numbers. Later, the Babylonians, Chinese, Greeks, and Romans advanced the writing of numbers to a high level.

The ability to handle numbers and their increased use went hand in hand. At first, man may have counted his economic resources—his cattle or measures of grain. Soon, rulers wanted to know the number of their soldiers; then, their taxpayers. The foundation was thus laid for the earliest known censuses.

It was not too long before the full number of their subjects became the object of their counting. It was from the population that the soldiers and taxpayers would be drawn. The results of these enumerations often became carefully guarded state secrets. Later still, as individualism emerged, the counting had another justification. People were regarded as assets. In addition to providing the soldiers and taxpayers, they became the manpower of an expanding labor force. The counting was done with hope.

In the nineteenth century a new element was introduced into the approach to population that has been the subject of debate to this day. Thomas Robert Malthus (1766–1834), theologian, philosopher, and founding member of the Royal Statistical Society in 1834, wrote *An Essay on the Principle of Population.* The essence of his argument was that population tends to increase in a geometric ratio, doubling itself every twenty-five years; "the means of subsistence," however, tends to increase in an arithmetic ratio. Ultimately, population must outstrip the food supply, and widespread famine results. Many of his calculations were based on returns from the first American censuses.

There were many flaws in Malthus's presentation, as well as imperfections in the statistics of his time. He could also not foresee the tremendous technological advances in agriculture in this century. However, his fundamental premise has been discussed ever since. Today, as the world's population increases at a rate higher than ever before in history, in many parts of the world the counting of people is done with fear.

As rulers and governments sought to ascertain the number of their people, it became evident that the results of the enumerations were often highly inaccurate. A census of population was more than a matter of adding "One and one and one. . . ." A realization of the enormous complexity did not come readily. In the early eighteenth century, Fénelon, François de Salignac de la Mothe (1651–1715), Archbishop of Cambrai and tutor to the eldest grandson of Louis XIV, could say naïvely, "It is as easy for a king to know the number of his people as for a shepherd to know the number of his flock. He has only to wish to know." However, even at the end of the nineteenth century, the Czar of Russia, although he wished to know, never did know, even approximately, how many subjects he ruled.

Today, statistical theory has reached an extremely advanced level. Its uses are widespread, and the results of its applications affect our lives in many ways. But in its social, economic, and political effects, no statistical activity is more important, or more complex, than the counting of people and their characteristics in a census of population.

Part I

THE CENSUS THROUGHOUT THE WORLD
*From the Earliest Counting
of Man to Censuses
in the Communist World*

Chapter 1

THE CENSUS BEFORE MODERN TIMES

Scholars have searched for the earliest recorded censuses with as great intensity as archaeologists probe for ancient cities and civilizations. The clues have come from clay tablets, biblical accounts, obscure documents, and early church registers. The discoveries show that, with varying success, man has been counting his kind for more than five thousand years.

As would be expected, the civilizations of the pre-Christian era that have left records of enumerations of their people were the most advanced of their time. Among other characteristics, all had stable, well-organized social systems, which were essential for carrying out as complex an undertaking as a census.

In addition, these societies had developed a system of mathematics and number notation of a high order. At an early time, each had men capable of making complicated astronomical calculations. The Egyptians had the necessary skills to plan and carry out the construction of the pyramids. As early as 1766 B.C., the Chinese were using a calendar. Each society had a system of taxation that had a mathematical foundation.

THE BABYLONIANS

The earliest records of counting population that can be called census taking come from the Babylonians, one of the peoples inhabiting the area called Mesopotamia. As far back as 3800 B.C., they had developed a system of revenue control that involved the enumeration of the tax-paying segment of their population. By 2500 B.C., based upon the census, Babylonian rulers could make fairly precise estimates of their revenue. Two hundred years later, by 2300 B.C., each district of the kingdom was able to calculate its own returns.

The information about the Babylonian administrative system is based upon clay tablets unearthed by archaeologists. As many as 30,000 of these were found. Many of them can be seen today in the British Museum in London. When the cuneiform script in which they were written was deciphered, the tablets were found to be records of administrative activities. They contain inventories of farm animals and farm products, as well as the results of counts of the number of households within districts. From these tablets it is also known that the earliest system of notation was to impress upon the tablet circles to represent tens and semicircles for units.

The Babylonian kingdom endured until its conquest by the Persians in the sixth century B.C. Although documents have been found that date to the fourteenth century B.C., there are no records of later censuses.

THE EGYPTIANS

The only civilization that can dispute the Babylonian claim to the origin of census taking is the Egyptian, the oldest for which substantial records exist. There can be little doubt that at an early stage in their development, the Egyptians had the mathematical and administrative ability for such an enterprise. The great age of pyramid-building came in 2900 B.C. These vast projects required the same skills as a census—organization, control, and exact timing of the activities of armies of men, as well as materials. The employment of such an enormous supply of manpower would seem to indicate the existence of reliable information about the human resources of the kingdom. However, in the absence of specific records of such information, this must remain as speculation.

Records do exist that indicate that counts of the population had occurred by 2500 B.C. Three hundred years later (c. 2200 B.C.), maps of the country had been drawn with statistical material relating to the areas they described. By the time of Ramses II, 1292–1225 B.C., the historical record becomes more precise. Under his rule a division of land took place. For this purpose, as well as for taxation and levying of work on public-work projects, Egypt was divided into administrative districts. Although births and deaths had been registered for some years prior to this time, there now took place a complete registration of the heads of households and the members of their families. In effect, a household census was carried out.

For many centuries after, the historical record is fragmentary. Therefore, it is not known how regular or continuous the registration was.

The world is indebted to the writings of Herodotus (fifth century B.C.) for much of its knowledge of Egyptian civilization from the sixth century B.C. This famous Greek, often called the "father of history," traveled widely throughout the ancient world and wrote about other civilizations of that era, as well as the Egyptian.

The registration of households that took place in the fourteenth century B.C. is related by Herodotus as part of Egyptian administrative activities in the sixth century. By then, it had become the responsibility of the police.

Egypt came completely under Roman domination in the first century B.C. The country was then fully incorporated into Roman census-taking activities. In each village the Romans stationed an appointed official whose sole responsibility was the collection of census information. With the' end of Roman domination, a three-thousand-year recorded period of census-taking, however much interrupted, came to a close.

BIBLICAL ISRAEL

Much of Babylonian and Egyptian history was interwoven with the fate of another people attempting to establish a civilization of its own in the same part of the world. These were the biblical Israelites, composed of the tribes of Israel and Judea. The society they created, distinct from that of either of the two great nations, never attained the stability of the latter. For extended periods, the history of the Israelites consisted of bondage, displacement, and wandering.

There is no record that the institution of revenue collection was ever developed to equal that of Babylonia or Egypt. Yet, despite the lack of such preconditions, the census-taking activities of biblical Israel had far greater effect upon the world's subsequent efforts in that field.

From the moment of their freedom from bondage in Egypt, they undertook to enumerate their people. The Old Testament, in which the accounts appear, is a storehouse of census information. Enumerations are reported with a rare concern, for that era, for exactitude of number. Some authorities have speculated that the Israelites' ability to conduct a census was a heritage of their long bondage in Egypt, where they must often have observed the process.

Virtually all of their enumerations had one objective: to determine the number of fighting men. As such, they had the same limitations as have all censuses conducted for taxation or military purposes. It is almost impossible to estimate the entire population from their results.

The first description of an enumeration occurs in Exodus (30: 11–14) at the point where the Israelites are freed from their bondage in Egypt. It opens with these resounding words:

"And the Lord spake unto Moses, saying,

"When thou takest the sum of children of Israel after their

number, then shall they give every man a ransom for his soul
unto the Lord, when thou numberest them; that there be no
plague among them, when thou numberest them.

"This shall they give, every one that passeth among them
that are numbered, half a shekel after the shekel of the sanc-
tuary: . . . an half shekel shall be the offering of the Lord.

"Every one that passeth among them that are numbered,
from twenty years old and above. shall give an offering unto
the Lord."

This "shekel census" was carried out in 1491 B.C. Although there
is no universal agreement among scholars upon the dates of biblical events, this date was in use for many years. Contemporary
research has tended to move these dates closer to our time but not
by a significant number of years.

The result of the census is announced later in Exodus (38: 25–
26) as follows:

"And the silver of them that were numbered of the con-
gregation was a hundred talents, and a thousand seven hundred and threescore and fifteen shekels . . .

". . . half a shekel . . . for every one that went to be
numbered, from twenty years old and upward, for six hundred thousand and three thousand and five hundred and fifty
men."

The total, then, was 603,550 of men "twenty years old and upward."

There are several interesting aspects of this enumeration. The
people "went to be numbered"; they were not visited by enumerators. And they were not counted directly; instead, their tokens—
the half-shekels—were counted. This is not unlike the methods of
counting pebbles or seashells cited earlier.

More significant, however, was that the census did not include
the entire population but only the men "from twenty years old
and upward." If one were tempted to estimate the entire popula-

tion of Israel on the basis of the likely proportion of this age group to the entire population, another difficulty arises. As will be seen later, the probability is high that not even *all the men* of this age group were included.

The next enumeration occurs one year later, in 1490 B.C., "after they were come out of the land of Egypt." It is told in the book of Numbers (1: 2–3, 19).

Again the Lord commanded Moses:

> "Take ye the sum of all the congregation of the children of Israel, after their families, by the house of their fathers, with the number of their names, every male by their polls;
>
> "From twenty years old and upward, all that are able to go forth to war in Israel . . .
>
> "As the Lord commanded Moses, so he numbered them in the wilderness of Sinai."

The results, this time, are reported with great precision by the numbers in each tribe, or "family." And, although it is one year after the first enumeration, the total is still 603,550.

If this is indeed another census, the similarity in the total may be explained by the hypothesis that those who died during the year were replaced by those who reached age twenty. The interesting fact, however, is that the enumeration was now of "all that are able to go forth to war"; in other words, potential soldiers. Since this is the basis, also, of almost all later censuses, it is a reasonable assumption that it was the basis of the first.

Among the men not included in the count were the Levites, the chosen attendants at the tabernacle. They were subsequently counted, but in their case the enumeration was of "every male from a month old and upward." The count showed about 22,000 members of this tribe in this age category.

Another count was made of "all the first born of the males of the children of Israel from a month old and upward," of whom there were 22,273.

Thirty-eight years passed before the next enumeration in 1452 B.C. This was taken "in the plains of Moab by Jordan near Jericho." The details are given in Numbers (26). Again, the count was of those "from twenty years old and upward . . . all that are able to go to war in Israel." The number of such men was now 601,730, with numbers by tribe.

Surprisingly, there were now fewer than there were thirty-eight years earlier. However, the years since the census of 1490 B.C. had been difficult ones, filled with afflictions visited upon the people. In one plague, 14,700 are said to have perished; in another, 24,000. In addition, some died in fire and in battle. An interesting comparison of the populations may be made on the basis of the two enumerations.

The Changing Population in Biblical Israel

Tribe	1490 B.C.	1452 B.C.	Change	
			Number	Percent
Total population[a]	603,650	601,730	− 1,920	− 0.3
Reuben	46,600	43,730	− 2,870	− 6.2
Simeon	59,300	22,200	−37,100	−62.6
Gad	45,650	40,500	− 5,150	−11.3
Judah	74,600	76,500	+ 1,900	+ 2.5
Issachar	54,400	64,300	+ 9,900	+18.2
Zebulun	57,400	60,500	+ 3,100	+ 5.4
Ephraim	40,500	32,500	− 8,000	−19.8
Manasseh	32,200	52,700	+20,500	+63.7
Benjamin	35,400	45,600	+10,200	+28.8
Dan	62,700	64,400	+ 1,700	+ 2.7
Asher	41,500	53,400	+11,900	+28.7
Naphtali	53,400	45,400	− 8,000	−15.0

[a] The "population" is of potential soldiers.
Source: Numbers, 1 and 26.

Between the two enumerations there was an absolute decline in the population where one would normally expect an increase. If one assumes that the population would have grown at an annual rate of about 0.3 percent (the use of this rate is explained later), the true decline was of about 75,000 men.

There was also a complete realignment of tribal strength. This was of the utmost importance because the objective of the enumeration was a fair division of the newly won land, to be apportioned on the basis of the tribe's number.

The next census undertaking described in the Bible was one of the most significant ever taken. Its implications later spread over the Western world, and its effects were felt for centuries. Today, the world is still not completely free of them. This is the census taken at the command of King David in 1017 B.C. The first account is in the second book of Samuel (24). It is repeated and extended in the first book of Chronicles (21, 23, 27).

The idea of taking a census was born when, according to Chronicles, "Satan stood up against Israel and provoked David to number Israel." David then called Joab, his army commander and instructed him, "Go, number Israel . . . and bring the number of them to me, that I may know it."

Joab, sensing the evil in the endeavor, said to David (Samuel 24: 3), "Now the Lord thy God add unto the people, how many soever they be, an hundredfold, and that the eyes of my lord the king may see it; but why doth my lord the king delight in this thing?"

In Chronicles (21: 3) Joab also asks David, "Why will he [David] be a cause of trespass to Israel?"

Joab's protests were useless against the king's insistence.

He and other captains of the armies departed on their mission and returned nine months and twenty days later. In the account in Samuel (24:9) his report is, "And Joab gave up the sum of the number of the people unto the king: and there were in Israel eight hundred thousand valiant men that drew the sword; and the men of Judah were five hundred thousand men."

The total here is 1,300,000 "valiant men that drew the sword."
But it is believed that the count was incomplete. The evidence is
in the first book of Chronicles (27:24), where it is stated, "Joab
. . . began to number, but he finished not, because there fell
wrath for it against Israel." Also, a greater number of men is now
reported: 1,100,000 in Israel and 470,000 in Judah, a total of
1,570,000. Neither enumeration included the tribes of Levi or Benjamin "for the king's word was abominable to Joab."

To express his wrath, the Lord decided to punish Israel, giving
David the choice of three years of famine, defeat in battle, or
three days of "pestilence." King David chose the last, "and there
fell in Israel seventy thousand men."

This census has intrigued students for many centuries. David
evidently sensed that an enumeration would be a sinful act. In the
first book of Chronicles (27:23) it is stated, "But David took not
the number of them from twenty years old and under: because
the Lord had said he would increase Israel like the stars of the
heavens." Could he, then, have committed the sin of pride? However, this is not the element of the census that has interested students of the subject.

The first fact worthy of note is that David instructed Joab, "Go
number Israel." But Joab brought back the number of *men* "that
drew the sword," or, fighting men. Undoubtedly, this was understood without having to be stated. Thus, far many more were uncounted than counted. The largest group eliminated were, of
course, the women; then, the children under twenty years. But,
were older men, those above sixty, for example, to be counted as
able to "draw the sword"? What of the sick, the infirm, the disabled of any age? Were they included? Certainly slaves were excluded, as were aliens.

These exclusions and unanswered questions make it virtually
impossible to estimate ancient populations, whether of Israel or
elsewhere.

It is worth comparing the total of 1,570,000 men, not including
the tribe of Benjamin, in the last census, with the total of 601,730

in the enumeration of 1452 B.C. In this interval of 435 years, there was an increase of more than 1,000,000 men, allowing for the Benjaminites. This represents a rate of population growth of about 0.3 percent per year, a fairly substantial rate for that era. It should be borne in mind that plague, famine, and frequent warfare were common conditions of life then.

However, of immeasurable demographic importance was the effect upon census taking, up to this very day, of King David's census. The feeling spread widely that the Lord's wrath was an indication of His displeasure with the counting of people. The resulting reluctance to being counted directly affected the introduction of scientific census taking. It was the opinion of the late Sir George H. Knibbs, who organized the first census of Australia, that David's census "had the effect of delaying the adoption of the census by Christian Europe for many years." Hugh H. Wolfenden, one of the world's most eminent demographers, added that it "had the effect of delaying the adoption of the census in England for many years." To the various superstitions in the world against being counted, David's census added the most formidable.

Subsequent to this, there were two other significant enumerations. First, King David and, two years later, his son, King Solomon, enumerated the "strangers," probably aliens, in Israel. The purpose was to estimate the labor force available for the construction of the Temple of Solomon. The total was 153,600, made up of men who cut wood and stone, men who carried, and their supervisors.

The second enumeration is cited twice—in the book of Ezra (2) and Nehemiah (7). The presumed date is 536 B.C. The result, given in detail by "family," is of the *men* of Israel who returned from Babylonian captivity. There were 42,360, not including 7,337 "servants and maids" and 245 "singing men and women." The animals that returned with them were also enumerated.

Except for passing references or enumerations of single tribes, this concludes the biblical census accounts.

ANCIENT CHINA

Several thousand miles away, in China, another civilization, contemporaneous with the three nations discussed above, was flourishing. The many written records that exist from the earliest years of Chinese history indicate that the necessary conditions existed for primitive census taking. Very early, the Chinese had a well-organized society, a knowledge of number, and a system of taxation.

Some authorities believe that there were counts of the population as early as 3000 B.C. Topographical data relating to parts of the country, the provinces of Yuking, are available from about 2300 B.C. Also from this period, there exist tax returns forwarded by local officials to the central government. It has often been noted by historians that the existence of maps and related information are associated with a well-developed system of taxation and probable enumeration of the population.

Many experts have attempted to estimate the population of China at that time from the tax returns. These attempts are made more difficult by the knowledge that many local officials were corrupt; they deliberately kept the counts low to cheat the central government of revenue. This practice was not unique to China.

Another source of confusion in estimating ancient populations, in China as elsewhere, is in the changing meaning of common terms. The Chinese word for "individual" or "mouth," for example, is *K'ou*. But this may mean "adult males," "adults of both sexes," or "persons of all ages, excluding infants." Another important term in any census, "household," is represented in Chinese as *hu*. This word, too, has had a variable meaning. Ancient records seldom give reliable clues to the definitions of terms then used. Naturally, the results of any estimates would vary widely with the definition used.

It is known that by 1200 B.C., topographic officials were appointed in China. This seems to provide a thread of continuity with the maps and descriptions of about a millennium earlier.

The next significant addition to the record of early counting of the population of China appears in a series of volumes called *shu-ching* (or *shu-king*). In translation it means "classic (or book) of documents." In 550 B.C., the *shu-ching* was compiled by the great scholar and philosopher known to the West as Confucius. However, over time, many scholars contributed to these classics. They contain reports of population censuses, as well as of surveys of the country with statistics of agriculture, industry, and commerce. The statistics they contain go back as far as 3000 B.C. However, it is generally believed that only the data relating to Confucius's own time are fairly reliable; the earlier information is regarded as pure conjecture.

The significant fact about the *shu-ching* is the evidence that even in 550 B.C. Chinese scholars believed that man had been counting man for thousands of years.

The question of the probable size of the Chinese population has always intrigued students of the subject. One authority, Professor Chiao-min Hsieh of the University of Pittsburgh, has estimated the population for the period of the Han Dynasty which lasted from 202 B.C. to A.D. 220, with only a brief interruption from A.D. 9-A.D. 25. His estimate, not too different from that of other demographers, is that at the close of the Han Dynasty there were just under 60,000,000 people in China. If China then, as now, had about one-fifth of the world's population, at the beginning of the Christian era there were between 250,000,000 and 300,000,000 people on earth.

ANCIENT GREECE

In view of the extraordinary heritage of literature, philosophy, and history left to us by the Greeks of antiquity, positive evidence of census taking is surprisingly sparse. The prerequisites were certainly present. The opinion of most authorities is that there were undoubtedly a number of enumerations, as well as regular registration of the citizenry. This view was best expressed by the late Professor August Meitzen, who wrote, "The distribution of real property, of classes of citizenship, of military and naval service, of taxes and public burdens, and privileges was arranged in many Greek states in a manner which presupposed many inquiries of a statistical nature."

Ancient Greece was not a single entity; it was made up of a group of independent city-states that frequently were at war with one another. They were united only by conquest, most completely under Philip II of Macedon and his famous son, Alexander the Great (356–323 B.C.). Even this imposed unity was neither complete nor long-lasting. Most commonly, when people speak of ancient Greece, they mean the city-state of Athens, the source of its cultural riches.

In comparison with the civilizations discussed earlier, Greek civilization was extremely short-lived. The earliest Athenian for whom there is authentic historical evidence is the great ruler Solon (c. 638–559 B.C.), who came to power in 594 B.C. By 146 B.C., less than 500 years later, Greece was completely within Roman power. The great period of Greek history was of much briefer duration.

The Athenian population was never large, although its exact number is unknown. It has been estimated that during the Golden Age of Pericles, 460–429 B.C., the city had about 50,000 freemen.

Census history in Greece begins in 594 B.C. with the election of Solon to the highest Athenian office, that of Archon. He received a mandate to reform the tax and landholding laws. In connection with these reforms, there was an enumeration and then a registration of the electorate. Solon adopted the latter practice from the Egyptians, in the opinion of the historian Herodotus. It was still in effect in Athens in the latter's own lifetime, about 450 B.C.

The census resulted in a classification of the population into four groups, based upon the value of property owned. Since it also resulted in a poll tax upon resident aliens, it is reasonable to assume that they, too, were enumerated.

Some unique registration lists have been preserved that date from the fourth century B.C. These contain the names of Athenian citizens engraved on stone tablets. Unfortunately, few remain. With a complete set, a roster of Athenian citizenry would be available and an estimate of the entire population would be possible.

The only other known census of Athens was made in about 309 B.C. when Demetrius Phalereus was governor of the city. It was rather comprehensive; it included *all* males, free as well as slave. There were, it showed, 21,000 citizens; 10,000 metics, resident aliens with some citizenship privileges; and about 400,000 slaves.

THE ROMANS

The census-taking activities of the Romans, like so many of their other undertakings, had elements of the modern in an ancient setting. The practicality, thoroughness, and efficiency of organization so characteristic of them was brought to bear on the enumeration of the population. In the opinion of many authorities, the Roman census was as exact and comprehensive as any until modern times.

The fundamental objectives of their census, always strictly adhered to, were an objective system of taxation and an estimation of military resources. From its very origin in the legendary days of ancient Rome, the basis was practical. It was a by-product of fund raising to pay for festivals and sacrifices accompanying public religious ceremonies. In later years, when the population of newly conquered provinces became subject to taxation and military duty, they were included in the census. Still later, when Italians were exempted from these burdens, they were, at times, not enumerated. Romans who were free but owned nothing, the proletariat of the time, were often ignored by the censors. There is no record that census returns were ever analyzed for any other purpose, such as economic planning.

The scope of the census was more comprehensive than any taken until the modern era. The general inquiry included such questions as: name and age; the class to which a free person belonged; the position in the family, whether father and husband, mother and wife, son, or daughter. Widows were sworn for by their guardians. Slaves and freedmen were counted but included with the personal possessions of the head of the household, so that their number could not later be estimated. Real property was evaluated, as was personal property, and both classified by kind. Resident foreigners were not listed, but their property was. The lists were based on the sworn statement of the citizen.

The Roman citizen took the census seriously. Evidence of this occurs in the Gospel of St. Luke (2:1, 3) of the New Testament. The year is about 5 B.C. and the account is as follows:

"And it came to pass in those days, that there went out a decree from Caesar Augustus, that all the world should be taxed. [Author: that a census be taken.] . . .
"And all went to be taxed, every one into his own city."

Joseph and Mary then made a notable voyage to Bethlehem to comply with the imperial decree.

The Roman censor was an important public official whose responsibilities were:
1. The official registration of all citizens—the census itself
2. The evaluation of their property
3. The collection of revenue
4. The overseeing of revenue
5. The guardianship over public morals. From this obligation stems the contemporary meaning of the word *censor*.

The first census under the supervision of the official censors was in 435 B.C. This preceded the census of Athens under Demetrius of Phalerum, cited above, by more than one hundred years. However, this is not the earliest Roman enumeration.

Servius Tullius (578–534 B.C.), the sixth legendary king of Rome, is credited with being the originator of the Roman census. In his time, one of the important annual religious ceremonies was accompanied by festivals and sacrifices to the pagan gods. In order to meet the cost, the population contributed money offerings—men, women, and children each a different piece of money. The counting of the money revealed the characteristics of the population. A form of registration existed, too, in that at three stages of life—birth, death, and arrival at manhood—it was mandatory that a coin be deposited. From this practice it was known how many men were available for military service. This is another example of a population being counted by its tokens or symbols, rather than by direct enumeration of persons.

The Latin word for a sacrifice or a ceremony of purification is *lustrum*. This eventually came to be the word for a census, and the act of enumeration was a *lustration*.

In the one hundred years between the reign of Servius Tullius and the first census under the direction of the Censorate in 435 B.C., there were about ten enumerations. One, in 457 B.C., is referred to in the work of the Roman historian Livy (59 B.C.-A.D. 17). He wrote, "The census commenced in the preceding year is completed, the number of citizens rated being 117, 319."

When the Censorate was established, the intention was to take a census every five years. Despite wars, rebellions, and other stresses upon the state, this timetable was adhered to with remarkable fidelity. In the following 470 years, there were 69 enumerations. From 443–318 B.C. there were fifteen censuses, an average of about one every eight-and-one-half years. From then to 86 B.C., a period of 232 years, there were 41, an astonishing average of about one each five-and-one-half years.

From early days there also existed a primitive form of registration of vital events. Births were reported in the temple of Juno

Lucina, arrival at puberty in that of Juventus, and deaths in the temple of Libitina. Whether meaningful records of these registrations were kept is, however, doubtful.

To the census cited above must be added a number of enumerations of the population of the provinces, notably in Sicily, Sardinia, and Spain.

Enumerations became more irregular after 86 B.C. The last census under the Roman republic was held in 69 B.C., followed by a lapse of forty-one years. The Emperor Augustus (63 B.C.-A.D. 14) revived the census as part of his reform of the tax structure that had fallen into virtual chaos in the last days of the republic. There were three enumerations during his reign—in 28 B.C., 8 B.C., and A.D. 14. The significant fact of these enumerations is that they were conducted throughout the entire Roman Empire.

After Augustus there was no census for thirty-three years until the Emperor Claudius ordered one in A.D. 47. And the last enumeration came in A.D. 72, in the reign of Vespasian. By then, Italian citizens were subject neither to taxation nor military duty, so that no practical purpose would be served by counting them. The population in the provinces, however, was enumerated. Although the tax reforms initiated by Augustus were extended and perfected by later successors, into the reign of Diocletian, A.D. 284–305, there are barely any further references to censuses of the empire.

This amazing record of consistent census taking over such a span of history has not been equaled by any nation in the world. As Professor A. B. Wolfe, a noted authority on population, has stated, "The periodical repetition of even a partial enumeration at relatively short intervals over a period of four hundred years, as well as the increasing area covered, gives to the Roman census a significance that no other ancient population record possesses."

In view of this, it is astonishing how little *detail* is available today about the results of the enumerations. Historians know that censuses were held, that detailed questions were asked, but the answers, except for occasional totals, are lost to history. The Emperor Augustus had the result of his census engraved on the Monumentum Ancyranum. But usually, although they were not regarded as state secrets, census figures were not made widely known. Much of what we do know comes from Roman literature, most notably from the works of the historians Livy and Tacitus.

Livy cites two other censuses in addition to the one quoted earlier. Of one enumeration, in 193 B.C., he wrote, "Cornelius now closed the lustrum, the number of citizens rated being 143,704." He said of the one in 188 B.C., "Campanians were directed by the Censors, in accordance with a decree of the Senate issued during the year, to be included in the general census of Rome." And further, "Marcus Claudius Marcellus, the Censor, closed the lustrum, 258,308 citizens being rated."

Writing of a later period in Roman history, Tacitus (c. A.D. 55–117) refers to three enumerations. Of the one in 14 A.D. he wrote, "In this year, during the reign of Tiberius Caesar, the German legions mutinied against Germanicus, their general, while he was carrying out the assessments of Gaul." This matter is referred to again when he states in A.D. 16, "Publius Vitellius and Caius Antius [were] appointed to continue the collection of the taxes of Gaul." His last reference is to the census under Claudius about which he says, "Emperor Claudius closed the lustrum in A.D. 48, the number of citizens enumerated being 5,984,072."

In addition to the one in Luke, there is one other mention of an enumeration in the New Testament. It occurs in the Acts of the Apostles (5:37) and refers to one carried out under Cyrenius, then Governor of Syria, in about A.D. 3. The reference is to a revolt of Judas of Galilee and his followers. It states, "After this man rose up Judas of Galilee in the days of the taxing . . ."

For no period in Roman history is it possible to construct a realistic estimate of the population under Roman domination. The inclusions within the census shifted. Definitions of citizenship changed. This appears in sharp focus from the fact that in the last census under the republic, in 69 B.C., the total enumerated was 910,000. Forty-one years later, in 28 B.C., the Augustan census of the empire enumerated a citizenry of 4,063,000. The census of Claudius, twenty years after that, counted 5,984,200. But this is believed to have included only males from seventeen to sixty years of age.

The Roman census, conducted as it was for purposes of taxation and military duty, undoubtedly suffered from the defects of all censuses with these objectives. Evasion and resistance must have been widespread at various times. In addition, the practice under the later republican governments of "farming out" tax collection to private agents resulted in widespread corruption in the enumeration itself and the consequent reports of revenue collected.

With all its limitations, the Roman census represents one of the most remarkable administrative achievements in human history. When it finally passed into decline, the enumeration of populations with such thoroughness and efficiency and on such a scale was not renewed for many centuries.

Chapter 2

APPROACHES TO THE MODERN AGE

In the world that Rome ruled, census taking practically came to an end in the first century of the Christian era. As internal rebellions and barbarian invasions became more common, the political and social structure of Europe began to fall apart. A long decline set in. From the last Roman census until the Renaissance, more than a thousand years later, the counting of people that took place was barely enough to keep alive this human activity.

At the height of Roman power, the proudest claim that a man could make was "Civis Romanus sum"—I am a Roman citizen. In the Christian world that replaced Rome, the individual became unimportant. Man's earthly existence was considered a brief episode on a journey to eternity. The effect of such an attitude was to eliminate the need for census taking.

The census, at this time, was identified with Rome. And all things Roman were regarded as pagan and vile. Also, in these intensely religious times, the plague upon Israel for King David's census was a warning that God frowned upon such activities. As the first attitude died away, the second became stronger.

Census data from the medieval period in Europe is composed of scattered bits and pieces. Until fairly recent times, there was not even a book that dealt with the population of Europe during the Middle Ages.

In the fifteenth century, the Renaissance began to spread over Europe, first in Italy and then elsewhere. Great interest developed in the Roman and Greek heritage. With the expansion of trade and commerce, there was a flourishing of art and ideas. Enumerations of population began again and became more frequent, especially in the Italian city-states. In view of the supremacy in trade, in art, and in the study of ancient civilizations in such city-states as Florence and Venice, their leadership in this activity is not surprising.

The most significant change, however, was in the nature of the counting. Although it was still primarily for tax and military purposes, more and more frequently *man,* rather than his land as a tax unit, was the object of the counting. At the time of the Renaissance, democracy as it is understood today was still far in the future. Although there was no equality of man, there was a renewed sense of man's worth. The counting of man by his kind resumed, however imperfectly and incompletely. It has continued without interruption ever since.

Although every country has its own census history, those discussed in the pages that follow illustrate problems and approaches that were typical for most of Europe in those years.

ENGLAND

In the Public Record Office in London, there is on view the outstanding statistical document of the Middle Ages. It is the original record of the *Domesday Book,* compiled for William the Conqueror in 1086. In its time it was often referred to as "the description of England," and despite some omissions, that is what it is.

It was begun by King William I on Christmas Day of 1085 for fiscal purposes. Its aims were to determine the extent and value of his land and to establish who were the actual occupiers of the land—the tenants-in-chief. The king appointed panels of commissioners, called *legati*, to carry out his orders. There were about eight of these panels, each responsible for a number of counties. The panels traveled throughout their territory, holding hearings in the most important town of each county. The hearings were public affairs, attended not only by a jury but also by various public personalities, including the reeve and the sheriff. Their presence undoubtedly contributed to the accuracy of the record. The landholders—lords, barons, and tenants-in-chief—appeared before the commissioners and, under oath, answered a long list of questions. Their answers were entered on official rolls in great detail.

The entries were made separately for each county, usually starting with the largest town. The name of the holder of any land, from king, to clergy, to the lowliest tenant-in-chief, was written down and his holdings described. The list of the manors and the name of each was entered both as of "now"—1086—and "on the day when King Edward was alive and dead"—1066. Under the landholder's name and assigned number were entered his lesser tenants (or subtenants), as well as the numbers of various categories of serfs and servants.

The detailed "descriptions" for each county were forwarded by the commissioners to the treasury at Winchester, then the capital of England. They were then summarized, and this summary is the *Domesday Book* that the king saw before his death in September, 1087.

This "description of England" omits four northern counties and part of a fifth, as well as London and Winchester. Some authorities believe that the two cities were actually surveyed but that the accounts met some unknown fate.

In view of the conditions of the time, it is impossible to overestimate the accomplishment of the *legati* of the king. There does not exist so comprehensive a statement of population and social conditions for any other country in the world during that era. On the basis of the documentation of the *Domesday Book,* several scholars, including the Englishman Henry Ellis, in 1833, were able to estimate the population of England at the time of William I as being somewhat under two million.

It served other purposes as well. It is a record of ancient customs and royal obligations for earlier services rendered. Many towns and villages were, in effect, "born" of the survey in the sense that their names were registered and boundaries defined for the first time. For many years after its completion, it served as evidence in the courts of England to settle disputed land claims.

Almost three hundred years pass before the next record of any enumeration. In 1377, Edward III (1312–1377) ordered a count of all persons subject to a poll tax. After his death it was completed by his successor, Richard II (1367–1399). The enumeration was fairly complete since the poll-tax rolls needed revision after the Black Death of 1348–1349.

On the basis of these returns, the British demographer, J. Topham, estimated the population to have been about 2,500,000. If one assumes that the population under William the Conqueror was 1,750,000, in the 291 years from 1086 to 1377, the rate of population increase was slightly more than .01 percent. In view of the frequency of the Black Death or plague, this low rate is not surprising.

The Tudor monarchs who ruled England from 1485 to 1603 were responsible for some new approaches to recording the population. Sir Athelstane Baines, former president of the Royal Statistical Society, said of this period, "The almost continuous unrest in western Europe rendered it necessary to take stock from time to time of the number of men capable of bearing arms, as well as of the fiscal resources of the country in anticipation of war." In 1537, Henry VIII, again following a siege of the plague, started the registration of deaths. In 1550, the maintenance of baptismal records by the local clergy was ordered. By the end of the sixteenth century, records of mortality by sex were published for the

city of London. A further refinement was added in 1629, when
women were employed to count the dead, estimate their age, and
state the cause of death. The findings were published weekly as
Bills of Mortality. The weekly publication of burial records continued without interruption until 1849.

As will be seen, these *Bills of Mortality* played a prominent part
in the work of John Graunt, a pioneer in the cause of scientific
census taking.

Other measures such as poll and hearth taxes enabled later
scholars to study the changing population of the country. And the
parish registers were still being maintained. From the results of
the hearth tax of 1690, Gregory King later estimated the population of England to have been 5,500,000 just prior to the eighteenth
century. Several decades later, from summaries of the parish registers, John Finlaison estimated the population in 1700 to have
been 5,131,516.

It was becoming evident that indirect measures for estimating
the population were inadequate. Each had serious shortcomings.
What Charles H. Wickens of Australia, a noted twentieth century
demographer, pointed out about the burial records could apply to
similar records. He said, "These records cannot be regarded as
furnishing any reliable estimate of the total number of deaths actually occurring in the area to which they relate. He cited the
following:

1. People who died in London often were buried in the countryside.
2. Burials of persons not members of the Established Church
   of England often went unrecorded.
3. Parish clerks often failed to forward registration reports.

It is Wickens's opinion that for the seventeenth and eighteenth
centuries the underestimates were as high as 44 percent.

Mid-eighteenth century England, already the world's leading
trading nation, was moving steadily toward its Industrial Revolution. A genuine census of population became more urgent. But
there were great obstacles to overcome. In 1753, Thomas Potter

introduced a census measure in Parliament. The debate on the bill reflected the attitudes within the country. One speaker opposed it on the ground that "a census would reveal England's weakness to her enemies." Another denounced census inquiries as "subversive of the last remains of English liberty." But the most serious charge was that a census would bring "some public misfortune or epidemical distemper." This charge, of course, referred to the biblical plague upon Israel. Many authorities have attributed the long delay in undertaking a genuine enumeration of England to this fear.

The bill finally passed the House of Commons but was defeated in the House of Lords.

In 1796, John Rickman wrote an article entitled "Thoughts on the Utility and Facility of a General Enumeration of the People of the British Empire" that was published in *Gentleman's Magazine.* In the article, Rickman discussed the possibility that the actual population exceeded most estimates. He cited the economic advantages in knowing the exact population. His paper reached Charles Abbot, an influential member of the House of Commons who somewhat later became its speaker. Abbot introduced a census bill in 1800; in 1801, the first general enumeration of Great Britain, not including Ireland, was undertaken. John Rickman was appointed Director of the Census.

Many scholars have speculated upon the reasons for the change in attitude that resulted in passage of the census bill. Some have pointed to the famous essay, "On Population," by the Rev. Malthus in 1798. This essay set in motion a reexamination of the traditional idea that a country should encourage as large a population as possible. In fact, the preamble to the Census Act of 1800 states that "in times like these, when subsistence of the people is in question, it is surely important to know the demand for which we are to supply."

Sir Athelstane Baines attributed the passage of the bill to the "new spirit" evoked by both the French Revolution and the Industrial Revolution in England.

Professor A. B. Wolfe expressed the belief that the first American census in 1790 had helped to overcome the religious superstition. He wrote, "The decision of Parliament to risk a general enumeration may have been influenced by the fact that the young United States had made a general count of the people, without to any notable degree suffering the displeasure of the Almighty."

FRANCE

More time has been spent by more scholars, with less result, in attempting to estimate the population of early France than for any other country. What drew authorities to this field is the rich collection of fragments of enumerations of every variety. It is known, for example, how many soldiers were due the king in 1190 from the commune of Paris. A few years later, the records show that Paris, Orleans, and Amiens sent him 6,270 sergeants and 153 chariots. In 1292, there were in Paris 4,159 artisans in the manual and mechanical trades; by 1300, other records show the number had grown to 5,800. The membership of other guilds has also been preserved. It is known how many butchers and butcher shops there were in the fourteenth century. Later, municipal records were kept of the amount of wine, wheat, and other commodities that were consumed. In addition to these, documents have been preserved of counts of parishes and households.

In attempting to put together these statistical odds and ends to estimate the population of France before the Revolution, French scholars have always been frustrated. There are three main sources of frustration. In the first place, there are missing pieces. Documents of enumerations were confidential, intended only for the eyes of the king and his minister of finance. They were not published, and the only known copies were the originals. Since the keeping of records was in a primitive stage, documents known to have been prepared cannot be found. But, much more important was the early recognition by French statisticians that any report involving finances was almost always a fraud. As the late Professor Fernand Faure of France's Conseil Supérieur de Statistique said, "Everything conspired to falsify the figures of financial statistics in this period from the fourteenth century to the sixteenth which was constantly confused by war, foreign war and civil, and in which over the head of our Kings the real sovereign was almost always anarchy." Almost all the officials involved with money were dishonest. "Its heads and clerks [of the Chamber of Accounts] did not hesitate to alter the figures when they saw a chance to profit."

As one example, Professor Faure says, "The Province of Burgundy (in 1484) reported annually 80,000 *livres*. The representative of the King ascribed to it a revenue of 18,000." If any person in the chain of authority, from clerk to minister, could profit from falsifying figures, they always turned out to be falsified.

The third source of frustration arises from the sheer incompetence of the administrators. France, as Gaul, had been one of the oldest, most loyal, and best ruled provinces of the Roman Empire. But by the time of the Frankish kings in the eighth century, there was no trace of Roman administrative talent.

One of the earliest records of any sort of counting is the *Brevis Capitolorum*, or *Breviary* of Charlemagne (c. 742–814), the great Frankish emperor. The *Breviary*, or summary, was compiled in 808 and was intended to serve the same purpose as the later *Domesday Book* of William the Conqueror—to "describe the land" for the king. But it was not collected with the same thoroughness as was the later document.

In the early days of his rule, the king had been able to know his free subjects from association with them on the fields of combat. But, with peace, they scattered over the kingdom, and the relationship was no longer personal. A kind of royal messenger corps, called *missi dominici*, was established to transmit the king's orders to the nobility and higher clergy. Then, local authorities were to carry them out. The *missi dominici*, constantly on the move, gathered the information, including a listing of land and other property, that went into the *Breviary*. The intention was that they were to keep the information up to date and make necessary changes.

From what is known of it, the *Breviary* was far from the thorough document that the *Domesday Book* became. But, more than this, the system of changes, based upon the unsupervised authority of the *missi dominici*, made for corruption, which soon set in.

Another fascinating document was begun at about the same time, in the year 806. It is called the *Polyptique de L'Abbé Irminon*. *Polyptiques* were land registration documents that became the principal source of information about the population of France in the Middle Ages. The *Polyptique d'Irminon* was a land registry for the area of the Abbey of St. Germain des Pres, then the equivalent of an average French *département*, or state. The details of land ownership, however, covered only about half the area.

Since it was assembled almost simultaneously with the *Breviary*, one can easily make the assumption that the *Polyptique d'Irminon* must have been prepared in connection with Charlemagne's orders. However, there is today, in fact, no known reason for its preparation.

Similar registers were prepared for other parts of France. However, Emile Levasseur, author of *La Population Française*, summarized them all by saying, "From these data it is not possible to draw an hypothesis sufficiently sound as to the numerical state of the population in the Frankish empire."

An interesting enumeration took place in 1332 in Pontoise, then the capital of a province. Its purpose was to determine the size of the dowry to be given to Queen Jeanne of France upon her marriage to King Louis XII.

In the fourteenth century, enumerations increased, but they were mainly of the kinds discussed earlier, of skilled workmen, commodities, or soldiers owing service to the king. They continued throughout the next two centuries but always of limited areas or of certain taxpayers. Not one provided a basis for estimating the population of the territory they included, much less all of France.

In the seventeenth century, due in part to the Renaissance and the ideas it generated, there slowly emerged a new approach to the enumeration of population. But in France, as in much of Europe, any undertaking of this kind was controlled by the Ministry of Finance and regarded as a by-product of the collection of taxes. At the heart of the system in France were the fiscal agents known as *intendants.*

The France of Louis XIV was divided into thirty-two provinces, each administered by an *intendant* who was known as *l'homme du roi,* the king's man. Each had a number of assistants. The *intendants* sent their reports, highly confidential documents, to the Minister of Finance in the form of *Mémoires. Les Mémoires des Intendants* are the basic records of population from this time to the French Revolution.

For the time, such an arrangement would have been ideal for the collection of population data but for one factor. The corruption of the *intendants,* and virtually everyone connected with the financial administration of the country, was limitless. In 1620, hundreds of fiscal agents of various ranks who were supposed to send in reports every three months had not submitted any for five years. In 1665, in the course of a reform of the system, some collectors of taxes were brought to trial. It was revealed that in a six-month period there had been *millions* of false statements and forged accounts.

In 1661, Jean Baptiste Colbert (1619–1683), an able man, was appointed to the Council of Finances; in 1665 he became its controller general, the chief financial officer of the kingdom. Under the loose moral standards that prevailed then, Colbert had become a wealthy man before becoming Controller General. Having become wealthy, he became honorable. He thus began a complete reform of the administration of the tax system. The more corrupt tax collectors were brought to trial and convicted. The reforms are significant here for their bearing upon the attempts to enumerate the population of France.

In 1663, Colbert sent his deputies, called *maîtres des requêtes*, throughout the provinces to obtain information about the population. His aim was a reorganization of the tax system. These inquiries were supposed to determine not only the size of the population but also whether it was increasing or decreasing. The instructions, however, were vague; the results were hopelessly incomplete. Like his tax reforms, which were undone by the wars of Louis XIV, his plans to enumerate the population could not overcome the deep corruption of the system.

However, Colbert did bring about one reform that lived beyond him. From 1670, he decreed for the city of Paris that the statistics of baptisms, births, and burials be published. From that year to the present day, with the exception of the years 1684–1709, for which the data are missing, there is an unbroken public record.

In 1694, Colbert's successor, Pontchartrain, sought to introduce a poll tax or "head" tax in France. But to his dismay, it was not known how many "heads" there were. To correct this omission, he decided upon an enumeration of the population. Needless to say, the primary agents to carry out his purpose were to be the thirty-two provincial *intendants*.

A formal questionnaire was drawn up. Aiding in this was Fénelon, cited earlier, and the Marshal de Vauban, a strong advocate of census taking but with very naïve ideas about it. Although it was hoped that Louis XIV and the Dauphin would be enlightened by the resulting description of their kingdom, one of the primary purposes was the enumeration of the population.

The final form contained the following questions:
1. The number of towns
2. The approximate number of men in each

3. The number of villages and hamlets
4. The number of parishes in each of the above and their populations

The instructions to the *intendants* made it clear that the object of enumeration was the individual. They were also told to "consult the old registers to see if the people were more numerous formerly than today; causes of the decrease; if there were Huguenots and how many of them have gone away." Some *intendants* went even further on their own. The one for Paris, for example, drew up a sixteen-column questionnaire with inquiries relating to individuals, income, and taxes.

Since the *intendants* themselves would not do the actual counting, it was expected that the enumerators would be the local clergy, or *curés*. These men had had the responsibility for registering marriages, births, and deaths since 1539. It was assumed that they would have a measure of experience. The hope also was that their "moral authority" would insure the accuracy of the enumeration.

The results bordered on farce. Of the thirty-two *intendants*, twelve enumerated households rather than individuals; fifteen counted nothing but merely copied the records of the earlier poll tax; five actually attempted an enumeration; the other two felt that an enumeration was too difficult to undertake, and they did nothing!

Of the *Mémoires* that became part of the record, some show that where individuals were counted, certain classes of people were excluded. Those that involved households often included only the taxable ones.

From 1776 to 1781 another energetic man, the banker Jacques Necker, was Minister of Finance. Finding himself in need of accurate population statistics but aware of the shortcomings of earlier enumerations, Necker used another approach. In a way, he was a pioneer in the use of scientific sampling to estimate population. Necker reasoned that if he knew the number of births, which he

called the "least uncertain index," he could arrive at an estimate of
the population.

His method involved a series of complicated steps. The ultimate
aim was to obtain, for all of France, the average number of people
per birth. After the selection of the sample, the counting of the
sampled population, and the counting of the registered births, it
was calculated that there were 25.75 people in the country for
each birth.

Necker multiplied the average number of births in France—
963,207—in the period 1776–1780 by the average population for
each birth—25.75— and estimated France's population in 1781 to
be 24,802,500.

Although the method was ingenious, it was not really scientific.
The *intendant* selected the sample as he pleased and then proceeded to count it.

As French society moved toward its revolution, there had not
yet been an enumeration of the French people. The demographic
historian, Levasseur, wrote, "The *Mémoires* of the *Intendants*
constitute . . . the only general view of French population before 1780 which has an official character."

The failure to complete an enumeration long after its importance in public affairs was recognized was true of other nations as
well as of France. In every country there were peculiar local conditions, but, in general, there was much in common. It may help
to shed light on all to analyze the reasons for the French failure.

The system of *intendants* seemed to be an excellent instrument
for the collection of census data. There was a direct line of responsibility above, and they controlled trained assistants. These
men were familiar with numbers. They also knew their territory
and its people. However, after years of exercising authority in the
name of the king, they had become virtually independent. They
were not easily subject to discipline. And their corruption led
them to forge and distort reports as they pleased.

However, there was another factor that was far more important than any of the above in limiting the usefulness of the *intendants* as census agents. Their basic function was to raise soldiers and collect direct and indirect taxes. They were responsible for public works, including the construction of roads. In connection with this, they could force people to perform involuntary labor. It has been historically true, even to the present day, that anyone associated with any of these responsibilities cannot be trusted to enumerate a population. People seek to evade such burdens, and even when such an official comes to call on another assignment, they try to escape his attention. Failing this, they will not hesitate to lie to him.

The French people hated the *intendants*. Professor Faure wrote that their failure "is due to causes which persist to the end of the eighteenth century . . . because of the resistance, frequent and difficult to overcome, which the people made to all investigations of authorized officials."

There were other handicaps in addition to the corrupt and incompetent *intendants*. Transportation was primitive. In France, a large country with high mountains, some parts were completely isolated for much of the year.

Deeply rooted in the society and people of France were customs, attitudes, and prejudices whose nature would have made even the best-organized census effort an impossible task. At the top of French society, there existed a large, privileged nobility whom there was no point in counting since they were generally exempt from taxation. At the other extreme were the Protestants, especially the Huguenots, who were persecuted and forced into exile. They became the object of a count when óne Minister of Finance tried to determine how many had been driven out.

France is a predominantly Catholic country. It was not until 1787, on the eve of the revolution, that a civil law granted Protestants the right to register their vital statistics. Since the Catholic clergy had acted as enumerators in the few census attempts, as well as having been the registrars of baptisms, marriages, and deaths, Protestants, Jews, heretics, and others were often not included in the enumeration.

There was also widespread superstition about the counting of people, most of it stemming from the biblical accounts. The Chevalier des Pommelles, in a study of population published in 1789, wrote, "The people have so many prejudices against such an enumeration that in 1786 the provincial assembly of Auch was obliged to stop it in the province on account of the disturbance it caused. It will take a long time to inspire enough confidence in the people to cure them of their prejudices in this respect."

Such superstitions were not limited to the common people. The Duc de Saint-Simon, a prominent member of the court of Louis XIV, who wrote a well-known account of life there, wrote in his diary about "those impious enumerations which have always outraged the Creator and drawn the weight of His hand on those who have had them made and almost always earned startling punishments."

One other factor doomed any census effort to failure from the very start. This was the unrealistic and naïve attitude toward the difficulties involved by men whose opinions carried weight in official circles. France, as early as the sixteenth century, had men who wrote about the need for genuine enumerations with great foresight. But their ideas were not influential at that time. The voices listened to by important officials were those like Fénelon, who wrote, "It is as easy for a king to know the number of his people (as for a shepherd to know the number of his flock). He has only to wish to know."

In like manner, Sébastien de Vauban, a marshal of the French army and author of an important political work, could say that it was possible to design a method by which he could complete "without confusion and with ease, in twice twenty-four hours, all the enumerations which it might please the King to make of his people." And the Abbé Terray, Controller General of Finance, in writing to the *intendants*, told them, "It is not an enumeration by persons, dwellings, or households that I ask of you, that enumeration, although easy . . ."!

It is little wonder then that instructions sent to the *intendants* concerning enumerations were always vague so that these men could make their own interpretations. The approach seemed to have been: If the task can practically complete itself, why bother with petty details.

Add to the above long periods of warfare during which territory and people changed countries and kings with regularity, and it is not surprising that as the revolution broke out, no one knew how many Frenchmen would be affected by its outcome.

ITALY

After the disintegration of the Roman Empire, armies were in almost continuous march across the plains and mountains of Italy. Until the twelfth century, the country was in virtual chaos and anarchy with warriors contending for its parts. In the thirteenth century, the city-states began to form; in the fourteenth, the economic prosperity that has been associated with the Renaissance spread widely. To balance the equation, the Black Death struck. Afterward, although local wars continued, they did not affect general conditions too seriously for several centuries. Then, important trade routes changed, and foreign intervention brought decline and continuation of disunity among the city-states. Italy did not become a unified state until the second half of the nineteenth century.

The trade of city-states such as Venice and Florence was worldwide; the citizenry of the Italian Renaissance was sophisticated; the country led the world in the arts. Also, Jakob Burckhardt, the great historian of the Renaissance, said that here and now "man became a spiritual *individual* and recognized himself as such." And, in addition, "This period . . . led the individual to the most zealous and thorough study of himself in all forms and under all conditions." In view of this, one would expect a new chapter in the history of enumerating populations. And such is the case. However, had it not been for the diligent research of one man, much of it would have been lost to history.

K. J. Beloch was a late nineteenth century German classical historian who became interested in ancient populations. In the course of his research in the archives of various Italian cities, he discovered many records of early enumerations. Among his discoveries were 1,416 volumes of records in Naples that were the original enumerated lists of hearths and population of Italian city-states during the sixteenth, seventeenth, and eighteenth centuries. His discovery created the same excitement among demographers as did the finding of the tomb of Tutankhamen by Howard Carter in Egypt in 1922 among archaeologists.

Enumeration in Sicily may have begun as early as 1241, when a registry of land was made. In 1442, a salt tax was imposed, and this, too, was probably accompanied by some record of the people. However, in 1501 there was a genuine enumeration, the so-called "descriptions" of the country that included details about households and their inhabitants. It listed the people by sex and enumerated separately the men from ages 18–50 and over 50 years.

The Spaniards came to dominate the island in the middle of the sixteenth century. But the enumerations continued. They were still being made well into the eighteenth century, but the later ones lacked the detail of the earlier. A very significant feature of these counts is that they were carried out by *officials appointed for this very purpose.*

Some demographers claim for Sicily the distinction of having conducted the first genuine, detailed enumeration of a whole population.

Since the Venetians counted a wide variety of commodities, including the amount of bread sold daily, it is not surprising that

they counted their inhabitants often. At times there were enumerations of the entire Venetian Republic, but many more exist for
the city itself. For the republic, the earliest, relatively complete
record is that of an enumeration of the mainland territory in 1548.

For Venice itself, a census conducted by the church in 1540
gave the population as 129,971. It grew to 158,069 in 1552, and a
similar census in 1563 recorded 168,627 people. The unusual feature of these censuses was the accumulation of detail. All people
were counted by sex; boys and girls under the age of sixteen were
shown separately. There were counts of the members of religious
orders, including those who worked in hospitals, of beggars and of
Jews. These enumerations continued irregularly until the end of
the seventeenth century and were then not resumed until 1760.
From then until the end of the eighteenth century there were six
more.

There are similar records for many other city-states. Their enumerations varied in detail and in the frequency with which they
were carried out.

These censuses are of historic importance even though they have
little in common with modern enumerations. Errors were plenti-
ful. Summaries were almost never made. Since they were usually
carried out for tax or military purposes, there were large gaps in
the information. At times entire communities that were exempt
from taxes for some service to a monarch were not enumerated at
all.

This was also an age in Italy when towns and villages were
bought and sold, won and lost overnight. Thus, it is impossible to
establish any kind of sequence of changes in the'size of the population.

With these gaps and faults, these censuses are among the earliest signs of rebirth of a vital human activity.

It was not until Italy was unified as a constitutional monarchy
under King Victor Emmanuel in 1861 that there was a complete
enumeration of the Italian people.

RUSSIA

One of the many contradictions of life in Czarist Russia was that a literature of world rank rose from an environment of general illiteracy, gloom, ignorance, and oppression but did not affect them. In like manner, mathematicians of outstanding ability flourished but did not affect an almost total absence of statistical data about a people occupying the world's largest land mass. On the very eve of World War I and the Bolshevik Revolution, a leading Czarist official could state, "We not only do not know the condition of life in the individual parts of the most extensive state in the world, but not even the condition of the different activities, the number of persons concerned with them, nor yet the growth of population in the Empire as a whole. We lack data not only in regard to the composition of the cultivated area but in regard to the total area. We have no complete account of the settlement of the Empire."

There are historical reasons for this poverty of information. The long isolation of Russia from European thought was a factor. There was official indifference to the individual. For much of early Russian history, statistics about people were the responsibility of the police or of the Ministry of Interior, which included the secret police. Added to all these factors was official stinginess. Even when an enumeration was approved, the appropriation for it was totally unrelated to its goals.

The early registers that were compiled here were, as elsewhere, for purposes of taxation and military service. There is a great body of literature in which the general dread of service in the Czarist armies is described. There was, therefore, widespread failure to register through hiding, lying, or bribery. The tax officials were at least the equal of the French *intendants* in corruption. In the vastness of the land, they were even more remote from the centers of control.

In 1802 a Board of Nobles was created to organize some kind of historical picture of the conditions of the provinces. Although the

Minister of the Interior requested pertinent information from the provincial authorities, the attempt came to nothing. In reality, there simply were no verified statistics that could be supplied.

One of the earliest of many reorganizations placed the administration of statistics under the Ministry of Police in 1810. In 1817, an "Institution of the Learned" was added to "extract" the statistical fallout from the reports of the provincial governors. Another reorganization in 1834, that lasted until 1852, placed statistics under the Ministry of Interior. Its stated task was to prepare the first statistical tables of the Russian government. It was also to arrange "statistical expeditions to the provinces."

In 1853 the first International Statistical Congress was called by Adolphe Quételet, a Belgian who was then the leading figure in the world of statistics. This, and subsequent congresses, had a tremendous effect upon activities in many countries. In Russia it resulted in the reorganization of the Central Statistical Commission along lines recommended by Quételet. In theory, its powers were great, *including the organization of enumerations*. In fact, it was powerless. At the beginning of the twentieth century, its budget was 57,000 rubles, about $65,000 today!

There was, in addition, a higher advisory Statistical Council consisting of government officials who had no interest in statistics whatever and who contributed nothing.

Many authorities begin the demographic history of Russia in 1897, the year of the first enumeration of the population. The events leading up to this census contain elements of comedy.

The story begins in the 1860's, when a man named Ssemenow, a statistician in the Central Statistical Commission who later became its director, began to draw up plans for a general census on his own initiative. Undoubtedly, he was carried away by the ideas of Quételet and the reports of censuses from many parts of the world that were delivered at the International Statistical Congress. Receiving no official encouragement, he set to work on his own.

Working in this way, almost semisecretly, progress was slow.

But by 1870 he was ready to discuss a preliminary plan with provincial statisticians. Nothing came of this. Four years later, a new commission was appointed to prepare registration methods for military purposes. Ssemenow went to the commission with his own proposal for a census, probably trying to convince uninterested officials of the superiority of his approach. His proposal was rejected. A register of those eligible for military service, largely the peasantry and the urban workers, was decided upon.

But Ssemenow was a stubborn man. In 1882, about twenty years after he had first put pencil to paper with his census plans, they were sent to the Statistical Council for study.

At that time, among the duties that Ssemenow had acquired was the preparation of the *Statistical Year Book*. In the edition of 1882, in a move that almost seems born of desperation, he wrote the following, "The Central Office had abundant opportunity to convince itself of the untrustworthiness of the current population figures; it has long since felt sure that one should use them only in anticipation of a census and that without it no partial test even under the most favorable circumstances will yield thoroughly satisfactory results."

His statement about the "untrustworthiness" of figures was not likely to win Ssemenow many friends in official circles. A few years later, Ssemenow had a quarrel with his superior, the Minister of Interior, and resigned.

But no "comedy" would be complete without a happy ending.

In 1894 the council again took the plan under study. And, in 1895 more than thirty years after Ssemenow's wild but beautiful dream, the Russian Duma passed legislation authorizing "the first general census of the population."

The date set for the enumeration was February 8, 1897. An appropriation of 3,900,000 rubles for the preparation and counting was granted. This was a trivial sum for so large a population in so vast a country. Although the population was not yet known, this turns out to be an allotment of one ruble to count thirty-three Russians. By contrast, in 1890 the United States spent one dollar to count fewer than six Americans. To oversee the census, for which neither tradition nor experience existed, a Chief Commission on Population Enumeration was created. Its director was a population expert; other members were government officials from various agencies. The superintendents of the direct enumeration were to be the existing rural officials.

Because of the illiteracy of the peasantry, the rural enumeration was to be made by direct interview. However, because of the low general level of education, the rural enumerators themselves were men of borderline literacy. The urban population and those "within the domain of the nobility" were required to submit written responses. However there were no existing lists against which to check the completeness of response.

The original plan called for the Commission on Population Enumeration to tabulate the collected data. However, the appropriated money had run out. The commission was dismissed and the responsibility for tabulation turned over to the existing Central Statistical Office. For this purpose, this agency was granted an additional 1,300,000 rubles.

At the outset, it had been expected that twenty tables, or volumes, would be published containing the census findings. This turned out to be too ambitious "considering the forces and means at hand." In 1905, two volumes appeared presenting the general results for such a huge multinational population. The total population was reported as 129,800,000.

The results of this census taking did not inspire confidence. There was no provision in law for another census. In 1913, a second enumeration became a topic for discussion. But, shortly thereafter, Russian history took a dramatic turn.

ELSEWHERE IN THE WORLD

Until Beloch's discoveries in the Italian archives, historians had given Quebec the distinction of having been the scene of the earliest complete census. In 1665, when it was called La Nouvelle France, an enumeration of the population was held that listed the inhabitants by name, sex, marital status, and trade or profession. The total population was then 3,215.

Soon after this pioneer achievement, there were similar censuses in Nova Scotia and Newfoundland. In the following ninety years, there were fourteen more in Quebec, as well as seven in Nova Scotia and six in Newfoundland.

Across the earth another settlement had been established at about the same time. The Dutch, through the Netherlands East India Company, controlled the Cape of Good Hope in Africa. There are indications that earlier enumerations had been made, but from 1687 to 1785, with some omissions, there were annual counts of the population. These counts, with details about the livestock and agricultural crops, were part of the progress reports sent back to the controlling company.

Later, under British rule, the enumerations continued from 1823 to 1856. After this long history, they were abandoned because the results were not considered trustworthy!

To complete the encirclement of the globe, it is reported by H. H. Risley, the British authority, that in the thirteenth century, at the time of Marco Polo's travels to China, Kubla Khan had completed a census of Tibet. Unfortunately, not more is known about this interesting historical fragment.

PROPHETIC VOICES

In the sixteenth century, influenced by the Renaissance, many writers appeared whose work affected attitudes toward the study of population. Within a brief period, such work was published in the most important countries of Europe. In their basic approaches to the subject, they fall into three groups.

The earliest writers were often official ambassadors of their state. Usually men of wide scholarship, they were sent to the lands of potential enemies or allies to estimate their resources. This was in an age when most statistical information was regarded as a state secret. They returned to write "descriptions" or "portraits," as they were then called, of the countries they had visited. For these men, any remarks on the population were important only as they related to the analysis of military and economic strength.

Niccolò Machiavelli (1469–1527), the famous author of *The Prince*, was typical of this group. In 1515, he wrote *Ritratti della Francia e della Allemagna*—Portraits of France and Germany—after official missions to those countries.

Such authorship continued for a long time and became more ambitious. In England, Thomas Salmon wrote *The Present State of All Nations* in 1724. And, as late as 1749, the German, Gottfried Achenwall (1719–1772) wrote descriptions of the important countries of Europe. Achenwall was one of the rare men who had some qualification for his task. He was a professional statistician and political economist who is credited with being the first to use the term *statistik*. James Gray Kyd, Registrar General for Scotland, claims that Sir John Sinclair, in 1791, introduced the word to the English language.

Of course, estimates of population by any of these men, including Achenwall, were nothing more than informed guesses. The significance of their work is in the recognition that a knowledge of population was an element in the administration of a state.

Scholars soon appeared who realized that the people were a vital resource of the state. They became advocates of genuine enumeration of the population.

Jean Bodin (1530–1596) of France, political philosopher and professor of law, represents a group of writers on population who differ from the men discussed earlier. His concern is still not primarily with population; it is with the nature of the authority of a state. The logic of his position led him to conclude that census taking was a vital activity for any government.

In 1576, Jean Bodin wrote his great work, *Six Livres de la Ré-*

publique—Six Books on the Commonwealth—in which he attempted to present a scientific approach to history and statecraft. In the sixth book, the first chapter, "De la Censure," deals with the justification for a comprehensive census. After a general statement that its uses are infinite, he says that an enumeration results in these specific benefits:

"1. Offers a way of insuring the defense of the country and of populating the colonies.
2. Makes clear the legal status of the individual.
3. Permits knowledge of the people's occupations and social rank.
4. Affords means of driving out vagabonds, loafers, robbers, ruffians who live in the midst of respectable people.
5. Provides for the just grievances of the poor against the rich.
6. Permits levying and collecting equitably the thousands of kinds of imposts.
7. Enables elimination of extortion by officials.
8. Puts an end to all rumors, appeasing all complaints, quieting all movements, suppressing all occasion for riot."

Points 5, 6, and 7 were sufficient for Bodin's ideas to be rejected in his time.

About forty years later, Antoine de Montchréstien (1575–1621), the famous dramatist and political economist, published his *Traité de l'économie Politique—Treatise on Political Economy* —in which he repeated Bodin's ideas without giving him any credit.

The modern age may be said to have begun with a modest volume entitled *Natural and Political Observations . . . made upon the Bills of Mortality* by John Graunt (1620–1674) of London. This pioneer work was the first to deal solely with population and to justify an enumeration as one of the most important administrative tools of the state. After Graunt, the subject of population could no longer be discussed meaningfully only in relation to armies and taxes.

Captain John Graunt was a London tradesman who spent his free time studying the birth and death records that the parish clerks had been gathering for years. He was part of a group of scientists, political economists, and other scholars who had become fascinated with experimentation and the analysis of observations. As Graunt studied the available vital statistics, he observed patterns of regularity. While today, about three hundred years later, some of the observations may seem simple or obvious, in their time they were revolutionary.

One of Graunt's observations showed that more boys than girls were born; he estimated the ratio to be 14:13. This statement of an inequality created great surprise. Going further, he correctly stated that, after a time, the number tended to equalize. This fundamental equality, he concluded, was not seriously disturbed by war or plague.

Graunt also observed that there was a relationship between births and deaths. He worked out the ratio and then stated that on this basis one could calculate the number of living persons, or the population. His analysis showed, for example, that of 100 individuals born in a given year, 36 would die within the following 6 years; 24 within the decade that followed; 15 in the decade next following; and so on, in decreasing number. At a time when general enumerations were unknown, this was a powerful tool for estimating population.

More than most men, Graunt knew how useful such estimates could be to a government. He reached the logical conclusion of his work by calling for a genuine census. In his book he wrote:

"It may be asked to what purpose tends all this laborious buzzling and groping? To know,

"1. The number of People
2. How many Males and Females
3. How many Married and Single
4. How many fighting men
5. How much London is and by what
   steps it hath increased."

To Graunt, an enumeration was justified on the grounds that "Trade, and Government may be made more certain and Regular, for, if men knew the People . . . they might know the consumption they would make. . . . a clear knowledge . . . is necessary in order to good, certain, and easie Government." Although he advocated, in addition, a census of land, cattle, and other goods, he further stated, "It is no less necessary to know how many People there be of each Sex, State, Age, Religion, Trade, Rank, or Degree. . . ."

A census based upon tax needs would be replaced by the desirability of "good, certain, and easie Government." Information about "fighting men" would have its place, as it does today. In short, Graunt was asking for an enumeration along modern lines.

John Graunt was one of history's fortunate in that his work was recognized for its importance when it appeared. He was widely read by the learned men of his day. There were even international effects from his work. His estimate of the population of London, showing it to be greater than Paris, aroused envy in the latter city and stirred a great deal of discussion there about the need for more reliable estimates of population.

King Charles II nominated Graunt for membership in the Royal Society. He entered that illustrious body in recognition of his pioneering work.

Another Englishman who became an advocate of a general census was Sir William Petty (1623–1687), a friend and supporter of John Graunt. Petty was one of those rare men who, in today's specialized age, have become almost mythical. Trained as a physician, he was, in the course of his life, professor of anatomy, physicist, inventor, professor of music, Member of Parliament, Surveyor General of Ireland, who drew the first detailed map of Ireland, and an economist who came to be called "the father of political arithmetic." He was a founding member of the Royal Society.

In 1672, William Petty published his *Anatomy of Ireland* in which he presented the first estimates of the population of that country. His great work, *Political Arithmetick*, was completed in 1679 but did not become widely available until 1690, after his death. "Political arithmetic" was the name then given to "the art of reasoning by figures upon things relating to government." In his work Petty estimated and speculated upon virtually all concerns of a government—the value of lands, manufacturing, commerce, fisheries, number of seamen, taxes and interest rates, harbors, shipping, sea power, and population. He criticized the lack of information that could be corrected by a genuine enumeration. His stature in British society focused attention upon the subject.

In 1693 there appeared a famous paper by Sir Edmund Halley (1656–1742), the discoverer of the comet named after him. Far afield from the primary interest of the great astronomer, it dealt with vital statistics. It was called *An Estimate of the Degree of Mortality of Mankind, drawn from the curious Tables of the Births and Funerals at the City of Breslaw; with an Attempt to ascertain the Price of Annuities on Lives*. It is significant that the "curious Tables," with notes, were sent to the Royal Society by the eminent Gottfried Wilhelm von Leibniz, who had also become interested in vital statistics. It was inevitable that men with logical minds such as theirs would see the need for more accurate data and advance their collection.

Elsewhere in Europe, two other distinguished men added their voices to the demand for genuine population censuses. In France, Sébastien de Vauban (1633–1707), Marshal of the French army and then the world's foremost authority on fortresses, published in 1698 a work called *Projet d'une Dix^me Royale*. In it, de Vauban proposed a reform of the tax system, claiming that the peasantry was unfairly taxed while the nobility was exempt. As a basis for reform, he demanded an annual, complete enumeration of the population. For these unorthodox views, his work was suppressed and de Vauban fell into disgrace.

In Germany, Johann Peter Süssmilch (1707–1767) applied the methods of Graunt's and Petty's work to his native Prussia. As had

Graunt, Süssmilch estimated the sex ratio at birth from the vital statistics data available in the Prussian provinces. His calculations showed the male-female ratio to be 21:20, with equality attained at the age of marriage. Süssmilch collaborated in what was probably the earliest serious estimate of the world's population, which was set at one billion at the beginning of the eighteenth century. Contemporary demographers place the population of the world at that time at a much lower level.

Chapter 3

WHO ARE PEOPLE?

A modern census of population is the only national undertaking, in peace or war, in which every person in the country plays some part. In an election many eligible citizens fail to vote; others are disqualified because of age, residence, or citizenship requirements. In any war a considerable segment of any nation remains uninvolved because of remoteness, indifference, or, again, age. Even a wartime rationing system has exclusions as, for example, men and women serving outside the country's borders. In a census, however, the infant born at the moment the census is taken is counted, as are the sailors thousands of miles away at sea. No other human activity is so comprehensive in its scope.

This is the intention or ideal. However, it is an astonishing fact that virtually no census in history has ever succeeded in matching accomplishment to ideal, despite generous appropriations of money, as in the United States, excellent communications, a literate population, vast resources of technical experts, and a long tradition of census taking.

The reason for the failure of a census to be completely inclusive lies in the fact that it is a social enterprise. It is affected by a nation's history, customs, and the patterns of thought of its people. Most of the failure can be traced to the answer that a nation gives to the question, "Who are people?"

The question seems to be an absurd one. The answer that springs naturally to the lips is "Everybody." Yet, throughout history, in almost every country, there have been groups of people who existed "outside the census." Consciously or unconsciously they have been excluded from the concept of "Everybody."

The common denominator of almost every enumeration prior to modern times was its limitation to taxpayers or potential soldiers. Women, children, and slaves were almost never considered "people." When King David asked Joab to "number the people," there was a bond of mutual understanding that excluded all except "fighting men that drew the sword." In later years, in France, as well as in other countries, there was a privileged nobility, free from taxation, that was never enumerated. In many lands the military and clergy, who often acted as enumerators, were themselves not counted. In China, according to Ta Chen, author of *Population in Modern China,* during the Ming and Tsing (or Ch'ing) dynasties that ruled from 1368–1912, "Certain social classes, either because of civil disabilities or of lower cultural development, were excluded from the population report." A general pattern emerges from the premodern enumerations. It is that of a privileged class and, at the other end of the social scale, women, children, slaves, and others without rights or privileges who, by general understanding, are not "people" in the sense intended by a particular enumeration.

As the modern census developed, exclusions were less frequently deliberate. However, deliberate exclusions persisted. The Constitution of the United States was the basis for not including the Indians until the census of 1880. Article 1, Section 2, describes the method of apportioning seats in the House of Representatives among the states according to population. It contains the clause, "excluding Indians not taxed." In 1880 the first enumeration of the Indians was undertaken. Until then, the answer to the question, "Who are people?" in the United States should have been, in all honesty, "Everybody—except the Indians." (The position of the Negro people before and after the Civil War in relation to the census is discussed in the section on the American census.)

The Indians of the United States are not unique in their exclusion. The one group most consistently omitted is the aboriginal population, the original inhabitants of any country before the arrival of the white man. In the Chinese population reports mentioned by Ta Chen, one of the excluded groups were the aborigines of southwest China.

Even in the twentieth century, provisions in the Australian Constitution similar to the American served to exclude its aboriginal population from the census. In the first complete census of the Commonwealth of Australia in 1911, the aboriginal population was counted. However, Sir George H. Knibbs, the chief statistician of Australia, whose report of that census is a classic, stated, "The cards relating to full-blooded Australian aboriginals were eliminated, owing to the provisions of Section 127 of the Commonwealth Constitution that 'in reckoning the number of people of the Commonwealth, or of a State, or other part of the Commonwealth, aboriginal natives shall not be counted.'"

The full-blooded Indians of Panama were not considered to be part of the civil population in the census of 1940. Mme. Beaujeu-Garnier, one of the world's most eminent geographers, says of almost all Latin-American censuses that "in some cases, the forest-dwelling Indians do not figure at all." In this part of the world, the Indian dwellers in the high Andes are often equally ignored. Wherever there is an aboriginal population, it has, at some time or other, including the present day, not been fully included in the concept of "everybody" in census terms.

Especially in the more advanced countries of the world, policies of deliberate exclusion from a census have virtually ended. What remained, however, were continuing and significant undercounts of large segments of the population. The reasons for this can usually be found in the history, customs, and prejudices of the particular nation. By and large, the groups undercounted are minorities within their country. They may differ from the dominant majority in color, racial origin, religious belief, tribal allegiance, or style of life. But, in some way, they are considered inferior or a threat to the majority. As a consequence, they are diminished in number in the census count.

When the aborigines of Australia were finally included in the census, it became evident that they were being underenumerated. In 1965 the chairman of the Aborigines Welfare Board of New South Wales, a government official, stated that his investigations had led him to the conclusion that there were closer to 250,000 aborigines rather than the 100,000 shown in the census.

It is well to consider the attitudes of the enumerator as a representative of the American people and the Indian at the time of the first enumeration in 1880. It is important because of the existence of almost parallel circumstances in many parts of the world today.

The earlier attitude of moderate Americans was perhaps best expressed by James Barbour, Secretary of War in 1826 under President John Quincy Adams. The historian, Leonard D. White, wrote as follows in *The Jeffersonians:*

"James Barbour had a plan, too, for the happiness of the Indians, and their civilization; but he closed its presentation with the somber words that if these efforts [Barbour's] 'should even fail, by the overruling influence of an inscrutable destiny whose fulfillment requires their [the Indians'] extinction, however it may fill us with sorrow, we shall be relieved from remorse.'"

In 1880 the general view was still that the Indian was doomed to die out. From this it followed that his views on legislation affecting him were not important. Soon after, in 1887, the Allotment Act was passed by Congress. As a result, the Indians lost 86 million acres of land of the 138 million still held by them before the act. A further cause for bitterness was added.

The mutual hostility was still being expressed on the battlefield about the time of the first census. In 1876 General Custer and his men were slain by the Sioux and Cheyenne Indians. And in 1890

Chief Sitting Bull was slain. Against such a background, an accurate census, which requires mutual acceptance between enumerator and enumerated, is highly unlikely.

It is a tragic fact that in the 1960's, in much of the world, hostility of long duration between groups within the same country broke out into warfare. The world's attention was on the war in Vietnam. But, perhaps to a lesser extent, citizen fought citizen in India, Indonesia, Laos, Malaya, and the Philippines; in Nigeria, the Congo, Ghana, the Sudan, Angola, and in other parts of Africa; in Algeria, Yemen, Saudi Arabia, and in other Arab countries; in the Dominican Republic, Haiti, Bolivia, Venezuela, and Guatemala. This list is not complete.

There was extreme unrest and hatred, short of open warfare, among parts of the population in South Africa, Rhodesia, Pakistan, Greece, Israel, and elsewhere. In the United States there was the special situation of the Negro and Puerto Rican people.

In some of these countries, there is a fundamental division in the population of long standing—the Arab, Moslem north against the black south in the Sudan; the Naga tribes and others against Hindu India; the eastern region (Biafra) of Ibo tribes against the Hausa of Nigeria—that is reflected in an undercount of the minority. Under such circumstances even if one wishes to count accurately, one can't.

Recent events in the Philippines illustrate this. There a rebellious group called the Huks has been waging guerrilla war since the end of World War II. Milton D. Lieberman of the United States Bureau of the Census went as an expert adviser to the Philippine government in a planned enumeration. In the *Journal of the American Statistical Association* of March, 1958, he wrote about his own experiences in the 1955 enumeration: "In the Philippines the difficulties of inaugurating a widespread sample survey are compounded by geographical problems, poor transportation facilities, some law and order problems. . . ."

In 1967 the *New York Times* reported that the influence of the Huks was increasing, especially on Luzon island.

Even when conditions within a country are far from a state of violence, minorities are usually undercounted. In the United States the Negro has been underenumerated throughout history, a fact acknowledged by the Bureau of the Census itself. Today, the count of the Puerto Rican people is incomplete. The Chinese in New York's Chinatown, as well as the Chinese in Indonesia, are not fully represented in the census totals.

The presence of a minority or of some other group that does not share equally in the rights and privileges of a society is often reflected in other ways in its census statistics. In the tabulation of the first American census in 1790, the white population was divided into male and female, with males also classed by age group. For slaves, however, only the total number was given, with no separation by sex or age group. In colonial Africa the white settlers were counted; the native population was merely estimated. In South Africa the "European" population is counted every five years; the black population is counted every ten years, and this only recently. In past Canadian censuses the white population was divided into twenty or so groups based upon European ancestry; nonwhites, including Indians, Negroes, Chinese, and others, were collected into a single group. In Hitler Germany there were Jews, Jewish mixtures of the first degree, and Jewish mixtures of the second degree. All other Germans were simply Germans.

In addition to those described above, throughout the world there are various "nonpeople" who almost never enter a census count. Sometimes their "nonexistence" is self-imposed; more often they cannot speak for themselves, nor is anyone likely to speak for them. As an extreme example, the ten most-wanted criminals on the list of the F.B.I. are hardly likely to be enumerated in any census.

On rare occasions criminals may form a significant part of the population. It is an historic fact that many of the original settlers of Australia were deported British convicts. In 1828 a census in the state of New South Wales showed a population of about

36,000. This total did not include the military forces. More interestingly, however, it also excluded an estimated 2,000 convicts who had run away from the census to hide in the bush. They would have represented more than 5 percent of the total population.

In the world today escaped convicts are not a significant proportion of the population. Even in countries where political opposition is a crime, the failure to count the people actually in hiding would not distort a census count. It is likely that in the American census of 1970, the so-called Hippie population, with a style of life likely to confuse census enumerators, will be an underenumerated segment of the population.

However, in many parts of the world, there are more substantial numbers of people who exist uncounted. On the Pacific island of New Guinea, a group of nomadic tribesmen were discovered in 1967 who had never before seen or been seen by any white man. Undoubtedly there exist similar groups in the inaccessible, little traveled parts of the world.

The *New York Times* reported in September, 1967, that in Japan each year an estimated 80,000 people simply vanish without trace. They leave their homes for a variety of reasons and disappear somewhere in the crowded islands, completely losing their identity. Such people anywhere in the world are likely to evade any official visitor, including a census enumerator.

It comes as a shock to most people to realize that in the second half of the twentieth century, human slavery should still exist in the world. It has been outlawed by United Nations convention and by every government in the world. However, traffic in human beings continues. In Saudi Arabia slavery was first made illegal in 1962 by decree of King Faisal. However, it is estimated that to this day 100,000 human beings are still kept in slavery in that country. Despite government efforts to suppress it, an estimated 40,000 people live in bondage in West Pakistan. The Human Rights Commission of the United Nations estimated in 1967 that there were still 2,000,000 slaves in the world.

Needless to say, the number of slaves must be "estimated." In the face of illegality and universal condemnation, slaves are not likely to be reported to an enumerator.

The population of India in 1967 was estimated to be almost 500,000,000. Within this vast concentration of human beings, most of them illiterate and poverty-stricken, can be found almost every condition leading to census underenumeration. One that invariably shocks every Western visitor is a scene in the streets of the industrial city of Calcutta. Its official population is placed at 3,000,000. But, as the American economist, Professor Robert L. Heilbroner, has stated, it could easily be 5,000,000.

Each night a human drama is played out in Calcutta. Several hundred thousand people, including families with children, bed down for the night in their only permanent home—the city's streets. The streets may be in middle-class communities, but the street dwellers are the city's poor. Mainly, they are not beggars. In the morning the men leave for low-paying jobs elsewhere in the teeming city. The meager possessions they own, the cooking utensils, and small stocks of food are stored in rented, foul-smelling cubicles in other parts of the city. The cubicles may also be used for cooking. This is not a new or temporary characteristic of Calcutta. There are families sleeping in the streets whose parents slept there before them.

This tragic phenomenon has obvious significance for any census. In the United States, after an enumerator has made several fruitless visits to an apartment in a city, he may ask a neighbor for information about the absent family. But the question, "Who occupies this part of the sidewalk?", would seem to be an unusual census inquiry.

The situation in Calcutta may be extreme. But in many parts of the world, segments of the population live in a manner that makes complete enumeration difficult or impossible. In the Puerto Rican community in New York City, more than one family, each with children, may share a small apartment. It is not rare for two or three men to share a single room, occupying it in shifts throughout the day. In the South Vietnamese capitol city of Saigon, as elsewhere, there are numberless small streets, unmapped, with unnumbered houses, and unnamed, as are, no doubt, many of the people living within them.

A census is a cooperative undertaking between the enumerator, who represents the government, and the enumerated, the people. Whatever stands in the way of full cooperation tends to reduce the completeness of the census. Laws, however strict, are never as effective as voluntary cooperation.

The question, "Who are people?", and the real, living response, "Not everybody," appear in many disguises. One of the most subtle is in the superstitions to be found among the people. There is hardly a country on earth, from the most backward to the most advanced, where some people do not regard the counting of human beings as filled with the possibilities of great misfortune. Its effect upon a census depends upon how deeply rooted are the fears and superstitions.

Several examples of the fear of being counted that stem from the biblical account of King David's census were cited earlier. The census in Great Britain is believed to have been long delayed due to the widespread fear of divine wrath. Such fears are not a thing of the past. There are religious groups today, in the United States and in other parts of the world, that have objections in principle to being counted.

Superstitions about being counted have shown themselves with particular force among the newly independent countries of Africa, usually in connection with the first census of a country. Most frequently it takes the form of underreporting young children, especially boys, and most commonly the firstborn. There is a fear of the "evil eye" and of offending one's ancestors.

In African society, children, especially males, are regarded as a blessing. A family with many is considered fortunate. But to a census enumerator, parents with five children may report only three. In this way they are not tempting fate or calling down the "evil eye" upon them; by not boasting about their riches, they are not offending their ancestors. An alert census taker may overcome this problem by arranging to have the entire family appear before him or by questioning neighbors. But this procedure is not always possible.

Very often a newly born infant is not reported. In most of Asia and Africa, infant mortality is very high. The first year or two of life are those of maximum danger. The feeling is, therefore, that it is wiser not to call attention to this sensitive life. Sometimes, since boys are more desirable, an infant boy, if reported at all, will undergo a change of sex.

Although the failure to report all children has been most evident in recent African censuses, it is by no means limited to that continent. To some extent it appears in almost every country, especially in rural areas. One can say, in general, that the degree of underreporting of children is proportional to the rural composition of a country.

Women, too, are generally underreported in a census. This is true mainly in Moslem and Asian societies. In Moslem lands women are still in a position far from one of equality. When an enumerator comes to call, the male answers for his family. While he would be likely to answer for his wife, he might omit his mother or mother-in-law who lived with him. He might also not report a daughter of marriageable age. Where polygamy is practiced, he might fail to mention all his wives. It would be an extreme violation of custom and tradition for an enumerator to enter the house and personally check the answers given to him.

In India there is great social pressure upon a young girl to be married. Girls approaching marriageable age go through special marital rites during which they call upon their gods to bless them with a husband and a large family. A girl considered to have passed the most desirable age of marriage without having wed becomes a symbol of shame to her family. In parts of India she will be hidden from all strangers, including a census enumerator.

Such practices can have important consequences in analyzing the results of a census. Demographers study the ratio between males and females in a society. It is important in forecasting the future birth rate, for example. In England there are approximately 1,069 females to 1,000 males; in the United States the ratio is 1,030 to 1,000. In India the ratio is reversed. Based upon 1961 estimates, there were 941 females to 1,000 males. Although Indian society differs considerably from that of America and England, there is reason to believe that the Indian ratio is influenced by the underreporting of women.

There is another interesting aspect to the fears and superstitions about being counted. This is the widely held belief in "lucky" and "unlucky" numbers. It has been shown again and again that if a person is asked to repeat number after number at random, the distribution of his choices will probably reveal his "favorite." The numerals from zero to nine will not appear with equal frequency. Superstitions about numbers do have important consequences for accurate reporting.

Social factors other than superstitions distort census results, particularly those having to do with age. The census of 1940 was the first after the passage of the Social Security Act in the United States. An unusually large group reported itself as having reached age sixty-five at the time of its passage. This was the age of eligibility for benefits. In Western societies there is a widespread reluctance, especially on the part of women, to enter the next decade of life. The women unexpectedly missing from the age-thirty group create a bulge at age twenty-nine.

In this connection, the following story appeared in the British publication, New Statesman, on March 24, 1967: "Miss Blanche Timothy received a telegram from the Queen yesterday—her 100th birthday. 'I was quite surprised; until then I thought I was only 98,' she said."

In technical terms, the worldwide social phenomenon of special, personal feelings about numbers leads to a result known as *age heaping.* In every society, the bulge at certain numbers in the distribution of ages of a population is a reflection of some of the basic attitudes in that society.

When tax officials, soldiers, or policemen act as enumerators, the results of their counting are likely to be poor. This has been true throughout history. People tend to fear them and either hide from them or are less than honest in their answers. This does not mean that their use as enumerators has ended. The action of the two thousand runaway convicts in the census of New South Wales (Australia) cited earlier is logical when it is realized that the enumerators were police officials.

Today, military men are seldom used except in special situations. Jonathan Schell, the author of a book, *The Village of Ben Suc*, about a village in South Vietnam in 1967, relates this interesting anecdote. A United States Army major, Allen C. Dixon, pointing to a map, is speaking:

"There's the Iron Triangle, and then there's the village of Ben Suc. This village is a political center, as far as the V.C. [Vietcong] is concerned, and it's been solid V.C. since the French pulled out in '56. We haven't been able to get a census taken in there to find out who's there."

In the Middle East, immediately after the war of June, 1967, the Israelis conducted several censuses in captured and occupied territories. Of the census in the Old City of Jerusalem, the *New York Times* of June 27, 1967, gave the following account: "Arabic speaking Israelis, accompanied by armed escorts, swarmed throughout the Old City of Jerusalem and its environs today conducting a census of the occupied city. At each house a soldier would hammer on the bolted door with a terrifying sound and then Mr. Liebel and his fellow census-takers would slowly unfold the layers of fear inside."

A receipt for having participated in the census later served as an identity card permitting free travel.

On December 15, 1967, Naomi Shepherd wrote the following

story in the British publication, *New Statesman*, "The people of Gaza have been counted and recounted like so many biblical tribesmen. The Egyptians made an estimate of the population last year; the Israelis carried out a census this year. The Israeli figure came out 22 percent lower; they say the Egyptians failed to register all the deaths."

Another possible explanation is that this was an undercount resulting from military participation in an attempt to count a hostile population.

An amazing variety of people with training in other fields have served as enumerators throughout history. Though in past centuries religious officials often were called upon, their use in the twentieth century has virtually ended. However, in 1918–1919 Protestant missionaries serving in China undertook to estimate its population.

It is not surprising that postmen have often been asked to serve as census takers. In fact, in 1920 and 1926 in China, they replaced the Protestant missionaries as enumerators. In the United States, E. Dana Durand, a former director of the census, in 1910 proposed that the mail carriers be given the sole responsibility for enumerating the population. The proposal was never adopted. However, they will play an important part in the census of 1970, which will be, in great part, a "mail out, mail back" census.

Schoolteachers have also served as census takers in many parts of the world. They counted the population in prewar Hungary and played a major role in the first census of the newly independent Republic of the Sudan in the 1950's, as well as in many other African countries. In the American census of 1960, teachers enumerated the population of the more remote parts of the state of Alaska.

In 1801, during the first census of England and Wales, the principal enumerators were the so-called "overseers of the poor laws" —i.e., those responsible for administering the laws relating to poor people. They were assisted by the more well-to-do householders in the parishes. This arrangement continued through the censuses of 1801, 1811, 1821, and 1831. As in the United States, the census was taken decennially, or at ten-year intervals. There was a reform of the entire procedure for the census of 1841.

The United States marshal and his deputies, made immortal in countless epics of the American West in movies and television, were the earliest enumerating agents. They performed this function from the first census of 1790 for almost one hundred years. At the other end of the legal scale, literate prisoners served as enumerators in the Sudanese census of the 1950's. The widespread illiteracy in the country forced census officials to use literate persons from every segment of society.

In countries where the illiteracy rate is high, the student, with his long summer holiday, has often been sought as an enumerator. An unusual, though not very productive, use of student talent was made in Burma in 1966. In an interview reported in the *Sunday Times Magazine*, Premier Ne Win complained about the lack of accurate statistics for his country.

"It is all very bewildering," he said. "We asked the students to gather statistics during their school holidays, but the figures are not correct. . . . We therefore find difficulties in drawing up plans."

Acting as an enumerator has often been a dangerous assignment. The American marshal and his deputies, frequently traveling through sparsely settled country, facing possible encounters with hostile Indians, were not free from danger. Today, especially in Africa where tribal antagonisms are strong and the fear of strangers is great, enumerators have been killed by angry mobs.

There is evidence to support the belief that, to a tremendous extent, the quality of a census depends upon the quality of the enumerator. The best enumerator is usually the person hired specifically for that purpose and then given adequate training and instruction to function effectively. The shortcomings of tax agents and military men as enumerators has been discussed. But even others whose primary interest and occupation is something else—

teacher or mailman—do not often perform well as census takers.

Very frequently, circumstances beyond the control of the most expert census planners determine the quality of the enumerator. In the United States the employment of an enumerator is of short duration; the pay is not very high. Consequently, when a census occurs during a period of full employment and high wages, the supply of capable people is limited. On the other hand, in times of depression, the job of enumerator is eagerly sought and the quality tends to rise. Thus, the level of prosperity determines the quality of the enumerator.

An interesting example of this cause and effect occurred in Thailand in 1964. Miss Patience Lauriat of the United States Bureau of the Census was sent there as demographic adviser to the Thai government. Her task was to set up a reporting system for births and deaths, which were known to be seriously underreported. Enumerators were hired to travel throughout selected parts of the country and to count these events.

Miss Lauriat and her team of experts soon realized that the enumerators were not making a complete count. In an attempt to correct this, three changes were made. Enumerators and supervisors were given higher status by being made part of the permanent civil service; the pay was increased from $1 per day to about $2 per day; the ratio of supervisors to enumerators was increased. The results were immediate and dramatic. From reporting about 1,500 births per round of visits, the enumerators reported 2,078, an increase of more than 38 percent.

The enumerator is truly the man on the firing line. All the antagonisms within a society, its fears and superstitions, come to a head when he faces the respondent—the people. Not only do their attitudes come to the surface but his own as well. In the final analysis, he is most important in answering the question, "Who are people?" As a member of the population, he will reflect its customs, prejudices, and the kind of mutual understanding shown between King David and Joab as to who are people. Where tribal loyalties are strong, he will share them. Where there is widespread prejudice against a minority, the enumerator may harbor such prejudice.

In the United States in the 1880's, as was indicated, there was mutual hostility between Indian and white man. The white man also believed that the Indian was doomed to die out. Under such circumstances, is it unrealistic to imagine an enumerator of Indians thinking, "What difference does one Indian more or less make?" Whether the thought is conscious or unconscious, the result is likely to be underenumeration.

A census is an expression of the society that carries it out. The most expertly planned and adequately financed enumeration must still come to terms with the question, "Who are people?" The census will approach a complete count only to the extent that in practice, as well as in theory, the answer is, "Everybody." On this imperfect earth, there are very few places where this answer can be given truthfully. As a result, *the actual answers to this basic question in the many forms it takes always point in the direction of an undercount of the population.*

This does not diminish the census. What other human activity on so broad a scale approaches perfection?

Most authorities regard the United States Bureau of the Census as the most efficient organization of its kind in the world. Its staff of experts is without equal. They are sought as advisers to many foreign countries. The bureau serves as a "university" for demographers and census personnel from every part of the globe.

On the whole, the bureau's activities are generously financed. It performs its functions among the highly literate population. Fears and superstitions about being counted are at a minimum. Transportation facilities are unequaled anywhere. However, the bureau's own experts admit to undercounts in the 1950 and 1960 censuses of from 2 to 3 percent. Other eminent authorities have estimated the errors to have been as high as 5 percent. Both agree that the undercount of the Negro population was higher than either estimate.

In 1966 the world's population was estimated to be 3.4 billion. This is based upon an accumulation, mainly by the staff members of the United Nations, of the results of national censuses and estimates. The total population reflects the *official* counts and estimates of the individual countries. Asia, not including the Soviet Union, has about 56.5 percent of the world's people; Africa, about 9.2 percent; South America, about 5 percent. In all, these continents, with probably the highest rate of underenumeration, have more than 70 percent of the world's population. Since almost all roads lead to official undercounts, one important hypothesis may be proposed. Scattered over the face of the earth there may be a great unnamed, uncounted "nation" with a population considerably larger than the 200 million people of the United States.

Chapter 4

AFRICA

COLONIAL CENSUSES

Shortly after the end of World War II, the most extensive transition to independence in mankind's history occurred. On the African continent alone, from 1956 to 1966, thirty-five new nations came into being. Their birth was the result of an awakened nationalism and the postwar economic and military weakness of their former colonial rulers, mainly Great Britain and France.

Freedom brought with it a tremendous burst of pride and joy. But even in the midst of celebration, the new governments, lacking experience, were aware of the problems to be faced. They may also have known, to their dismay, that there was an almost total lack of facts or statistics about their country upon which intelligent decisions should be based.

It comes as a shock to many Western people to learn that before independence most Africans knew almost nothing about each other. Colonial policies were founded upon the maintenance of tribal structures. This served to enforce isolation.

Robert K. A. Gardiner, Executive Secretary of the United Nations Economic Commission for Africa, described the situation as follows: "As the colonial period ended, African countries were strangers to one another. The only links between them most often went through Europe. There was no African transport, whether by air, rail, or road. The only way to telephone from Kigali, the capital of Rwanda, to Bujumbura, a mere 100 miles away, was to call Brussels."

Even within a country there was little movement or mingling of people. After the war there was some migration from village farm to city. Migratory workers sometimes even crossed borders seeking temporary employment. And, of course, there was the age-old movement of nomads, usually over well-worn routes. In the main, however, it was a static society, with travel limited to the clan or tribal area.

With independence, the tribal structure of African society presented many problems. When they had carved out the continent, the colonial powers had drawn arbitrary boundaries across native tribes and their traditional areas. With nationhood, tribal aspirations for unity made for restlessness in many of the new countries. Also, under colonialism, there had been favored tribes. Now, often as minorities within their own country, they faced the hostility of the majority. In several countries there were divisions between Moslem-Arabic tribes and Christian-Animist ones. The division was sharpened by the frequent association of the former with the slave trade, even into the twentieth century. The Fulani of Northern Nigeria, for example, were notorious in this connection. Independence brought with it a heavy residue of old scores to settle.

This is part of the general background of the continent that has a bearing on the story of the census. There were other concerns of greater and more immediate urgency. Among the first was the almost complete void of information about each country that the colonial powers left behind them. The first United Nations development plan for Somalia, which became independent in 1960, included the following statement:

". . . certain [other] necessary data are either not available at all, or if available are unreliable and incomplete. This is true of population, birth and death rates, age distribution, immigration and emigration, labor force, employment and unemployment, wages and salaries, areas under different crops, agricultural holdings, livestock population, livestock products, livestock trade, forestry, fisheries, small-scale and handicraft industries, building construction, electricity, wholesale and retail trade, price indices, road transport, education, health, personal income, and housing."

The game of guessing Africa's population was a very old one. In the eighteenth century a widely accepted estimate was that Africa had 150 million people. One hundred years later the pendulum swung; estimates, based mainly on travelers' reports, fell as low as 40 million. This was the period when large areas of Africa were almost depopulated by slave raids. Toward the end of the nineteenth century, there was a sharp upward revision based upon testimony from a respected and eminent source. The famous explorer, Sir Henry M. Stanley of "Dr. Livingstone, I presume" fame, estimated the population of Africa to be 180 million.

The colonial powers, especially Great Britain, had made attempts at censuses in various countries. In the nineteenth century, there were enumerations in some of the provinces of the later Union of South Africa. In the rest of Africa, census taking did not begin until the twentieth century. These later efforts have one thing in common—they were all almost total failures. *There was not a single census during the colonial period that did not turn out to be a gross undercount of the population.*

The history of these censuses is instructive in trying to understand part of the heritage of the newly independent nations.

In 1911 there was a census of Northern Nigeria. No special preparations had been made for it. The results of the census were forwarded to the Secretary of State for Colonies in England on a single sheet of paper. This was for an area that then had a population that was probably close to 20,000,000.

Ten years later Great Britain adopted a policy of decennial censuses for its African territories. There were counts in that year and another series in 1931. Those scheduled for 1941 were postponed because of World War II. Some were taken after the war, in 1948 and 1952.

The British geographer and authority on African populations, R. Mansell Prothero, analyzed the results of the 1931 censuses. In discussing the official estimates of the error of the census, he wrote, "However, neither the provincial Census Officers nor the Census Superintendent seem to have considered the possibility of the error being in excess of the actual population."

This statement was not as outrageous as it may sound. The 1952 census of Western Nigeria, under British auspices, estimated the population to be about 4,600,000. In 1963, after independence, the Nigerian census counted almost 10,300,000 people in this area. The same census of 1952 in the eastern region had an error of at least 34 percent. The 1952 census in the northern region showed a population of about 16,800,000; in 1963 it was almost 30,000,000. With all allowances for a high rate of increase in population, the undercount was still extraordinarily high.

One of the sharpest shocks experienced by the independent Nigerian government came when it discovered that instead of a population estimated at 30,000,000, it was actually responsible for about 55,000,000 people.

Colonial census taking was so erratic that in 1948 the East African Statistical Department, a British institution, did not know whether the populations of Zanzibar, Kenya, Uganda, and Tanganyika were rising or falling. A conference of African statisticians, of whom there were only a few dozen on the entire continent, in 1957 stated, "No African censuses can be classified as being in all cases universal, nominative, and simultaneous."

The failure of these censuses was due in part to the widespread superstitions about being counted, the suspicions about the motives of the colonial administrators, and the ignorance of the counters and the counted. The population was almost entirely illiterate with the result that there were not enough enumerators available. The administration, on the other hand, was incredibly ignorant of the country it governed. But the fundamental reason for failure was simpler. It was just not important for a colonial administrator to know the size of the population and its composition.

One way in which the unimportance of census data revealed

itself was in the consistent failure to provide enough money to collect it.

Professor William O. Jones of Stanford University in 1955 described census efforts as follows: "Administrative budgets in the colonies have tended to be tight, with little money available to support even the most elementary statistical services. There has never been a census of population. . . . Estimates of the population . . . are usually built up from reports of District Commissioners on tour. The population estimates made from 'tour counts' are very rough indeed and during the years to which the study applies there had been very little touring."

Exactly how tight the budgets were was disclosed by J. R. H. Shaul of the Central African Statistical Institute. The 1948 census of all of central Africa was to be done by a sample of 2,561 villages out of an estimated total of 23,270. Aside from the fact that the exact number of villages was never known, that many were forgotten and others omitted, the intriguing statistic is this: The entire outlay, including analysis, for a census of a large part of a continent was about $16,000!

In sharp contrast was the expenditure by Ghana for its 1960 census, the first after independence. To count about 7,000,000 people, the government spent about $850,000, not including the services of foreign experts.

During the years of England's rule in India, certain stereotypes developed about the British civil servant there. The picture was not flattering. He was shown as a man striving desperately to create "a little bit of England" wherever he was. His life centered around his "club," completely isolated from the Indian people. He did not bother to learn the language, and what he observed about their customs amused him.

Africa was a less desirable place of service than India. Undoubtedly it attracted a less competent official. Since the environment was also more hostile, the isolation of the British was more complete. This fact and the lack of interest in census data brought about some glaring errors of planning.

A British author, R. Mansell Prothero, wrote about the 1952 census of Northern Nigeria, the last before independence, as follows in his *Population Census of Northern Nigeria 1952; Problems and Results:*

"The *Census Handbook* for the use of enumerators was most unrealistic in suggesting that maps should be drawn to assist enumerators in delimiting their areas. There are virtually no maps showing the boundaries of Village Areas and it can be safely said that none of those which exists is accurate. In any case the suggestion ignored the inability of the majority of enumerators to understand a map even if one could be provided."

In addition, the rainy season was misjudged in many areas.

Perhaps the shortcomings are best summarized in the words of Jonathan Swift, the early eighteenth century satirist:

> ". . . *geographers, in Afric maps,*
> *With savage pictures fill their gaps,*
> *And o'er unhabitable downs*
> *Place elephants for want of towns.*"

Had colonial efforts been well planned and generously financed, there would still have been great obstacles to complete enumeration of the African people. Difficulties of transport and communication would have remained. Superstitions had deep roots. The suspicions of the people as to the motives for counting them could not easily have been overcome, given the heritage of colonialism. The almost universal illiteracy was a serious problem even to post-independence census planners.

It is difficult for many to comprehend the extent of illiteracy on most of the African continent and the problems that it creates. The definition of literacy is, in most cases, a very flexible one. It includes many with a very limited ability to read and write any language. Despite the loose definition, in most African countries more than 90 percent of the population is illiterate. Attendance at school is the exception, rather than the rule. Robert K. A. Gardiner pointed out that, in the 1960's, "only 2 countries—South Africa and the United Arab Republic—counted more than seven students per 10,000 inhabitants. In the United States, the corresponding figure was 210."

Attendance at school does not necessarily produce literacy. Some children attend religious schools, especially Moslem, where the main emphasis is not upon teaching reading and writing. Others, in state or Christian missionary schools, leave before they have acquired any language skill. Still others, who had once reached some degree of literacy, lose it because of a lack of libraries or reading material.

As a result of the widespread illiteracy, problems multiply. In any enumeration it is impossible to ask the people to fill in all or part of a census schedule by themselves, as is done in many Western countries. Therefore, in proportion to population, more house-to-house enumerators are needed. But, due to the illiteracy, *fewer* are available. An additional difficulty arises from the fact that a really literate person is usually employed in a responsible position. He cannot be released for census work without sacrifice.

The shortages were even more extreme at higher levels, especially of experts who could plan, administer, and analyze a census of population. In the 1950's, as stated earlier, there were only a few dozen statisticians on the entire African continent. This is fewer than can be found at any large American university. After independence, some African nations discovered that they had less than several dozen college graduates in *all* fields.

The new nations had to call for outside assistance in planning their first censuses and economic development. The United Nations, the United States Bureau of the Census, and many other agencies sent experts throughout the continent. The *New York Times* reported in 1967, "The Algerians, in a gesture of impartiality, asked both the Soviet state planning agency and the International Bank for Reconstruction and Development to make surveys of development possibilities. But a Cabinet minister concedes that the basic statistics needed for long-range planning either do not exist or are unreliable."

The basic illiteracy included unfamiliarity with numbers as well as with words. Birthdays and ages, among other numbered things, were seldom known. This created special problems. In the Nigerian census of 1963, after independence, the official instruction booklet for census officers contained the following:

"A list of national historical events will be included in *Instructions to Enumerators* and these events may help the enumerator in estimating a person's age. A list of more local events at provincial and divisional level would be useful and should be issued to enumerators if the provincial and divisional authorities have time to prepare them."

In 1952, Professor J. E. Goldthorpe was teaching a freshman class at Makerere College, the University College of East Africa in Uganda. Forty-nine members of his class wrote essays on the topic: "Describe the difficulties of doing a census, and maintaining birth-and-death registrations, among your people. Suggest how they may be overcome."

The young men came from twenty-two tribes in what were then Tanganyika, Zanzibar, Kenya, Uganda, and Nyasaland. Although now only freshmen, eight of the forty-nine students had acted as enumerators in the 1948 census series. Their essays form a remarkable record, on the part of the enumerated, of the obstacles to census taking created by poor transport, illiteracy, superstition, and suspicion.

In their essays, thirty-six of the forty-nine discussed the nature of the problems arising from superstitious fears, and a report of this project was carried in an article by Professor Goldthorpe in *Population Studies.*

One student, a member of one of Africa's larger tribes, wrote, "Amongst the Kikuyus, counting people is superstitiously considered a terrible thing. The parents think that the children would die if they were counted, and they normally abstain from strict veracity when census questions about their families or ages are presented to them."

The most frequently mentioned factor interfering with census taking under a colonial system was suspicion of the motives for conducting the count. It was cited by forty-two of the forty-nine freshmen.

Professor Goldthorpe presented his own views. ". . . unhappy memories of events in the not-too-distant past still tend to create suspicion of the Europeans' motives. . . . Indeed, fear of the further alienation of land is possibly the major political factor in the whole East African situation at the present time."

Many essayists wrote about the fears encountered everywhere in the world in earlier times that the census would be used for military recruitment and taxation. There had been serious riots in Nigeria because the people feared that a colonial census was a step toward increased taxation.

The suggestions for change included, most often, broader educational opportunities, improved transport, propaganda as to the real motives for census taking, and the use of native census officers. After making these suggestions, one student added, "At present any enthusiastic person fails because the bulk of the people would shout at him rudely telling him that he was 'determined to sell them to the Europeans.'"

Deeply rooted suspicions lingered on after independence in many countries. The Algerian government had to assure its people that no harm would follow the answering of census questions. The instructions to enumerators stated, "For those who tend to distrust official interrogations, there is assurance that nothing they say will be used in evidence against them." This assurance was repeated on the schedule itself, with the exact provision of the law that protected the enumerated person.

After independence certain suspicions, although not new, became more prominent. In Nigeria, for example, many literate Ibo tribesmen lived and worked in the north, in industry and government. Their tribal homeland, however, was in the southern part of the country, called the eastern region. In 1967 this area seceded and formed the independent state of Biafra. Civil war followed. Ibo tribesmen could not be used as enumerators in the north because of the suspicion and hostility of local tribes, mainly Hausa. Such intertribal suspicion was not limited to Nigeria.

The experiences cited above are mainly from British colonial experience. This was deliberate because, by and large, the British were the "best" administrators. In the colonial territories of other countries, enumerations, illiteracy, suspicions, and other factors discussed above were not better and frequently worse.

THE FIRST CENSUS OF THE
REPUBLIC OF THE SUDAN

In industrialized societies, it was said, a population census is an inventory of its human resources. At this stage in history, the periodic census seldom reveals startling changes. In the United States, for example, trends that began in the past usually continue. The urban population rises; the rural declines. The proportion of people engaged in agriculture diminishes further. More people are going to school and for a longer time. Elevator operators are disappearing; computer programmers are increasing rapidly. For the most part, only the statistician and demographer sense the real drama and excitement in the census results. The people join in the excitement only when a truly historic event is revealed, such as when the population of California passed that of New York, or, on November 20, 1967, when the Bureau of the Census estimated that the population of the country had passed the 200 million mark.

The taking of a first census in a newly independent African nation is an altogether different matter. Its primary purpose is usually the allocation of seats in the national legislature. But it is also a human inventory, often with saddening overtones. It is as if a man had suddenly undergone a sharp change in the conditions of his life; with merciless honesty he must evaluate the resources with which he must face the future.

A country's first shock is to realize that it does not even have the means to analyze itself; strangers must be called in to assist. The results themselves show only enormous shortages—in skills, in literacy, in every human resource except sheer number. Their first census disclosed to the Nigerians that they had to provide for about 55,000,000 people rather than the 30,000,000 or so that they had anticipated. Their first census showed Sudanese leaders that, considering the extent of illiteracy and the current rate of school construction, it would take five hundred years to provide each child with a place in school!

Equally grim facts have been disclosed by virtually every first census in an underdeveloped country.

The first census of the Republic of the Sudan was not significantly different from that in other developing countries. It will be discussed in some detail to illustrate the difficulties and complexities of a first-time national self-appraisal.

Like a giant presence, the Republic of the Sudan dominates the eastern part of Africa. It sprawls over almost one million square miles, the largest country on the continent and the tenth largest in the world. Because of its central position, in the past it was often referred to as the "crossroads of Africa."

The land is not very hospitable. Vast desert covers the north and northwest. Treeless plains are the landscape of much of the central part. The south is, in large part, wooded savanna, tropical in climate, uninhabited over vast areas. In all, almost a quarter of the country is uninhabited.

One of the chronic problems of the Sudan is water, both in its lack and in its sudden, overwhelming abundance. Large areas of the country receive virtually no rainfall; in others, the earth does not retain what little there is. Elsewhere, except for coastal areas along the Red Sea, more than 75 percent of the annual rainfall comes down during the three summer months in thunderous cloudbursts. It creates widespread floods and forces villagers to abandon their homes. Little of the rainfall is captured, so that later in the year there may be water shortages in the same places.

Water is the dominant factor in the life of the people. As many as one of every seven Sudanese is wholly nomadic, traveling with family and cattle in search of water. Others become nomadic for a period each year when existing water has become depleted. Some agricultural tribes, in a cycle that repeats itself in five- to fifteen-year intervals, abandon home and village entirely and settle elsewhere. It is estimated that from 40 to 50 percent of the Sudanese are nomadic to some degree.

There is ample room to roam in this immense land. The population density of the Sudan, about ten people per square mile, is among the world's lowest. It is about one-fifth the world average. The country is mostly rural, with four main urban concentrations: Khartoum—the capital—Khartoum North, Omdurman, and Port Sudan on the Red Sea. There are also scattered towns that serve primarily as market places. Most people live, however, in what were called, during the first census, "well-defined villages" or in clusters of widely separated homesteads called "tukls." In addition, there is the nomadic population that is either on the move or in small tribal groups temporarily gathered at well-established watering places.

The population of the Sudan is composed of about six hundred distinct tribes, with additional subtribes. These, in turn, can be classified into about sixty broader tribal groupings. Approximately two-fifths of the tribes are Arabic. In addition to the diversity of tribes, there is a great diversity of languages. Although at least half of the Sudanese speak Arabic to some extent, there are more than one hundred distinct languages spoken in the country. Most of them have never been written down in a script of their own; others have been set down in some formal arrangement by Christian missionaries. These facts were officially established by the census of 1955–1956.

There is a fundamental division in the Sudan between the Moslem, Arabic-speaking North and the partly Christian, partly pagan South. Today, to refer to the inhabitants of the Sudan as "the Sudanese people" does not have any real significance. There does not yet exist a population with a common language, culture, and heritage, where one inhabitant feels a sense of kinship with another regardless of where he makes his home.

The Sudan has a long and fascinating history, but for many centuries the record is shrouded in mist. However, from 1820–1885, Egypt administered the Sudan as part of the Ottoman Empire. The Sudanese resisted this foreign domination, and there are records of many revolts, all crushed mercilessly. Those that resisted most successfully were the nomadic tribes who never accepted Egyptian rule. Toward the end of this period, however, many Sudanese had entered the army and government.

In the 1880's, new forces emerged that were to play an important part in molding modern Sudan. A religious leader, titled "The Mahdi," appeared and won many followers. The Mahdists, as they were called, advocated a return to a primitive form of Islamism and the ousting of all foreigners. At this time, a fabled figure known to history, novels, and movies as Gordon of Khartoum offered his services to Egypt to fight the Mahdists.

By 1885, the Mahdists were powerful enough to attack and occupy Khartoum, the capital. In the battle, Gordon was killed. But the British, who had earlier established their power over Egypt, soon dominated the Sudan. The first governor general was another famous Englishman, Lord Kitchener. British domination continued until independence in 1956.

As in many other parts of the world, after World War II Sudanese demands for independence became more insistent. Events now moved rapidly. In 1948, an Executive Council with Sudanese participation and a Legislative Assembly were established. Three years later, local government was made more democratic. In 1952, Egypt declared its support of the Sudan's right to self-determination. And, one year later, Britain and Egypt agreed that the Sudanese should have a choice between union with Egypt and independence. The Sudanese voted for the latter. During this period, Sudanese affairs became their own responsibility. On January 1, 1956, independence was proclaimed. The Republic of the Sudan was born.

In the interval, the Sudanese leaders had been forced to ask themselves: How many are we? What are our people like? What skills do we possess? How old are we? How many among us can read and write? How many of our people have ever been to school? What myths and superstitions do they believe in? How many farm and how many raise cattle? How many work outside a farm, and what do they produce? How many nomads roam the land? What tongues do we speak, and what kinds of homes do we inhabit? What gods do we worship? In sum, who are we?

Not one of these questions then had an answer!

Never in its history had there been a count of the people of the Sudan. Guesses had been made by nineteenth century explorers and colonial officials. In 1905, based upon highly unreliable birth and death records, there was an estimation of the population of Khartoum. Then, in 1944, for the purpose of establishing a food rationing system in Omdurman, the largest city, a population estimate was made. Within the next ten years, counts were attempted in limited areas for a variety of purposes.

There was recognition of the need for a census in the late 1940's, but the planning was left to two inexperienced officials as a spare-time assignment. In 1952, with independence assured, a decision was made. The responsibility for planning a census was assigned to the Department of Statistics of the Ministry for Social Affairs. One can imagine the sense of excitement and anticipation.

But reality had to be faced. Nowhere in the Sudan were there professional experts to plan, conduct, tabulate, and analyze a census. Only about one person in ten past the age of about twelve had *ever* been to a school for *any* length of time. But this "one out of ten" was not a literate group. Many were in and out of school for very brief periods. Others attended religious schools, where reading and writing were not taught. Still others were once literate but, without exposure to any kind of reading matter, again became illiterate. In the Sudan there are large areas where over 99 percent of the boys and girls never attended any school. In all, about 3 percent of the population may be regarded as having a minimum level of literacy.

Under such conditions, a really literate person is very much in demand and may not be readily available for census taking. Foreign experts had to be recruited.

The Director of the Department of Statistics, C. H. Harvie, was British. Professor Karol J. Krótki, an internationally known expert of Polish birth and British citizenship, became Controller of the Census. In addition, there were Egyptians, Indians, Swiss, an Anglo-Burmese, an Austrian, a Dutchman, and men of various other nationalities. All were under contract to the Sudanese government, not the United Nations.

Working with the foreign staff were four Sudanese professionals. Other lower-ranking Sudanese were invited to participate in the planning.

The staff of experts made two fundamental decisions. The first was that the census would be taken on the basis of a sample rather than a complete enumeration of the country. The second was that, before the main effort in 1955, there would be an enumeration of selected areas of the Sudan. This limited count, started in 1953, came to be known as the Pilot Census.

In the world of demographers, the Pilot Census attracted more attention than did the wider count that began two years later. This was undoubtedly due to its dramatic aspects. A newly independent country, poor in material and technical resources, about which very little was known except its poverty, was on the threshold of self-discovery. But the obstacles were formidable.

The Pilot Census and the later national sample census of 1955–1956 will be treated as two phases of the same project. Areas that were enumerated in the Pilot Census were not included in the later sample.

There were important reasons for the decision to count a sample rather than the entire population. Tribal loyalties are deep in Sudan. There is also a widespread fear of strangers. Therefore, enumerators would have to be recruited locally. The enormous variety of languages reinforced this. In addition, a country as poor as Sudan could not afford to pay and transport over its vast territory the army of enumerators that would have been necessary for a complete count. But, more compelling than these was the reason given by Dr. Krótki, who said, "In certain areas in Sudan the available number of literate enumerators is so small, that it would take them years to accomplish a full count census."

The use of a sample was not a statistical compromise. It was felt that it would probably result in a more accurate estimate of the population. Since these estimates were to be used as a basis for apportioning seats in the national parliament, they had to be acceptable to many factions in the country. Elsewhere in Africa, where an attempted full-count census taken with limited resources was suspected of having been rigged in favor of one group, rioting and loss of life occurred when the results were announced.

The Pilot Census aimed to achieve the following goals:

1. Test the headquarters organization in Khartoum and in the field.
2. Train a corps of supervisors and enumerators.
3. Test the census questionnaire. Into how many of the Sudan's languages should it be translated? Did the questions have meaningful answers?
4. Determine how long it would take to count a given number of people; at what cost?
5. Find out the time of year that was best for enumeration in different parts of the country.
6. Make a preliminary classification of tribes; estimate how many there might be in the country.
7. Learn about the superstitions and objections to being counted that existed; how widespread was the fear of strangers?
8. Obtain answers to some technical problems of sampling; determine desirable size of sample for the later national count.

The Pilot Census was to be a training ground, but it developed a life of its own. It became an important historical event.

The legal justification for the enumeration was identical to the constitutional provision that is the basis of the American census: to apportion seats in the national legislature. Parliamentary districts were to be drawn approximately equal in population. They were also to be shaped so that no tribe would be divided. As a by-product, boundaries were also to be drawn for local government districts. For these reasons a person was to be included in the count of the area where he lived rather than where the enumerator happened to find him.

The census results were also supposed to serve the purpose of intelligent economic planning, as they do elsewhere in the world. The Sudan, hoping to attract foreign investment, had to have information about the size and composition of its population. Its rate of growth was completely unknown.

At this time, the best estimate of the Sudan's population was 8,750,000. This turned out to be wrong by about 17 percent. A similar error for the United States would underestimate the population by about 35,000,000 people!

Among industrialized nations, many characteristics of the way of life that are essential to a successful census are taken for granted. It is assumed that maps exist, that villages and streets have names and houses numbers. None of this was true for most of Sudan. The country was not unusual in this respect. Labels were pasted on enumerated dwellings. But nomads were enumerated and then vanished.

Another distinction between the two worlds is in the use of numbers as an accepted part of daily life. In industrial countries, aside from schooling, people go shopping, make and receive change in some currency, dial telephone numbers, and pay the bills for doing so. In the Sudan, these activities are virtually unknown outside the few cities. The people live outside a money economy, which means that they do not trade or sell for money; exchange is in the form of barter. Numbers play little part in their lives.

When asked to report in terms of number, such as stating their age, or the date of birth of a family member, or the year someone died—common census questions—they are at a loss. Add to this number problem the fact that births are seldom recorded and deaths almost never. Such questions do not relate to their experience.

In Western societies, family relationships follow a clearly defined pattern. When one says "my cousin," the relationship is understood in Canada as in Norway. In Africa, they are more complex and do not follow Western patterns. Also in the Sudan and elsewhere, the situation is further complicated by the existence of polygamy and the inheritance of a dead brother's wife. The word "brother" itself cannot be translated literally into English. The Sudanese word has a more general meaning. Thus, in a universal census question—the relationship of members of a household—an enumeration based upon Western tradition and experience creates problems.

The same complexity occurs in asking a man his name. When an American says he is "John Henry Taylor," his given, middle, and family names are easily distinguished. It is expected that he will always spell "Taylor" in the same way, as will his wife and children and his son's children. If he decided to change the pattern, he would run into trouble with any license renewal, with Internal Revenue, and a host of other agencies. He might not even be able to cash his paycheck.

But in the Sudan, except perhaps in university circles, the pattern of names depends upon the occasion or circumstances or to whom it is being told. The order changes. Names of relatives are added or dropped. There is no family name in the Western sense. Children may go for a long time without any given name. The spelling of a name, if it is known at all, varies from time to time or with use. There has never been a need for the kind of precision that others never question.

A more fundamental difference between the two types of societies is worth considering. In industrialized societies, the idea of a census could be "sold" to the people in the name of progress. This is a word to which most people respond. In large parts of the Sudan, this appeal often had the opposite effect. They were told, for example, that a census would help to determine where schools were needed. But, since most schools were boarding schools, the people were afraid that their children would be taken away from them, that their loyalty to tribal ways and customs would be affected.

The temptation is strong in the first census in a country such as the Sudan to attempt to find out everything, to erase centuries of ignorance in one mighty effort. However, reality had to be faced. There were only a limited number of census takers, many of only elementary literacy themselves. The population they would visit would be overwhelmingly illiterate, frightened, indifferent, or hostile. Each interview was likely to require a great deal of time, especially in view of the language differences and the need for translation.

The census planning staff decided upon the following questions as an essential minimum:

1. *Number* (to be assigned in sequence)
2. *Name*
3. *Father's name*
4. *Grandfather's name*
5. *Relationship to head of household*
6 and 7. *Nationality, tribe, and country of origin*
8. *Number of months in village or with sheikhship during last 12 months*
9, 10, 11, and 12. *Place of birth: country, province, district, town, or village*
13. *Sex*   14. *Married or single*   15. *Number of wives*
16. *Primary occupation*   17. *Secondary occupation*
18. *Highest school attended.*
19. *Age* (in one of the 4 or 5 groups, depending upon sex)
20, 21, 22, and 23. *Children:*

       All live births
       All live births during last 12 months
       Died during last 12 months:
         Of above, when still under 1 year

24. *Language spoken at home*
25. *Number of persons in family who died during last 12 months*
26. *Whether on the tax list of another sheikh*
27. *Whether on the tax list of this sheikh*

Although these are basic census questions with a Sudanese orientation, they turned out to be too ambitious. The results of some were unreliable or completely useless. Sometimes the fault lay with the enumerators who brought their own prejudices to bear upon the answers. In others, especially when their women and children were involved, the answers reflected common male biases and superstitions. The responses became vague and unreliable. In many cases, people did not know the answers but were too ashamed to say so.

The question of "household"—what it is, where it is, the people who make it up—is basic to a census. In countries with a tradition of census taking, it presents minor problems for special groups. But, in the Sudan, where the definition had to take into account nomadism, polygamy, inheritance of wives, and other customs that are part of the way of life, this was the official definition of a household: "Any family group who share the same cooking pot, including all its servants (but not employees sharing another cooking pot) and all boarders and visitors, provided they have slept the night before within the premises of the household under enumeration."

It may be interesting to note that in the census of 1870 in the United States, a "family" was defined as follows: "Under whatever circumstances, and in whatever numbers, people live together under one roof, and are provided for at a common table, there is a family in the meaning of the law."

In 1960, the American census definition of a household was still not entirely independent of the kitchen and cooking facilities.

The Sudanese definition was satisfactory for some of the population, but tribal customs are so varied that many changes had to be made. Some were made during the interviews to take into account local customs. The examples that follow indicate some of these.

In northern Sudan a newly married wife usually remains with her parents and shares their cooking pot. Soon after marriage she is allowed to prepare simple meals. Her responsibility increases until, after about a year, she is allowed to cook for herself entirely. If she has gone to live with her husband before this, she often returns to her parental home to give birth to her baby. She and the baby then live with the grandparents for a time. During this period, she goes home to cook her husband's meals.

Of which household are she and her child members?

In other parts of Sudan, the male members of a family eat together by age groups. The groups are made up of the children under seven years, those from seven years to puberty, adolescents who have acquired their tribal markings, and the grown men. The household was clearly defined but not by cooking pot.

When a husband and father dies, his son, brother, or uncle may inherit his wife and children. They move in with their new "father" and share his cooking pot. In African society, this is a form of social security, but it complicates census taking.

The practice of polygamy provided other problems. A man with five wives, for example, could shelter them all under one roof. If he were wealthy, he could maintain a separate home for each. Whatever his style, by custom each wife is entitled to her own cooking pot. Of which household is the husband a member?

The decision was that he would be considered head of the household of his most recently acquired wife. But this did not go unchallenged. It was pointed out that wealthy men often took additional wives solely for prestige. Therefore, the argument ran, he should be counted as head of the household where he kept his pillow.

One would imagine that the simple choice "male or female" could not present any difficulty. But pairs such as male-female, man-woman, boy-girl, and son-daughter that are specific in the West have subtle shades of meaning in many African countries. Often, the meanings of pairs depend upon age.

In the Bari language, a common pair of words equivalent to male-female began with the same letter of the alphabet. And there was no room on the form to write out the words.

Problems with "name" were almost endless. Most people had never had a need to write their names and could not spell them. This became the responsibility of the enumerator. The order of names changed with the circumstances. In Arabic, a man might decide to add the names of ancestors to his own. A woman did not always take her husband's name upon marriage. She might use her father's name or her grandmother's. But she would never use both simultaneously. Within some tribes the names of members often sounded alike. An enumerator not familiar with the tonal shadings might think them identical. Or, he might introduce difference where none existed.

Moslem men were reluctant to mention the names of female members of the family. In the town of Tokar, for example, it was almost impossible to obtain the names of the women. In the rare case where a Moslem woman would even talk to an enumerator in the absence of her husband, she would only refer to him as "he."

The problems of spelling and writing answers in a land of many languages, few of them written, carried over to almost every question. Under "town of birth," for example, there appeared these entries: Lalanga, Leilang, Lohilang. No one could say whether they were three different places or the same place spelled in three ways.

One can imagine the difficulties of trying to arrange Sudanese names in alphabetical order!

The United States encountered similar problems in early enumerations of the Indians. The enumerator was asked to record the following:

1. Indian name
2. English translation of Indian name

These were his instructions: "The spelling of the Indian name will be according to the alphabet provided in the 'Introduction to the Study of Indian Languages' furnished to the enumerator."

Census questions requiring numerical responses created even greater difficulties. Ages or dates of birth were hardly common knowledge. To complicate matters, there is no uniform calendar in the Sudan. Depending upon the area, its history, and its religious composition, the Mohammedan, Coptic, or Roman calendar may be in use. Only the few educated people are familiar with it, except for the religious holidays.

In order to simplify matters, broad age groups were established, and the head of the household was to answer for his family. These were the groups:

Male	Female
1. Under 1 year	1. Under 1 year
2. 1 year to under 5 years	2. 1 year to under 5 years
3. 5 years to under puberty	3. 5 years to under puberty
4. Over puberty	4. Over puberty but not past childbearing age
	5. Past childbearing age
	6 (instead of 4 or 5). Over puberty, exact category not specified

Within these broad groups, some exercise in numbers was still necessary. And where the requirement was most demanding, at the separation at five years of age, the results turned out to be most unreliable.

The enumerator was instructed how to attempt to overcome the problem of determining age. He was told to try to gather the entire household around him. In this way, one member might refresh another's memory. Where there were infants, he was told *not* to ask, "How old is the baby?" but to ask perhaps, "Was the baby born at exactly this season last year?" The hope was that a time relationship to an event or an agricultural cycle might be established. If there were still no agreed-upon answer, he was to use the baby's ability to walk as a guide!

Puberty is regarded as the beginning of sexual maturity. In tribal life this is a highly significant stage of growth and not likely to be mistaken. On the average, it takes place several years earlier in girls than in boys. For example, in English Civil Law, it is set at twelve years for girls and fourteen for boys. But, in either sex, there can be several years' variation in a population. Thus, in the Sudanese census, these classes represent a stage in the life process rather than an age.

Few women would admit that they were past the age of child-bearing; nor would their husbands. Dr. Krótki later stated in his report, "The question of past child-bearing is a very delicate one and asking it, in most cases, caused offense. However, it was usually possible to find out the correct answer discreetly from neighbors."

The questions on "primary and secondary occupations" have their roots in the industrial countries. There is, however, little specialization in the Sudan. A family most often consumes what it produces, or engages in barter. A seminomadic family may grow crops for part of the year and then move out with its herd. On what basis, then, was a man to determine his primary and secondary activities? The time spent on them? The value in money? It was decided that the man himself would decide on whatever basis he wished.

The measure that was sought from the responses to these questions was the number of people who were "economically active or productively employed." And the starting point was the age of five! At that age, boys not only help in the fields but also work as full-time shepherds or goatherds. The census disclosed that more than half the boys between the ages of five and puberty were "economically active."

Even the enumerators had difficulty with terms beyond their experience. It was found later that some women of the Dinka tribe had been classified as "professional and administrative" workers. Since the Dinka are a rather backward tribe whose women almost never attend school, this classification caused some surprise. Investigation showed that they were witch doctors and rainmakers. In other tribes, the midwives were classified as "professional" workers. In Sudanese society these people occupy respected places.

This incident again recalls experiences in the early enumeration of the American Indians. Enumerators in the census of 1880 were told, that "Special attention is to be directed to reporting 'medicine man,' as it is the only occupation among Indians resembling a profession in civilization."

The planning staff had to decide which areas of the country to include in the Pilot Census. Reliable maps were almost nonexistent. Available lists of people, such as the tax lists of local sheikhs, were expected to be incomplete and out of date. This expectation was fulfilled.

The selection of areas should have been on a random basis, giving each area an equal probability of being chosen. But one of the aims of the Pilot Census was to get a "feel" of the country, to obtain clues to its diversity of people and languages and customs. Therefore, the selection was not made on the basis of strict statistical theory. The selected areas were intended to represent a cross section of the country. They included a town, nomadic as well as agricultural people, varied tribal structures, languages, and terrain.

The governmental structure, formed long before the British came and left intact, also was a factor in the choice. The main divisions are:

> The Republic of the Sudan
> 9 provinces
> 5 districts in each province
> omodias, of varying number
> sheikhships, of varying number

An omodia may be defined as an area ruled over by an omda, who is roughly equivalent to a mayor. A sheikhship is dominated by a sheikh. The number of his subjects varies widely throughout the country. There are other spheres of authority in between. After the selection of provinces and districts, the sampling of omodias and sheikhships was random.

The one town included in the Pilot Census was to be completely enumerated. Elsewhere, the count of households was to be either complete, every other one, or one out of five. How many would be counted was to depend upon the type of living arrangements within the selected sheikhships.

For one reason or another, there were wide departures from the basic sampling plan.

Some idea of the diversity that the Sudan contains may be obtained from the chart on pages 108 and 109 that shows the selected areas and their characteristics.

After public announcement of the areas selected for the Pilot Census, there were two withdrawals. Central Nuer of Upper Nile province withdrew because of a misunderstanding that could not be settled before the census began. The Beja area of Kassala province would not participate because tribal unrest had shown itself due to superstitious fear of being counted.

The schedule for the Pilot Census was printed in three languages—English, Arabic, and Bari. Dinka and Nuer, two other widely used languages, were added for the national census of 1955–1956. Although these languages were spoken or understood by a majority of the Sudanese, provision had to be made for the more than one hundred other languages spoken in the country. The arrangement was that in such language areas, local translators, would accompany the enumerators.

The training course for the census personnel was very thorough. There was an intensive three-day course for census officers and supervisors. The subject matter was explained to them. There were also lectures on the training of the enumerators. At the completion of the course, they were given booklets that contained the material they had covered during training. Originally, the booklets were printed in English. Later, an Arabic version was distributed. However, Professor Krótki later wrote, "This proved to be of limited use because of the vagueness of technical and other terms when translated, the lack of precision in words even of generally acceptable meanings, and the tendency of translators to use different words to describe the same thing in different parts of the training program."

Areas Selected for the Pilot Census

Province	Location in Sudan	Area	Dominant tribe	Language Spoken	Used in census
Bahr El Ghazal	South	Aweil	Dinka	Dinka, Arabic	English
Kordofan	North Central	Jebels	Nuba	Arabic, tribal	Arabic
Kordofan	North Central	Kababish	Kababish	Arabic	Arabic
Northern	North	Merowe	Nubiyin	Nubiyin	Arabic
Blue Nile	East	Northern Gezira	Mixed	Arabic	Arabic
Darfur	West	Southern Darfur	Rizeigat	Arabic	Arabic
Kassala	Northeast	Tokar	Mixed	Tigre	Arabic
Equatoria	South	Torit	Latuka	Latuka	English
Equatoria	South	Yei	Bari	Bari	Bari
Kassala	Northeast	Beja	Amarari	Tigre	a
Upper Nile	Southeast	Central Nuer	Nuer	Nuer	a

a See narrative for explanation.

From Pilot Census, Republic of the Sudan, 1953

in the Sudan, 1953, and Their Characteristics

Characteristics

People live in scattered tukls. Nomadic part of year. At first, English was official language. Later, Arabic also introduced.

People live in scattered tukls. Use of Arabic is elementary.

Nomadic people with reputation of distrusting strangers.

People live near rivers and have village life. Men often away as railroad workers or servants. Little known before census about area or people.

People live in well-defined villages. Better off and more sophisticated than average. Men often work as migrants in newly developed cotton-growing areas of the Gezira.

Nomadic people with some homesteads. Area is geographically almost inaccessible.

A large town by Sudanese standards. Population changes.

It was assumed that people lived in well-defined villages. Found to live in scattered tukls.

Area has several missionary stations, and there is a degree of literacy. Only people living in scattered tukls were enumerated.

Nomadic people with weak tribal organization.

People live in scattered tukls but are nomadic part of year. During most of the year, the area is geographically inaccessible.

The enumerators were given a longer training course. Later, in evaluating the achievements of the Pilot Census, a great deal of credit was given to the effectiveness of the training program.

It was considered very important that the enumerator be a native of the area where he would work. Where two enumerators worked together, they had to be from the same tribe. Within these conditions, other qualifications, such as the level of literacy, could not be too rigid.

Many enumerators were students, some from the University College at Khartoum. Others came from intermediate schools that provide the fifth through eighth years of primary school study. Some were teachers in the unofficial subgrade schools. Many came from government offices; some were clerks in the courts or on the staffs of tribal chiefs. Any literate person who could be spared from other employment was sought as an enumerator.

But the really remarkable feature was the use of literate prisoners as enumerators. These were not, as might be imagined, desperadoes awaiting execution in death row. Professor Krótki later said of them, "It is necessary to realize that prisoners . . . were often respected members of the society. Often they were merely in breach of an alien social order, in a manner neither important nor unethical in their own society." Their use merely indicates that all resources of the country had to be drawn upon.

Women were not used as enumerators. It would have been unthinkable, in a predominantly Moslem society, for a woman to travel around alone or in the company of a male outside her immediate family. Some were later used locally in a limited way to interview other women in a post-enumeration check.

Government officials and the census planning staff realized that a united, national effort would be necessary to insure the success of the census. People in all parts of the vast country must be made aware of the undertaking to minimize fear, prejudice, and superstition.

Two major sources of difficulty were anticipated. The first revolved around the place of women in a largely Moslem society.

They are normally very much in the background. In the absence of her husband, who might be seminomadic or working in a distant place, a Moslem woman would be likely to refuse to talk to a male enumerator. She would certainly not talk about her husband in public.

Much more important were the problems expected in enumerating the children. Many superstitions center around them. In one form or another, they have to do with avoiding the "evil eye." Children under one year are often not even mentioned in conversation to avoid "endangering" them. Boys are talked about as if they were girls; boys are more desirable, and the "evil eye" is more likely to seek them out. A man with five children may say that he has three; his good fortune will then be less likely to attract misfortune. These are some of the strongly held superstitions that had to be overcome if the census was to succeed.

In a sense, the propaganda campaign began with the enumerator's training. He was urged to make the enumeration a social affair. A man should be urged to have his entire family present. This would not only create a friendlier atmosphere; it could also result in one member prompting another with a correct answer.

What often happened later was that the enumeration became a village social. Everyone gathered around the enumerator!

Another instruction was that in *no* case was he to ask a person whether his name was on any tax list. Tying the census to taxes in people's minds could only result in a lack of cooperation. Since the enumerator carried the tax lists, he could complete these entries later, perhaps with the help of the local sheikh.

For the Pilot Census, the propaganda started in low gear. Tribal leaders were told through official channels that enumerators were on their way. The official channel was often "a naked runner with a cleft stick to hold the paper in the absence of a pocket." The tribal leaders were the ambassadors between the government and their people.

Clever census takers found their own means of smoothing their way. As one suggested, "It is a good idea for the observing official [from the Statistical Department] to take along a present of smoking tobacco for the Headman."

An unprecedented technique of getting cooperation was used in Tokar, the only town to be included in the Pilot Census. The announcement of the census coincided with that for a public lottery. Prizes were to be in money or cattle. A great deal of interest was aroused. The "tie-in" sale was that the prizes would be awarded only if the winner was found to have given an accurate account to the enumerator.

The really big propaganda guns were rolled out for the national census of 1955–1956. The intensity was described by Dr. Krótki after the census:

". . . visualize the country in those twelve months . . . echoing from north to south and from east to west with the cry 'Where are the babies? They are your future. They are the hope of your beloved, newly-independent country.' This was the theme of the radio and the press, this was written by the Population Census Office into the speeches of the Ministers and Leaders of the Opposition, it was put onto the agendas of the legislature . . . of tribal gatherings. It was suggested to local notables, that whatever their problem, whether a new school, or a dispensary . . . the easiest solution lay inevitably through the reporting of all persons, particularly women and babies. Religious leaders were more cautious in their response . . . but otherwise the need for reporting babies was selling well. The fiercest anti-Khartoum politician would be disarmed when the'talk turned to babies."

Did this outpouring of men, money, and emotion yield worthwhile results? During the Pilot Census of 1953, approximately 52,000 people in 10,500 households were enumerated. They represented samples in areas with a total population somewhat under 1,500,000. The cost was about $31,200, not including the salaries of permanent employees of the Department of Statistics and machine analysis of the results.

Many of the stated objectives were achieved. The enumerators were found to be satisfactory. The census schedule was judged to be well designed and, with minor changes, would be used in the national census.

Estimates of the population based on the results of the Pilot Census for the nine districts in the sample proved how unreal earlier estimates had been. The table below shows this, as well as the incompleteness of the tax lists.

Population Estimates Before and After Pilot Census, 1953, and Percent of Population on Tax Lists

District	"Guessed" population before Pilot Census	Estimates based on Pilot Census	Percent difference	Total names on tax lists	Taxpayers as percent of Pilot Census population
Aweil	191,000	332,608	+74.1	43,553	13.1
Jebels	284,200	136,558	−52.0	26,609	19.5
Kababish	104,100	67,881	−34.8	3,473	5.1
Merowe	113,600	170,480	+50.1	55,167	32.4
Northern Gezira	368,125	357,711	− 2.8	45,149	12.6
Southern Darfur	69,900	103,260	+47.7	14,003	13.6
Tokar Town	17,500	12,451	−28.9	931	7.5
Torit	102,500	122,711	+19.7	25,137	20.5
Yei	112,700	135,372	+20.1	17,089	12.6

There were some negative findings that were no less important in planning future census activities. The most important were:

1. *Lists.* Lists of names of villages were either "incomplete, fictitious, arbitrary, outdated." Often, when a village was found, its boundaries were unknown. Some villages classed as "well-defined" turned out to contain scattered tukls. Almost all lists of names turned out to be out of date.

2. *Government subdivisions.* These, too, were outdated for census purposes. Districts, omodias, and sheikhships often lacked uniformity and real stability. All were in a state of

change. A sheikh could have less than twenty followers or thousands.

3. *Definitions.* It was impossible to define any census term that did not leave exceptions. Technical terms could not be translated in some areas. The languages in use were often primitive and basic. With an illiterate population, simple terms often became "technical." Meaningful occupational groupings were impossible in such a poorly developed economy.

4. *Post-enumeration check.* A careful post-enumeration survey provides a check upon the completeness and accuracy of enumerators' reports. In the Pilot Census, it was almost a complete failure. For one thing, it is impossible to recheck nomads. Once counted, they vanish. In some areas it had been impossible to check upon the number of children given by women. A few women were employed in the post-enumeration survey, but, especially in view of their small number, their contribution was trivial. The recheck did uncover one surprising fact. Many old people had not been counted. The very old and the very ill had simply been ignored. The feeling seemed to have been that, since they would die soon, why bother to count them? This attitude was found to exist not only among the general population but also among the enumerators as well.

Some criticism has been directed at the sampling methods of the Pilot Census—that it was poorly planned and that there were too many departures from the plan during the enumeration.

The national census took one year to complete and cost about $3,000,000, a very large sum for a poor country. On the basis of the census sample, the country's population was estimated to be 10,250,000, a considerable difference from all previous estimates. It was also learned that the rate of population growth was about 3 percent a year, among the highest in the world.

These findings alone, in a country without statistics, were very important in themselves. The rate of growth aroused a great deal of discussion. The question was whether, in a country as poor as the Sudan, such a growth rate of population was desirable. The common view among demographers was that it tended to slow down economic development. Many in the Sudan argued that, on the contrary, the growth of population would help to settle the vast unsettled areas, develop them, and contribute to economic growth.

In 1964, a commission of the United Nations agreed that, in the long run, the Sudan would need a high rate of population growth to develop the country.

The census also revealed that there were more than 570 tribes and that about 110 different languages were spoken in the country. It was found that about 93 percent of the estimated 1,565,-000 children from 7 to 14 years of age were not attending regular schools. From this followed the startling statistic that it would cost almost $1,000,000,000 to provide schools for them! At the rate of school construction then in process, this would take about 500 years.

One finding that has not been mentioned was the popularity of polygamous marriages. It was found that about 15 percent of the men over the age of puberty had more than one wife. About 4,000 men were able to afford and get along with five or more wives. Since the Holy Koran allows a Moslem no more than four wives, it may be assumed that these were not Moslems.

It is quite possible to analyze the census in the Sudan and find serious shortcomings. Such criticism could be valid. But the practical difficulties in places such as the Sudan are on a scale totally incomprehensible to anyone thinking in Western terms. Other standards must be used to judge success or failure.

A United Nations report in 1964 stated, "The success of this census was a remarkable achievement in the face of the great difficulties resulting from the vast size of the country, the cultural and economic diversity of the people, the presence of large numbers of nomads, the shortage of persons qualified to act as enumerators, and the scarcity of preexisting information on the numbers and locations of the persons to be enumerated."

In terms of *new* knowledge acquired, the enumeration succeeded. It is well to bear in mind that a huge, richly financed, carefully planned enumeration such as that in the United States provides relatively less *new* knowledge.

Although not measurable, there were other gains. The withdrawal of two areas from the Pilot Census was evidence of division within the country. The census itself became a unifying factor. The universal propaganda and the fanning out of enumerators over the entire country, all in a common cause, would tend to be a force advancing the new idea of nationhood. This was a substantial gain. The census also tended to increase the maturity of the country's leaders.

It did provide a basis for apportioning seats in the parliament. In a newly independent country, this has often been an explosive issue. It was present in the formative years of the United States. The Sudanese census provided, in this way, a measure of political stability. In a developing nation, this is a considerable gain, although one not usually found in textbooks.

Since the national census, some modest steps have been taken to improve the registration of births and deaths. Until now, the registration of births has been very spotty and that of deaths practically unknown. This is mainly true of the rural population, but the Sudan is primarily rural.

These events are supposed to be registered with an assistant registrar of the Ministry of Health. But *one* registrar may be responsible for an area of 25,000 square miles! C. H. Harvie has estimated that in some provinces, if the registrar were located in dead center, a man would have to make a round trip of 170 miles to register the birth of his child.

A step toward improving the registration of births has been to attempt to reduce illiteracy among midwives, who usually bring the child into the world. It is hoped that a rise in literacy will result in improved reporting. Almost no improvement is foreseen in the registration of deaths. It is likely to be a long time before the Sudan's vital statistics can be used as a basis for estimating the population or the rate of its growth.

Based upon the findings of the population enumeration, there were later sample censuses of income and agriculture. But there has not been another population enumeration, nor was one being contemplated by 1970.

Chapter 5

THE COMMUNIST WORLD

In a world inhabited by almost 3,500,000,000 people, more than one-third are living in countries ruled by Communist governments. Their population in 1967 was close to 1,200,000,000. The two Communist giants, the People's Republic of China and the Soviet Union, together had more than 1,000,000,000, close to 30 percent of the earth's population.

Mainland China, as many Western demographers refer to it, is by far the world's most populous country. According to most estimates, in 1967 its inhabitants had passed the three-quarter billion mark. Two of every nine persons on the earth live in Communist China. Each year it now adds about 20,000,000 persons, or more than the entire population of Canada. In the very near future, barring a major catastrophe, there will be 1,000,000,000 Chinese within its borders. The population has reached such staggering dimensions that errors of estimation or enumeration of a few million people do not make a significant difference.

The Soviet Union ranks third in the world in population, after China and India. Its population, approaching the one-quarter billion mark, is about 6.8 percent of the world's total. Almost every fifteenth person on earth lives somewhere within its vast territory.

Whatever their political differences, Communist China and the Soviet Union have much in common in their attitude toward population and its enumeration. Both arrived late on the census scene. The first Russian enumeration was not carried out until the very eve of the twentieth century, in 1897. In China there had never been a direct count of the entire nation until the Communist government carried one out in 1953. Neither nation conducts a census at regular intervals, as do other large industrialized countries of the world. The first complete census of the Soviet Union, after Communist authority had been established, occurred in 1926. Thirteen years later, in 1939, there was another. Then, following the enormous loss of life in World War II and the subsequent need to restore the economy, there was a full-scale census in 1959. A census scheduled for 1969 was postponed until 1970. In China, since the census of 1953, no plans have been announced to hold another.

Despite their enormous populations, neither the Soviet Union nor Communist China considers itself an overpopulated country. This part of the story will be discussed later.

RUSSIA: UNION OF SOVIET SOCIALIST REPUBLICS

The Russian population can only be understood in relation to the enormous territory it inhabits and the turmoil that has occurred within it for much of the twentieth century. The Russian land sprawls over one-sixth of the earth's surface, forming a massive land bridge between the Asian and European continents. Within it there is a tremendous diversity of peoples and languages as well as topography. To count people spread out over about 8.7 million square miles is a physical undertaking of great magnitude.

As a result of wars and revolutions, Russian territory has gone through many stages of expansion and contraction. However, the Russian land, like the Chinese population, is basically so vast that most changes did not make a significant difference. What did matter, over the years, was the area of effective control by the central government. This has often led to demographic confusion. Prior to the Communist consolidation of power in the 1920's, it was possible to find varying estimates of the population of "Russia." Although they differed, none was right or wrong. Each may have been an estimate for a different territorial combination.

At the time of Peter the Great (1672–1725), any reference to the "Russian people" was usually to those who lived within "the original land base," as it has often been called. This consisted mainly of the central and northern parts of western Russia. The great cities of Moscow and St. Petersburg, later Leningrad, were the focal points. After Czar Peter's death it came to be known as "Peter's realm." This territory has also been called the Russian "heartland." Professor Frank Lorimer, probably the outstanding American authority on the Russian population, estimates that the population of the country at Peter's death was about 20,000,000. About 85 to 90 percent dwelled within "Peter's realm." The Asian part of the empire contained perhaps 2 percent of the total population.

The only basis for estimating the population then, and for almost two centuries to follow, was the official list of males subject to taxation. The shortcomings of this method have been discussed. In Russia, it took many years to revise the complete tax list. Between start and finish, many were born and many died. The interval between revisions averaged fifteen years, but there was no regularity. The result was that the population *at any given time* could only be a crude estimate.

During the reign of Peter the Great, in about 1710, there was an official revision of the tax list. But the Czar rejected the results as unreliable and ordered it redone. The results were presented to him in 1724, one year before his death. This effort came to be known as the "first revision."

The "tenth revision" was made in 1859. The population in the "original land base" had more than tripled since 1724 and was estimated to be just under 60,000,000. The Asian part of the population, although still small in absolute number, had increased more than eight times. The relatively greater increase in the population residing in this part of Russia has continued into present times.

The first actual enumeration of the people of Russia was undertaken in 1897. The events leading up to that census, and some of its limitations, were discussed earlier. Whatever its faults, it was to assume an importance far beyond the dreams of the men who planned it. Before the next census would be taken, the Russian people would live through more than two decades of turmoil almost unparalleled among contemporary nations.

The unsuccessful revolution of 1905 was a dress rehearsal, in its way, for the greater upheaval to come. But it brought death and injury to some and imprisonment or exile to many. Then, World War I caused the loss of millions of Russian lives, in battle, in enemy prisons, or of war-caused wounds. The Bolshevik Revolution of 1917 completely altered the nature of the Russian state. There followed about six years of foreign intervention and counterrevolution, with death as a constant accompaniment. The chaos produced famine, and the world-wide influenza epidemic of 1918 struck a people weakened by hunger and the dislocation of life and lacking medical facilities. In 1920 a typhus epidemic swept part of the country. When the Union of Soviet Socialist Republics (USSR) was formed by the act of the All-Union Congress of Soviets on December 30, 1922, a measure of order had been restored.

At this time the borders of Russia had been drastically changed by great loss of territory. The population had been reduced by great loss of life, loss of territory, and by emigration. The *structure* of the population had been changed. Homeless people roamed over the land. Some nationalities had suffered more than others. And the enormous number of deaths was not distributed equally over the age groups but had struck some more severely than others.

The problem that faced demographers was to attempt to determine how many lives had been lost during this nightmarish period. Also, what effect had there been upon the Russian population from a long-range point of view? How many children who would normally have been born were not because men were in the army and life had been dislocated? How many people who would now be at the age of marriage and childbearing had died or had fled the country? The only base from which to make these calculations was the census of 1897.

It should be understood that an actual count of population becomes a landmark. This is especially true of a first attempt, whatever its faults. A census, once taken, can be adjusted, for example, for underreporting of infants, but it cannot be replaced by any system of estimation. There is no way to verify the results of a projection or estimate except by a census. There is certainly no way to prove that the estimate is superior to an actual count. This may help to explain the present value of the earlier enumeration.

The two men who made the most important contribution to estimating the human devastation were the Russian demographer, E. Z. Volkov, and the American, Frank Lorimer. The latter often extended the former's work. Their results, in rather close agreement, make up a fascinating story in demographic detective work. What they did, in brief, was to calculate what the population was in 1897 for the *new borders* of the Soviet Union and reconstruct the population by age and by nationality. On the basis of the reconstruction, they estimated what the population would have been under normal circumstances—in 1914, 1923, and at the time of the first Soviet census of 1926.

Professor Lorimer's conclusion was that there had been a loss of 28,000,000 people. They were distributed in the following groups:

Basis of loss	Estimated number (in millions)
Total loss	28
Military deaths	2
Civilian deaths	14
Emigration	2
Deficit of children who would normally have been born	10

One of the first acts of the new Soviet government was to transfer responsibility for registering births and deaths from the church to civilian authorities. The registration of vital events had always been poor and incomplete. But the sudden, drastic change in a country that had been deeply orthodox aroused great resentment. Without any period of transition, it was a "stupendous undertaking," as Frank Lorimer has stated.

Old ways did not die easily. However, the Soviet government placed great emphasis upon the program; there was a steady educational campaign, as well as penalties for those who did not comply. By 1926, the time of the census, the registration of vital statistics was general in the European territories of the Soviet Union.

The stress upon the accuracy and thoroughness of registration had a solid foundation. In a planned economy, Soviet experts wanted a system of continuous reporting of many aspects of life, demographic as well as economic. In its simplest and ideal form, a population can be estimated from the following formula:

Population based upon a census	+	Number of births	+	Number of immigrants	−	Number of deaths	−	Number of emigrants	=	Population at a given time

When immigration and emigration are so small that they can be ignored, the formula is simplified. Also, among demographers births minus deaths represents the *natural increase*. The formula that Soviet experts hoped to use in the future was therefore:

$$\text{Basic population} + \text{or} - \text{Natural increase} = \text{Population at a given time}$$

The vital element is the *basic population*, which must come from a census, and at the time of the introduction of the civil registration system, the only census information available came from the census of 1897. That data had almost no relation to present reality.

The Communist leaders recognized almost immediately that a census was essential. The first attempt was made in 1920. At that time, there were still battles raging within the country. The transportation system, primitive as it had been in the past, had been thoroughly disrupted by war and revolution. Much of the population had left traditional homes and was wandering over the countryside. A general air of chaos prevailed.

In addition, there was the heritage of Czarist days to contend with. The population, especially that outside the great metropolitan areas, was largely illiterate. Superstitions were many and widely believed. There were minorities with a long history of oppression by Czarist governments. As Professor Lorimer has said of some of them, "At the beginning of the Soviet period the position of the indigenous groups in Siberia was even less favorable than that of the North American Indians in the United States." Such groups were not likely to trust any authority at this stage.

Although the prestige of Lenin, the father of the Russian Revolution, was used to support the census, it was a complete failure. Hostility toward it was met in many areas. Some enumerators were killed; many were attacked. Census centers and material were destroyed. No results were ever published.

By the time of the first complete Soviet census on December 17, 1926, a large measure of stability had been established. Many governmental measures were designed to win the support of the people. Land had been distributed to the peasants, gaining their confidence. The previously oppressed nationalities had responded to promises of self-government, the free use of their languages, and the increase of educational opportunities. The unusual step was taken of assuring the population that all census information would be kept completely confidential.

The census was preceded by a tremendous barrage of publicity. The entire weight of the well-organized Communist party was thrown behind it.

All these steps did not mean that opposition was completely eliminated. Rumors were spread that the enumeration was for the purpose of increasing taxes. There were charges that it was an

ungodly undertaking. But, on the whole, there was public acceptance. There were no reported acts of violence, as there had been
in 1920. The general opinion of experts was that the census had
been well planned and carried through. The results were accepted
as reliable.

The Soviet census had the same constitutional justification that
it does in many Western democracies. Although its parliament of
that time—the Congress of the Soviets—did not have the same
role that it does elsewhere, the census was to determine representation within it. The Soviet Constitution of July 6, 1923, stated
that the *Council of the Union* was to be composed of 371 representatives. These were to be elected by the Congress of the Soviets *in proportion to the population in each republic.*

The enumerated population was 147 million. On the basis of the
calculations by Volkov and Lorimer, there would have been 175
million under normal circumstances. The shortage of 28 million,
or 16 percent of the "expected" population, reflected the loss of
more than a decade of violence, pestilence, and chaos.

A disturbing finding with great significance for the future
population was the shortage of men. Again, under normal circumstances, there would have been 98 men for each 100 women at age
30 and over. The census results showed only 88 men. In the age
bracket below this, from 25 to 29 years, there were only 84 men
for each 100 women. This meant that there would most likely be
fewer marriages, with fewer children to replace the lost population.

The Soviet Union had at that time about 188 nationalities. Of
these, Russians, or *Great Russians*, as they are often called, represented about 53 percent of the total population. Approximately 21
percent were Ukrainians. No other nationality had as much as 10
percent. The Jewish people, of whom there were about 2,681,000,
were about 1.8 percent of the population.

The census disclosed that about half the Russian people were
literate. In cities such as Moscow and Leningrad, the rate of liter-

acy was well over 80 percent; in rural areas it was considerably below 50 percent. The lowest level was found in the Asian republics, to no one's surprise. In the Tadzhik Soviet Republic, less than one person in twenty-five knew how to read and write.

The way of life of most people was still primarily agricultural, with 78 percent of the people dependent upon the land or the products of the sea. Only 18 percent of the Russian people lived in an urban environment in 1926. During the years of greatest turmoil, many peasants had left the land. Some, after leaving the army or revolutionary forces, had not returned to it. They had inflated the urban population. However, for some years prior to 1926, the government distributed land it had seized from the large landholders. There had then taken place a great movement of peasants to claim land now available to them.

The table below shows the age distribution of the Soviet population found in the census of 1926. There has been some minor adjustment for the underreporting of infants, but this has made relatively little difference.

The Soviet Population by Age in 1926
(In thousands)

Age group	Total population		Male		Female	
	Number	Percent of total	Number	Percent of total	Number	Percent of total
Total	147,608	100.0	71,336	100.0	76,272	100.0
0– 2 years	14,713	10.0	7,432	10.4	7,281	9.5
3– 7 years	17,822	12.1	8,922	12.5	8,900	11.7
8–12 years	15,473	10.5	7,830	11.0	7,643	10.0
13–17 years	17,979	12.2	8,823	12.4	9,156	12.0
18–22 years	15,044	10.2	7,253	10.2	7,791	10.2
23–27 years	12,989	8.8	5,972	8.4	7,017	9.2
28–32 years	10,312	7.0	4,823	6.8	5,489	7.2
33 years and over	43,276	29.2	20,281	28.3	22,995	30.2

From *The Population of the Soviet Union* by Frank Lorimer, League of Nations.

The Soviet people were then a young population. Almost 55 percent were under 23 years of age. Fifteen years later, when Hitler would invade the Soviet Union, the people in these age groups would provide the bulk of the defense forces upon which Soviet survival would depend.

The twelve years between the first two Soviet censuses were crowded with historic events that had important effects upon the growth of the population. Some tended to accelerate it; others, to slow it down. Government policy depended upon what had top priority during the period.

Shortly after the census of 1926, two major policy decisions were made that have become associated with the late Joseph Stalin. The first was that the economy of the country would be rapidly industrialized. The second aimed at changing the agricultural system in two fundamental respects: the small, individual farms would be transformed into huge complexes, called collective farms; and the nomads would be settled on the land. These goals were outlined in the famous Five-Year Plan, the first of which covered the period from October, 1928, to September, 1933.

Even without complete cooperation and model orderliness in accomplishing these objectives, they had important effects upon the growth of the population. Rapid industrialization meant rapid shift of people from farm to factory and city. It is a universal fact that the urban birth rate is lower than the rural. In the process of industrialization, the foundations were laid for giant new cities. Sleepy villages were suddenly transformed into great metropolitan centers by the construction of huge factory complexes. During the period of construction, and often for years afterward, living conditions were primitive. The result could only have been a higher death rate.

Of greater significance was the need to attract women into the new factories. To accomplish this, government policies were directed toward delaying the formation of families. The policies were extraordinarily effective. During 1926 and 1927, more than

6.5 million babies were born each year. This, called the *crude birth rate* by demographers, represented a rate of more than 40 infants for each 1,000 population. During 1935, although there was now a larger population, less than 5,000,000 babies were born, a birth rate of about 30 per 1,000. W. Parker Mauldin of the Population Council has said, "This represents the sharpest decline in the birth rate of any country in the world except that of Japan after World War II."

As a matter of deliberate policy, the Soviet Union was exchanging infants for industry.

The greatest resistance was toward the agricultural policy, both on the part of the individual peasant and the nomad. Most peasants had only recently come into possession of their land, as a result of land distribution after the revolution. They balked at entering huge agricultural combinations, despite threats and incentives. Many withheld their produce from the government-controlled markets; others let the crops rot in the fields. There were reports of widespread famine in 1933, especially in the southern European areas of the Soviet Union.

The nomads, mainly in the Republic of Kazakhstan and other parts of the Asian steppe, had for centuries roamed over the land with their livestock. Compelled by government policy to change their way of life, they rebelled by slaughtering their herds. This, as well as the resistance of the peasantry, led to meat and grain shortages throughout the land.

Such conditions not only do not encourage births and family building; they also lead inevitably to a higher death rate. The results of these policies were reflected in the population counted in the census of 1939, as will be seen.

Population policy began to change in 1935, and, one year later, there was a complete reversal of the earlier tendencies. Laws were enacted whose sole purpose was to encourage population growth by increasing the birth rate while lowering the death rate, especially among infants.

Although the government never gave reasons for the change in policy, some important ones stand out. By 1936 most of the opposition to the government's industrial and agricultural programs had been overcome. The first Five-Year Plan had accomplished its goals in both parts of the economy. Another had gotten under way. On the whole, life was somewhat easier. There was also some suspicion in government circles that the loss of life during the period of collectivization had been substantial. However, of far greater significance than either of these, war was in the air. Hitler had come to power in Germany, and part of his avowed program was to crush the Soviet Union. The change in population policy may have had its origin in the desire to insure a future population in the event of extensive losses.

The law of June 27, 1936, included the following sections:

1. Extra family allowances were granted for large families.
2. The number of maternity hospitals was greatly increased.
3. Expectant mothers were granted maternity leave for a period of eight weeks both before and after the birth of a child.
4. Social insurance for mothers was expanded.

In order to care for the children after their birth, there was a great expansion of child-care centers, nurseries, and kindergartens.

Divorce proceedings, which had been rather free and easy until now, were made stricter and more complicated in an attempt to strengthen family life.

The whole weight of the government, the Communist party, and its leaders was thrown into the campaign to increase the population. The propaganda was intense. It became patriotic to bear a child. Not unexpectedly, the results were dramatic. The birth rate, which had dropped to 30 per 1,000 in 1935, rose to 38 per 1,000 by 1938.

Many programs were started in the field of general health whose purpose was to reduce the death rate. In the years between the censuses, the number of persons described as engaged in "health work" was multiplied three-and-one-half times. There were now 1,267,000 such persons, mainly doctors, nurses, and technicians, as against 365,000 in the earlier year. There was a three-fold increase in hospital beds and an expansion of specialized health centers. Broad programs were started to eradicate such diseases as tuberculosis and malaria.

Another significant health factor was the greatly increased literacy of the population, which made it possible to carry out extensive programs of general health education.

The first attempt to measure the changes in population came in 1937. A full-scale census was planned, carried out, tabulated—and then completely suppressed! The only reasons ever given by Soviet authorities for throwing away the results of this great expenditure of money and manpower was that the census results were inaccurate and that there had been "ideological errors in the formulation of questions and the development of data."

According to Professor Lorimer, Soviet experts had expected to enumerate a population of about 180,700,000. Their estimate was based upon the 1926 census and the vital statistics since then. Instead, fewer than 170,000,000 were enumerated, although the exact number was never announced. (Two years later, 170,467,-000 people were counted in the 1939 census.) This may have been the source of the suspicion of inaccuracy. The "ideological errors" had to do with the content and wording of the questions dealing with occupation and social class.

The census of January 17, 1939, twelve years and one month after the first Soviet enumeration, was carefully organized and supported by a great publicity campaign. The campaign, carried on throughout 1938, often took on a strange tone. There were appeals to patriotism and there were threats. These were directed at the enumerators, as well as at the respondents. The suspicion in official circles that the results of the 1937 census were wrong would not die.

The atmosphere surrounding this census cannot be understood without an awareness of the political situation. The fear of impending war filled the world. Hitler had already taken the first of his aggressive steps. Within the Soviet Union, enemies, real or imagined, were being arrested. Most were denounced by the collective name of the "Trotskyist-Bukharinist elements." Sensational trials had taken place or were in progress. Amidst all this, the census became a political act and accuracy a political commitment.

The respondent who was "unconscientious" was threatened with punishment. So were the enumerators "guilty in divulging personal information collected in the census." This, as well as other pleas and threats, appeared in *Izvestia,* the government newspaper, during 1938. The following quotations from the same paper, collected by Drs. G. V. Selegen and V. P. Petrov, are fairly typical.

"The remaining Trotskyist-Bukharinist elements may try to harm the census, appearing in the role of subversive agitators, by spreading rumors, distorting the rules and misinterpreting the purposes of the census."—September 6, 1938

"One should know that the masked enemy may try to arouse distrust for the census. It is necessary to watch closely for their hostile machinations while this mass political work is conducted." —October 3, 1938

Citizens were urged, in the same issue, "to prevent appearance, in the role of enumerators, of some imposters, coming from the ranks of remaining criminals still at large."

It may be said that the Russians were about to count the human resources with which they would have to fight a war that they regarded then as inevitable.

The accuracy and thoroughness of the 1939 census have been widely accepted. However, in view of the tension surrounding it, one would not be likely to describe the event as a "fun thing."

The population of the Soviet Union in 1939 was 170,467,000, according to the census. As stated earlier, this was far below expectations. Many Western authorities believe that during the twelve years between censuses, the period of industrialization, collectivization of agriculture, and settlement of the nomads, there had been more than 5,000,000 deaths in excess of normal expectations. To this figure must be added the considerable loss of births.

The analysis of the 1939 census was interrupted by the outbreak of World War II. Only a few bare, descriptive tables were ever published. The results of twelve years of almost superhuman strain were reflected in the tables. In 1926, more than three out of four Russian people were dependent upon agriculture. Now the proportion was little more than one-half. Inevitably, the urban population rose—from 18 to about 33 percent in 1939.

The urban growth took two distinct forms. Moscow, for example, with 4,000,000 people in 1939, had doubled in population. The number of cities with 200,000 or more residents had increased from 12 in 1926 to 39. More significant for the future, however, was the creation of completely *new* cities in the more remote parts of the vast country. Karaganda and Magnitogorsk had grown from nothing to cities of about 150,000 people. Komsomolsk, a city constructed by 4,000 members of the Communist Youth Organization, now had a population of 71,000. All were to grow considerably in the years to come.

Dramatic changes in the level of literacy throughout the country were revealed by the census. In 1926, barely half the people could read and write; in 1939, about four out of five had acquired these skills. The most startling change was in the Republic of Kazakhstan. In 1926, less than 4 percent of the people were literate; by 1939, the percent of literate people had risen to 71.7!

Much of the increase was due to the education of women. In 1926, there had been nine literate men for each five literate women. By 1939, the ratio had been reduced to five men to four women.

An interesting disclosure by the census was the increase in the "Great Russian" segment of the population. This national group now represented 58 percent of the population, an increase from the 53 percent reported in 1926. Ukrainians, on the other hand, declined from more than 21 percent to about 16.5 percent. These changes, however, did not reflect any real differences in birth and death rates. In the Soviet census, one "chooses" his nationality; there are no objective standards. Since the census followed a period of official attacks upon Ukrainian "nationalism," many people probably thought it wiser to declare themselves as "Russian."

The Jewish people, now numbering about 3,000,000, were still about 1.8 percent of the population in this last census before the German invasion.

There were separate census tables describing the population by sex and by age but not in combination. However, Professor Lorimer was able to make a reasonable construction of such a table. The table showed, among other things, that there were now only 81 men for each 100 women in the part of the population that was at age 30 or older; in 1926, there had been 88 men. Even for the entire population, there had been a decline in the proportion of men to women. Part of the decline was undoubtedly due to the upheavals in the period between censuses. As the day of the German invasion approached, the Russians had almost 47,000,000 men between the ages of 15 and 59 upon whom to depend for duty at the front and at the factory. But an enormous responsibility would fall to the 52,000,000 women of the same ages.

At the end of World War II, Soviet demographers again faced the depressing task of estimating the dead. The actual number will, of course, never be known. It is estimated, for example, that during the German siege of the city of Leningrad alone, 1,000,000 persons, soldiers and civilians, died. In this war, civilian and military losses were equally high, often mingled. Perhaps 25,000,000 Russians lost their lives from causes traced to the war. When the loss of births is added to this figure, it may well be that the total loss of population was between 40,000,000 and 50,000,000.

Some demographers have calculated that if the Soviet Union had gone through a "normal" period of growth since its birth, its population today would be almost 100,000,000 greater than it is.

There were great internal shifts of population during the war and the immediate postwar period to further complicate any estimates. The Soviet Union gained 98,700 square miles of territory

on its western borders as a result of the war. From this area, however, about 1,500,000 million Poles left to reside within Poland's
new boundaries.

Even in the midst of war, the Soviet government began to take
steps to offset its huge losses. The first decree was issued in July,
1944. The date is significant. Any measures to increase births
would mean that the younger women would leave farm and factory, at least for some time, with a loss of their labor power. But,
one month earlier, allied armies had landed in France; Russia's
armies had reconquered its territories; and an offensive was about
to begin that would in nine months batter at Berlin. Victory appeared to be a virtual certainty.

The decree of July 8, 1944, raised family allowances substantially. Even more important in a wartorn land, food rations were
increased for pregnant women, mothers, and babies. The income-
tax rules were changed so that people with no family or small ones
had to pay more than a proportionate share.

At the end of the war, measures were introduced that would
tend to reduce the death rate as a means of increasing the population. Medical personnel were doubled, and the number of health
stations throughout the country were tripled. In addition, a campaign was begun to raise the level of general sanitation. There
was a considerable extension in public water systems to replace
the traditional village wells. Soap production was increased by 80
percent.

Expectedly, population began to rise substantially. But after a
decade or so, it settled down to a normal rate of growth for an
industrial nation. By 1958, one year before the next census, the
birth rate was 25 per 1,000 population. At the same time, the
United States had a rate of 24 per 1,000. The large Russian family
of old, especially in the cities, would soon be found only in literature. Only 8 percent of urban families now had six or more members; in 1926, about 13 percent of the families were of that size.
The general attitude toward population had changed.

Another sign of a return to normalcy was the appearance again of an important publication, the *Statistical Handbook*, in 1956. It had last appeared in 1939. It now contained the first postwar estimate of the population, which it placed at 200.2 million. Many Western demographers thus had their first insight into the enormous war losses. They had anticipated a population at least 20,000,000 greater.

The Soviet census of 1959 was identical in almost all respects to those conducted in the highly industrialized nations elsewhere in the world. The census plans were reviewed at a conference of statisticians as early as June, 1957. The proposed questions and procedures were pretested in various parts of the country during August, 1957.

The enumeration began on January 15, 1959. Eight days later, on January 22, the 500,000 enumerators had counted the 208.8 million people of the Soviet Union. One of the unique features was a complete recheck, or post-enumeration check, of all returns. A recheck of such proportions is extraordinary. One can only speculate as to the reasons. One may have been that, on the basis of the census returns, Soviet statisticians planned to make the first adjustment in the vital statistics registers in more than thirty years. Another reason may have been a desire for certainty about the size of the population in view of the huge war losses. It may also be that Soviet statisticians were still haunted by the rejected census of 1937.

War losses were reflected in several ways in the census results. Slightly more than one person out of three (34 percent) was now seventeen years or younger; in 1940, about two out of five (41 percent) were in that age category. This meant that for years to come fewer people would enter the work force than had in the past. It was a warning of possible future labor shortages.

There were in 1959 only 83 men for each 100 women. An even more shocking finding was that at age 32 and over, there were only three men to five women. This was a reflection of the tremendous war losses, greater than those of any other power involved.

Other results showed that trends whose origin was in the past had continued. The population was now almost equally divided between urban and rural. Also, of every ten Soviet citizens, three now lived east of the Ural Mountains, the geographical Asian boundary of the Soviet Union. Those citizens who declared their nationality to be "Russian" were now only 55 percent of the population, somewhat below the percent reported in 1939. Ukrainians, on the other hand, were 18 percent, an increase from the earlier 16.5 percent.

The extermination of the Jewish population in Russian areas captured by the Germans was also reflected in the census. They were now only 1.1 percent of the population rather than the 1.8 percent they had represented in 1939.

There was no general literacy question in the census. Rather, as in the United States, the aim was to find the level of "educational attainment." Only those who had not completed at least four years of school, called "functional illiterates" in the United States, were asked about their ability to read and write.

It is generally accepted that Soviet censuses and statistics are of a quality equal to any. Much of them may not be published, but that is a political decision.

The next census had been scheduled for 1969. However, in 1968 it was announced that it had been postponed until 1970 for more thorough preparation. Another reason was that a critical question had not been resolved. Population experts want to include questions relating to the birth rate. Statisticians within the Central Statistical Administration oppose this idea on the grounds that it is unnecessary and that it will prolong the census.

However the question is resolved, the census of 1970 will provide demographers with a rare treat. For the first time in history, the world's two great powers will be taking a census almost simultaneously. Their populations have been compared in the past, but always on the basis of projections. Now the results of actual enumerations may be available. Demographers throughout the world will spend many hours matching the characteristics of the two peoples for whatever significance they may contain for the future.

CHINA

In the past, population experts had as much fun estimating the population of China as radio astronomers have today in speculating about life elsewhere in the universe. The answers have been equally inconclusive. The basic cause for uncertainty in either area has been the absence of real, verifiable evidence. In such situations the imagination is free to take flight.

Ta Chen, a leading authority on China's population, has said, "Among all the historical nations in the world, China alone possesses a long and unbroken record of population estimates." But, in 1931, the Director of the Department of Statistics in China said that his country was "a land without statistics." Both were right!

The "unbroken record" dates back to long before the Christian era. Since that era there exist written records of more than one hundred registrations of the population. Between A.D. 2 and A.D. 155, there were at least ten occasions when the people were subject to enumeration. However, until the census of 1953, almost every enumeration had some limitation that brought into doubt the estimates derived from it.

In most cases, the counts were made in connection with taxation, work, military service, or some other burden to be placed upon the people. In China, as elsewhere in the world, such counting resulted in widespread evasion. Perhaps because they are a people with a long history, the Chinese developed some ingenious techniques for evading enumerations and the burdens that went with them.

At other times, emperors made it clear through their agents that they regarded an increase in population as a sign that their reign was prosperous. They were obliged with large increases, often inflated or imaginary. In some Chinese provinces, there were long periods when the population grew with the rhythm and regularity of a healthy child.

Often, differences in population within a region could be traced to inconsistent definitions. The names for various taxes, for example, changed over the years. Different groups of people became subject to them. In one case, a tax paid in actual labor service changed gradually to one paid in money, but the *name* of the tax remained unchanged. The composition and social level of the households subject to tax changed, however. The estimates of the population derived from the same tax, paid at different periods in different ways, bore no relation to one another. At times, it was impossible to state with certainty that the population had gone up or down, much less to estimate its total.

Prejudices against groups within Chinese society also affected the results of enumerations. Some excluded groups were discussed earlier. The aboriginal people in China, as in every other part of the world, were either excluded or only partially counted. The people who live on sampans, or houseboats, and form the colorful background in travel films of China were always considered inferior members of society and traditionally undercounted.

The special position of women in China made it a certainty that every past enumeration was deficient. The practice of infanticide, the killing of infant girls, until almost the present day was common in many regions. Where their deaths was not direct, they often came about early in life because of neglect. In such an atmosphere, merely understating their number would not bring criticism.

China is not only a very ancient land; it is also one with a long cultural tradition. The scholar ranked high in the social system. Since records were scholarly works, they were well preserved. Many exist from thousands of years ago. They are massive and voluminous. The three major historical records—*T'ung Tien*, *T'ung K'ao*, and *T'ung Chi*—cover periods from the eighth to the fourteenth centuries. They range in size from 200 to 348 volumes. These records summarize the existing knowledge of their times. Buried within this huge mass are estimates of the population at various times, including years prior to their writing. However, modern scholars who have studied them have found glaring inconsistencies in their population estimates.

These are some of the reasons why it was possible to say that, although China had had many population registrations, it was "a land without statistics."

The land and people of China have always had a strong attraction for Westerners. Although it was a "closed society" until about the middle of the nineteenth century, many Western adventurers, businessmen, writers, and others traveled across China. All who wrote or spoke about their experiences agreed upon one thing: the country contained an enormous population.

Professor Walter F. Willcox, a former president of the American Statistical Association, was an authority on China's population who exerted great influence upon other scholars. He was under no illusions as to the value of any of the early population estimates. In 1930 he stated quite frankly: "The outstanding fact is that no one knows what the population of China is within many millions." He attributed this to the limitations of the men working in this field whom he described as follows:

1. Westerners who had lived in China and spoke the language but who had no training in demography or statistics.
2. Westerners trained in statistics, attracted to "this puzzling and important demographic problem" who did not speak Chinese or know the customs of the country. They could not use original sources even when they suspected their existence.
3. Chinese scholars without statistical training who were attracted to the population problem as it related to political, social, or economic affairs.

Willcox added, "They [Chinese scholars] know almost as little of what Western scholars have written as the latter do of what Chinese scholars have written."

After World War II, Chinese-speaking population experts appeared in many parts of the world: Ta Chen, Professor Chiao-min Hsieh of the University of Pittsburgh, and several Americans, some working in the China Section of the Bureau of the Census. In 1959, with the publication of *Studies in the Population of*

China, 1368–1953, by Professor Ping-ti Ho of the University of British Columbia, a powerful beam of light was thrown on almost six hundred years of Chinese population records.

Professor Ho worked with original historical documents, including many local histories. His interest was in the "changing institutional context" within which past population records were assembled. This means that he analyzed the structure of the government of the time; the parts of the country it controlled; who the enumerators were and to whom they were responsible; the nature of the taxes leading to the enumeration of households; the attitude of the people to the taxes; the techniques used to evade them; the changes in definitions; the prejudices that were common; the famines, floods, pestilences, wars, and rebellions that occurred and their likely effects upon the growth of the population.

It is evident that without a knowledge of these conditions, no ancient records can be evaluated.

In theory, the Chinese people should have been readily enumerated despite their number and the vastness of the country. Mainland China is about twice as large as Europe, excluding the Soviet Union. However, its territory has been fairly stable. Parts of the mainland have been occupied by foreign powers during the last century, but real changes in territory occurred in the past only in the sparsely settled areas.

The population is concentrated. More than 95 percent of the people live in the eastern part of the country, spread over about 40 percent of China's total area. This area includes the populous coastal cities, as well as the richer agricultural lands.

Despite their number, the Chinese are a remarkably homogeneous people. About 94 out of 100 identify themselves as being of Han nationality. In China, the term "Chinese people" has more than one meaning. But a Westerner speaking of the Chinese people usually has in mind those of Han nationality. There are many minorities, but they are small in number in relation to the total population. The largest, the Chuang people, are only 1.1 percent of the total; Tibetans, less than one-half of 1 percent.

Many myths exist in the West about the Chinese language. A common belief is that there exists an enormous variety of dialects; that, although they both speak Chinese, two people from adjacent villages can hardly communicate. Actually, there are only about eight dialects that are truly distinct. Of these, what was formerly called Mandarin is by far the most common, spoken by about seven out of ten people. The term Mandarin had been associated with the emperor and then with aristocracy. After the revolution that deposed the Manchu in 1911, it was dropped. The Nationalist government renamed it the "national" language. Today, the Communists, in order not to offend national minorities, call it the "generally understood" language.

The dialect of Shanghai, called Wu, is spoken by about 45,000,-000 people. Cantonese, the dialect of the majority of American Chinese, is spoken by about 35,000,000. The remarkable thing about the language is that in its written form it is uniform everywhere.

There are also about fifty or so non-Chinese minority languages. More than half were first put into written form after the Communists came to power.

The most common religious beliefs of the people are fundamentally humanistic, or man-centered. They presented no obstacles, as Christian or pagan beliefs often did, to the enumeration of people. Chinese philosophers and religious leaders did encourage the formation of large families. According to Confucius, "to die without offspring is one of the gravest unfilial acts."

In theory, the structure of government was ideally fitted for enumerating a population, especially during imperial times. The emperor issued decrees to his ministers. They then filtered down through successive layers of the pyramid. Finally, the orders reached the villages, where, for centuries, there was a carefully calculated system of control.

When the Ming Dynasty was founded in the fourteenth century, the machinery for counting the people was established. It was known as the *li chia*. In outline it was extremely simple. A *li* was a unit of 110 households. From these, the ten heads who paid the most taxes and had the most male members were selected. These headmen formed a basic administrative unit. The remaining households formed ten *chia*, each with a headman. This structure of "ten and ten" assigned the taxes that were then paid in the form of labor service to the state.

Usually, in each self-contained community, there were widows, orphans, and others not subject to taxes. They were tacked onto other *chia* arbitrarily and given the name of "odds and ends."

In connection with the taxes, a register was kept. Copies were sent up the pyramid to ever higher authorities. The registers were supposed to be revised every ten years to reflect changes in taxes and in the number of adult males. These registers were the basis for estimating the population of the villages, the county, the province, and, finally, all of China.

The Ming emperor, T'ai-tsu, a reformer who sought a fairer distribution of labor service, developed the *li chia* system. Professor Ho says that the first registration was preceded by a ringing declaration in the name of the emperor that said, in part:

"You, officials of the Board of Revenue, will send out proclamations ordering the provincial and local authorities to get all the population . . . officially registered, and all the names of the people entered into official registers. The number of persons of each household must be written down without falsification. . . . Since my powerful troops are no longer going out on campaigns, they are to be sent to every county, in order to make a household-to-household check of the returns. Those households whose tallies agree will be treated as subjects in good standing; if they do not agree, the family will be placed on the list of those liable for military service. If it is discovered in the course of checking that some local officials have falsified the returns, those officials are to be decapitated. Any common people who hide from the census will be punished according to law and will be drafted into the army . . ."

The results of the first registration showed that in 1393 there were 10,652,789 households and 60,545,812 *mouths*, the term for persons used in China for centuries. The books in which the local records were collected for the entire country came to be known as the *Yellow Registers,* many of which still exist.

Professor Ping-ti Ho believes that because of some underenumeration, especially of the aboriginal people, the true population at that time was closer to 65,000,000.

Although the *Yellow Registers* were compiled for centuries, they quickly became useless as indicators of the size of the population. Since, in one way or another, this happened again and again in China's history, the principal reasons for the decline are worth noting.

1. The registration became more and more a tax list, with the enumeration of people merely incidental. This led to evasion of registration. Soon, the registration of women and children was all but forgotten.

2. The emphasis on the ten-year cycle made the system rigid and artificial. Artificial households were created out of the "odds and ends" as families moved, died out, or became too poor to be taxed.

3. The burden of taxes was shared by a village on the basis of tax-paying families. Ways of cheating became cooperative and ingenious. Clans joined and called themselves one household in order to share one family's tax. The rich began to pay the poor to perform their labor service. Soon, the tax changed to a money tax. Then the rich bribed local officials so as to escape paying taxes altogether.

4. As the taxes began to fall more heavily on the poor, they left the villages. Whole villages were depopulated. In other villages, a powerful patron protected the villagers so that they went unregistered and untaxed. Some villages that were prosperous reported the same population for decades so that their taxes would not be increased.

5. In some villages, where the headman wanted the approval of his neighbors, he underreported the population. In others, where he sought approval from higher authority or promotion, he overreported. An accurate report became a rarity.

In 1590, almost two centuries after the founding of the *li chia*, a county historian wrote, "The changes in the numbers of households and mouths are all unauthentic." The official enumerations had certainly deteriorated since the time when the Emperor T'ai-tsu had decreed, "Off with their heads!" to those who falsified reports.

The Ming Dynasty was overthrown by the Manchu in the early seventeenth century. The Manchu emperors, as the Ch'ing Dynasty, ruled China until the revolution of 1911. They installed a new system of enumerating the people known as the *pao chia*. Again, the basic unit was ten, and the household was the building block. It was arranged as follows:

10 households	formed 1 p'ai
10 p'ai	formed 1 chia
10 chia	formed 1 pao

At the head of each unit of ten was a *chang*, or headman. It is significant for their future to realize that the *pao chia* was also expected to function as the local police.

Under the new system, each family was to maintain a door placard listing all its members. It was to be kept up to date to show births and deaths. An extremely complicated routine was established for copying the information from the door placards onto official government forms, sending them up to ever higher steps in the chain of command for tallying, and then returning duplicate forms down the many-stepped imperial administration. In addition to population, the official forms contained a record of grain kept in storage in the event of famine.

The first important enumeration under this system was in 1741. The official population was given as 143,411,559.

The census of 1741 became a landmark for later Western demographers. They regarded its findings as relatively reliable and used it as a base from which to estimate later populations. What influenced them was, first, the intelligence and seeming efficiency of the then emperor, Ch'ien-lung. Also, the emperor's orders indicated a desire for an accurate census. As a sign of this, apparently, the Board of Revenue had decreed that women and children were to be included and that there must not be "any omissions and evasions."

However, the decision of a higher body was unknown to scholars until revealed by Professor Ping-ti Ho. He reports that a conference of cabinet ministers reviewed the orders of the Board of Revenue. They then issued a report stating that a complete census was impractical and that there was "no need to make a door-to-door enumeration." In their opinion, only the stored grain had to be fully reported. Obviously, such a negative attitude at the highest levels of government is not likely to produce an accurate enumeration.

The *pao chia* system became as ineffective as the *li chia* and for many of the same reasons. In 1775, the emperor, noting only trivial increases in the population of Hupeh province, declared:

"This is absurd. The purpose of the annual report of population . . . is mainly to use as evidence in the examination of economic prosperity. . . . How could it be that, in an area as large as hsien [county], the increase is only several persons a year? It is evident that local officials take it as a mere formality, and governor-generals and governors let them arbitrarily make reports without inquiring. What has been carried on is not a proper matter. . . ."

The emperor's criticism "worked." The population of the province leaped from 8.5 million in 1771 to 14.8 million five years later. From then on, there was always a sufficient "increase" to please an emperor.

On the other hand, elsewhere in the country, in times of flood or famine it was often found that more people applied for relief than were on the population registers of a locality.

Toward the middle of the nineteenth century, great political events occurred that many historians believe led inevitably to the victory of Communism one hundred years later. In the 1830's and 1840's, a series of wars, first with Great Britain, led to unequal treaties for China. Soon, other foreign nations established spheres of influence on the mainland. China's humiliation and general peasant dissatisfaction with the Ch'ing Dynasty resulted in rebellion in 1850. Its aim was to unseat the dynasty.

The rebellion was called the Taiping, which means "Great Peace," something China was not to know again for a long time. The rebels soon captured Nanking, the capital at that time. The conflict was a cruel one on both sides. There was tremendous disruption of life with devastating effects upon the population. In the fifteen years that it lasted, it is estimated that 30,000,000 lives were lost from causes directly related to the rebellion.

Eventually, the Western powers intervened to save the Ch'ing Dynasty. In 1864, an army commanded by the famous Englishman, Charles George (Chinese) Gordon, recaptured Nanking. But Manchu rule was never again to be complete or secure. In some provinces powerful governors arose who became almost independent of the central government. They paved the way for the warlords who followed them.

In the early twentieth century, the Manchu began a reform movement in a desperate attempt to save themselves. As part of it, they created a Directorate of Statistics with authority to conduct a regular census. The Directorate announced a six-year plan for one and completed it in four years. In 1911, it stated that the population of China was 341,913,417. Western authorities tended to accept the results.

Contemporary analyses of the conditions of the time, as well as of the results themselves, have cast doubt upon the accuracy of the census. The *pao chia* system had broken down. In some places it had been transformed into a militia; in others, to a police force. By 1902, it had been abolished.

The machinery for taking the last Manchu census was put together from bits and pieces. In some areas, the police were supposed to be the enumerators. In others, the county director was instructed to "select some local gentry of proven integrity" to undertake the census. The unreality of the whole enterprise was that in some places there were no police; in others there was no local government!

The highest ratio of police to population anywhere in the country was one policeman to 9,000 people. Unfortunately, many of the police were illiterate.

Since opposition to the Manchu was already nationwide, rumors spread that the census was being taken to increase taxes and to draft men into the army. An official report from the populous province of Kwangtung stated:

"From the beginning of the census-taking disturbances have repeatedly broken out in Kwangtung. In localities . . . the agitation developed into open riots which were put down only by the provincial army. . . . [Serious disturbances] were due partly to the ignorance and misunderstanding of the rustics who . . . believed that adult males would be drafted and taxes increased. . . .

"As a result, in most cases the census registers so compiled contain omissions and are unauthentic. Local officials for fear of punishment had to manipulate skillfully in order to comply [with regulations] and higher authorities had to forbear in order to save face. There cannot have been more self-deception and deception of others."

The Republican government that followed the Manchu overthrow in 1912 inherited the census results. It knew its shortcomings, but its own efforts were also frustrated. From then until 1949, when the Communists came to power, there was never another census, although "estimates" were issued. In 1934, Chiang Kai-shek restored the *pao chia* system. In justifying this, he said of earlier Nationalist attempts at enumeration that "the result is that *population figures are absolutely inaccurate.*" However, in the same statement he added that the *pao chia* headmen would serve "for local defense."

At this stage in Chinese history, no organization could have enumerated the population. No central government, until 1949, would again control the mainland. Warlords scattered over the country ruled independently. In 1934, when Chiang Kai-shek restored the *pao chia,* pockets of Communist control already existed. In 1937, the war with Japan started. As Professor Ho stated, "For most provinces, therefore, the population figures of the Nationalist period were almost pure guesswork."

How large, then, was China's population at any time in its early

Some Estimates of the Population of China
(In millions)

Year or Period	Official population from imperial enumerations	"Best" estimates according to Ping-ti Ho	Estimates by Warren F. Willcox	Estimates by A. M. Carr-Sanders	Ta Chen's "Five Cycles"	Chiao-min Hsieh's "Selected Periods"	
						North China	South China
208 B.C.–A.D. 25 (Western Han)						46.6	13.0
A.D. 2					59.5		
A.D. 25–220 (Eastern Han)						30.2	19.0
618–907 (Tang)						31.7	17.9
742–756					52.9		
960–1279 (Sung)						11.6	21.7
1098–1100					43.0		
1391		60.5					
1573–1620 (Ming)					60.6		
1650			70.0	150.0			
1710			140.0				
1741	143.4						
1750	179.5						
1760	196.8						
1770	213.6						
1779		275.0					
1780	277.6						
1790	301.5						
1800	295.3						
1810	345.7						
1820	353.4						
1830	394.8						
1840	412.8						
1850	429.9	430.0	342.0				
1910			342.0				
1930			342.0				
1933				450.0	400.0		

history? The question will continue to fascinate scholars. Contemporary authorities, almost all bilingual, have shed much light upon certain periods for Western students. Perhaps some day Chinese archives may again be open to the world.

There are three early enumerations that, by general agreement, are considered more reliable than others. Ping-ti Ho cites the following:

1391	65,000,000; adjusted from the official 60,500,000
1779	275,000,000
1850	430,000,000

Most authorities consider any estimates after 1850 as lacking any real basis.

Thus, when the Communists came to power in 1949, the most recent acceptable population enumeration was almost exactly one hundred years in the past.

The enumeration of the people of China in 1953 was an historic achievement in the counting of human populations. Like the first American census of 1790, it is a landmark. Within one year the equivalent of about every fifth person on earth was enumerated. It is difficult to imagine the scope of such an undertaking.

As with other enormous endeavors, it has almost become part of mythology. On a television show in April, 1967, the black comedian, Dick Gregory, said, "Those Chinese. There are 688 million of 'em. Think of that! Why, man, they got more census takers than we got people!" Actually, the census involved more than 2,500,000 enumerators. This exceeded then *the entire population* of more than one-third of the present countries that are members of the United Nations!

There had never been a direct enumeration of the entire population of China in its thousands of years of history. One reason was that few emperors or governments had ever controlled the entire territory. Another was the remoteness between any administration and the people. The absence of direct relationship was expressed in a traditional saying: "The sky is high up and the emperor is far away."

The Communist government, on the other hand, controlled mainland China completely. More important, however, through the Communist party and a variety of organizations, it had completely penetrated Chinese life and society. It had "made the existence of individuals as individuals extremely difficult," wrote Professor Ho. Another authority, Dr. Warren S. Thompson, said that the Communist organization was better equipped to obtain accurate census data than any other government for a century and a half or longer. Dr. S. Chandrasekhar, the present Minister of Health in India and a leading demographer, visited China in 1958. He was impressed by the thoroughness of organization that reached into every village and in every city street.

The only population estimates available to the Communists when they came to power in 1949 were those that had been made by the Nationalist government. Premier Chou En-lai reported to the United Nations in 1950 that China had 475 million people. Similar estimates continued to be used by government officials and agencies. Soon, from a variety of activities, suspicion arose that these estimates were seriously in error.

In the course of land distribution, local populations were often enumerated. These counts always revealed underestimates in the existing records. A check on the *pao chia* found their work to have been untrustworthy. The organization was abolished. Dramatic new evidence was uncovered by Professor Ho. According to him, the Communist government conducted two sample surveys before 1952 about which the rest of the world knew nothing at that time. These surveys pointed to a population of about 565 million, almost 100 million more than any previous estimate! Gradually, in government reports, the population estimates moved upward.

The decision to conduct a census in 1953 was made in 1952. The timing was very important. For one thing, registration of voters for a nationwide election had to be started. In addition, China was planning to introduce its first five-year economic plan. Accurate population totals, as well as other census information, had become a necessity.

Plans for the census were made late in 1952. Several advisers from the Soviet Union participated. Among them was Sergei K. Krotewich, who later acted as an observer. His later analysis of the census is the only one by a non-Chinese participant. It was decided that the Soviet enumeration of 1939 would serve as a model for census procedure.

The agencies involved in the census, including a special census administration, were responsible to the Ministry of Internal Affairs. This agency was to be in charge of the elections to which the census was directly related. A leading economist from the Academy of Sciences, Pai Chien-hua, was appointed Commissioner of the Census.

The census law was published in the Chinese press on April 6, 1950. Article I stated that the purpose of the enumeration was "to acquire an accurate census figure for the nation's economic and cultural construction." The next article placed responsibility in the Ministry of Internal Affairs. However, it stated that in the provinces and at lower levels the census was to be "under the charge of the department [bureau] of civil affairs." A significant feature of the census was the absence of tax officials, police, or soldiers, except that the armed forces were to count their own members.

Article VI set the "critical moment"—the time to which all information would be related no matter when it was collected—at midnight of June 30-July 1, 1953. For those who calculated time by the lunar calendar, it was the twentieth day of the fifth moon of the Kuei-szu year.

Another article of interest was that providing for the counting of the large population that resided on the water. An ingenious scheme for registering and tagging these floating, mobile homes was worked out that insured against either omissions or double-counting.

With the publication of the law, the newspapers also printed the slogan for the census. Stated as originating with Premier Chou

En-lai, the watchword was: "No omissions, no duplications, complete coverage, and accuracy." This slogan was to be repeated again and again during the census year by every means of communication.

As soon as the census was announced, the vast propaganda network that the Communist party had created went into action. By every conceivable means, including the ever-present loudspeakers all over the country, the people were told that it was their patriotic duty to be registered in the census. Theodore Shabad, a former correspondent for the *New York Times,* described another method. " 'Activists,' i.e. responsible, trusted persons from among the rank and file, were assigned to every large residential building or group of smaller buildings in cities and to every ten or twenty rural households." It would have been a rare person who remained unaware of what the government expected of him.

The 2,500,000 enumerators were, in the main, civil servants, teachers, upper-level students, and workers. Although the "activists" were not usually enumerators, they performed an important function. They visited people in advance to alert them to the arrival of the enumerator in places where the census was taken on a door-to-door basis. Where people had to go to be registered, the "activists" led them to the census station.

The planning staff's original intention was to obtain the following information:

1. Exact place of residence
2. Name
3. Relationship to head of household
4. Sex
5. Age
6. Nationality
7. Literacy
8. Occupation
9. Place of work
10. Social class

Questions 7 to 10 were eliminated for a variety of reasons. For example, the literacy question was judged to be too unmanageable because of the nature of the Chinese language. Literacy is related to familiarity with a sufficient number of Chinese characters. There was uncertainty as to how high that number should be. It was also doubted that many people would know, when asked, exactly how many characters they could recognize and write.

Two different census schedules were prepared—one for families and another for single persons without family. The latter were mainly soldiers and students. The schedules were printed in several non-Chinese languages to convince national minorities that the enumeration would be free from discrimination.

Some of the census questions of the few that remained presented problems unique to Chinese life. The census schedule itself was designed to meet one of the major problems. The official instructions stated that a person who had lived away from home for the past six months or more was not to be counted as a member of the family he had left. However, in China, family ties are strong and enduring. It is common for members who have been away for years with no intention of returning to be considered part of the "family." It was considered important not to offend these feelings. The enumerator was instructed to list the offered names of long-absent members on the family schedule—but on the left side. Before processing in the central office, however, the left side was torn off and not used.

The left side of the schedule also served as a check against omissions and duplications when the absent members of the family were registered elsewhere. See the chart on the next page.

After listing the place of residence on the basis of the *permanent* address, the head of the household had to be identified. In the West, this person is usually the main breadwinner; in China, it is almost invariably the oldest person in the family. As with "members of the family," here, too, Chinese tradition was very deeply rooted.

Other traditional Chinese practices came into focus in relation

Form A

Location of Town	Location of Rural District
Province	Province
Town	Administrative Area
County	County
Street	Village
Lane	Hamlet
House Number	

Absent population (family members living permanently in another place)				Resident population (persons living in the place in question)							Category of population
										Head of family	Relation to head of family
											Surname and given name
Total number of persons living in another place	Women			Total resident population	Women						Sex
											Age
	Men				Men						Nationality
											Additional remark

Person completing census sheet:_____ Date of filling form: 1953, __ Month __ Day to the question of "name." Up to the time of the census, it was possible for a woman to go through life without any given name. At various stages in her life cycle, she was known as "Mr. Wu's daughter," then "Mr. Sung's wife," and, later, "Kung-ti's mother." She had no identity of her own. At census time she was compelled to complete her individuality and select a first name.

In China, as in a large part of the world, one of the most serious and persistent census errors was the underenumeration of women. In an effort to eliminate this bias, enumerators had to follow two instructions. First, every female name had to be preceded by the Chinese character for "nü," or "female." No shortcuts were permitted. Second, if several female members were listed in succession, the enumerator was not allowed to use the character "t'ung" for ditto marks. "Nü" had to be written each time.

There were also problems with children's names. Quite often, a child was called by one given name during childhood and another later in life. Sometimes he might simply be called "Hsiao-erh," for "Little one, number two." At census time, the family was instructed to register the child by the most commonly used given name.

The greatest complexity arose in connection with determining the age of the person enumerated. The census planning staff had decided that all ages would be calculated in terms of the Gregorian calendar, that used in the West. Further, they were to be as of the "census moment," midnight of June 30, 1953. However, there were other ways of calculating age in China, especially in rural areas. And China is mainly rural.

Many Westerners have heard of the Chinese lunar calendar. It moves in a twelve-year cycle and includes Years of the Dragon, the Ox, the Tiger, and so on. This calendar is used by many Chinese-Americans to celebrate their New Year.

A third "calendar" was used by many older people. They dated their birth in terms of the emperor during whose reign they came into the world. Since the census was taking place only forty-one years after the overthrow of the last Ch'ing emperor, many people would say, "I was born in the thirtieth year of the reign of the Emperor Kuang Hsü." They would be only forty-eight years old since that emperor ruled from 1875–1908.

In China, a two-day old infant could have been called a "two-year old" without anyone's having a lapse of memory. An infant born on the day before the New Year became "one-year old" at birth. The following day, entering a New Year on his second day of life, he was called a "two-year old." Such practices, if accepted in an enumeration, could seriously distort the age distribution of a population.

To meet these problems, each enumerator carried an age-conversion chart. These charts, including the lunar calendar, listed the years back to the reign of Emperor Hsien Feng during 1851–1861. Thus, all ages, however reckoned, even for people one hundred years old, were changed to a common base without relying upon anyone's questionable arithmetic.

"Nationality" was a matter of personal choice, as in the Soviet census. Younger children were assigned their parents' nationality. However, children over the age of eighteen whose parents were of different nationalities were allowed to make their own choice. Members of minority nationalities were urged to register truthfully. As an incentive, they were told that their representation in Congress would be proportional to their number.

The original target date for completing the enumeration was November, 1953. But it moved very slowly. By the end of 1953 only 30 percent of the population had been counted. One reason was that the government did not want any disruption of agricultural work during the summer months. It kept advancing the planned completion date.

Despite the slow progress, enumerators were constantly urged to do careful work. As late as March 11, 1954, *Jên min jih pao*, the Communist party newspaper, told the enumerators, "The population figures are an important basis for the country's planned economic construction. All types of careless work will . . . mean that there will be no accurate population data in a considerable period of time. . . ."

In June, 1954, one year after its start, the first census results were announced.

The principal finding of the census, and the one of greatest interest to the world, was simply the number of people in mainland China; the number was somewhat more than 582,000,000. Although the government had earlier indications of the true population, a total that so far exceeded half a billion came as a shock to authorities all over the world.

The Han people were about 94 percent of the total population, according to the census. Some demographers believe that the proportion should be even higher. Often, people who call themselves "Hui," the old Chinese Moslems, or "Manchu," are today not different from the Han people. Many have even adopted Chinese names.

The enumeration revealed that the ratio of men to women was about 108:100. In the United States, as in most Western countries, the situation is reversed; there are slightly more women than men. The ratio in China may be the result, to some extent, of centuries of female infanticide. Almost all authorities agree that this practice has been eliminated by the Communist government.

The Chinese, in 1953, were a young people. About 45 percent of the population was under 20 years of age. Another 35 percent were between 20 and 44 years old. Already, children up to the age of 4, who were born during the period of Communist rule, where 15.6 percent of the total, or almost one-sixth of the population.

The population is still overwhelmingly rural. In China, as in Russia, the classification of urban and rural does not depend upon the size of the population of a place. Rather, the nature of the activity carried on there determines the classification. For example, a mining town, whatever its size, is defined as "urban." In these terms, only 13.3 percent of the people live in an urban environment.

The urban population is expected to grow steadily. Government policy favors it, especially in the western part of the country. By 1957, several cities there had doubled and tripled in size. The speed of westward movement will depend upon two factors:

1. The government's ability to hasten industrial development.

2. The success of its agricultural policies.

The Chinese claim that the amount of good unused agricultural land is equal to the amount in use. There is some disagreement about this estimate but little doubt that unused farm land does exist. The western population of China is bound to grow substantially in the years ahead, as has the Asian population of the Soviet Union.

The government is interested in speeding this process as much as possible. China has always felt vulnerable to attack because of the great concentration of people and industry on its eastern coast. Its frontier, once in the north, is shifting westward.

How accurate and complete was this historic census? If the Chinese evaluation is accepted, it was probably the best census in the long history of man counting man. A post-census check of about 52,000,000 people was made. After balancing extremely small undercounts and overcounts, there was a net underenumeration of only about 750,000 people. They repeated this claim as late as 1958.

Most world authorities agree that the census seems to have been well conducted. However, they are skeptical about the claimed level of error. Dr. John S. Aird, Chief of the China Branch of the Bureau of the Census, has analyzed the factors leading to accuracy or inaccuracy. Among the former he includes the strong leadership and careful planning, the use of the Soviet model, the seeking of minimum information, the anticipation of problem such as "age" and the solutions adopted, and the constant check of the work of the enumerators.

Among the negative factors he includes the limited time for planning as well as for training supervisors, the length of time it took—one year—to collect the information, and the fact that some families were registered at census stations rather than at home.

One other practice that was criticized by almost everyone was the fact that enumerators were given checklists of the estimated population based upon old censuses.

Dr. Aird concluded that the factors that could have led to an undercount were greater than those pointing in the other direction. In his opinion, the undercount may have been as great as 3 to 9 percent of the total population. Other authorities doubt that the error was so great. Throughout the world the Chinese census is accepted as reliable with a reasonable, if uncertain, degree of error.

At the time of the census, a sample survey of 30,000,000 people showed that the population was increasing at the rate of 2 percent each year. The Chinese later introduced a registration system for births and deaths from which they planned to estimate their future population. In 1959, the government announced that the mainland population at the end of 1957 was 647 million.

Since the rate of natural increase of 2 percent has probably changed since 1953, the game of guessing China's population has again attracted many players. By the end of 1967, even by conservative estimates it has undoubtedly passed the three-quarters of a billion mark. This is greater by 25 percent than the population of all Europe, excluding the Soviet Union.

The Chinese do not usually announce their plans to the world. No one outside China knows whether another census has been discussed. As the 1960's approached their close, the country seemed to be trying to recover from the turmoil of its "cultural revolution." On one of its borders, a war was being waged in North Vietnam. China felt itself menaced. Such conditions do not encourage census taking. However, China seems to be in full control of its own economy. The devastating floods and famines that, in the past, killed millions of people do not seem to have recurred. Barring great disaster, there is little doubt that in the 1980's the vast human sea that is China will contain one billion people.

Part II

THE CENSUS IN THE UNITED STATES

Chapter 1

COLONIAL AMERICA

In 1970, the nineteenth census of the people of the United States will have been taken. This will complete 180 years of unbroken, periodic enumerations. At ten-year intervals in years ending in zero, throughout the country's history, the population has been counted. No nation in history has achieved such regularity in this sphere over such a long span of time.

The American census has, in its way, had a charmed life. No scheduled enumeration has ever been postponed, much less canceled, due to unexpected circumstances. The War of 1812, although it resulted in the destruction of some earlier census records, occurred after the third census. The Mexican War ended in 1848, before the seventh census. The Civil War was bracketed between the eighth census in 1860 and the ninth census ten years later.

The Spanish-American War preceded the twelfth census in 1900. The United States entered World War I after the thirteenth census was history; the war ended well before the start of the fourteenth in 1920. The bombing of Pearl Harbor on December 7, 1941, that threw the United States into World War II occurred after the returns from the sixteenth census had been collected. By the time of the seventeenth census in 1950, the country had returned to normal. The wars in Korea and Vietnam did not involve the country sufficiently to affect any census activity.

Very rarely in the course of American history did the census fail
to reflect an important event. The one notable exception was the
Great Depression of the 1930's. At the time of the fifteenth census
in 1930, the full effects of the economic catastrophe had not yet
appeared. By 1940, when the sixteenth census began, war had
begun in Europe and economic recovery in the United States. The
two censuses enclosed the depression without revealing its terrible
effects. This was an historic exception. There have not been many
events in the nation's history whose characteristics are not, in
some way, part of the decennial census record.

The first enumeration of the people of the United States in 1790
was regarded in many parts of the world as a revolutionary undertaking. Great Britain, then the world's most industrialized nation,
would not count its population for the first time for another eleven
years. In the nineteenth century, a leading French statistician
called the provision of the Constitution that made the census possible a remarkable achievement. He stated, "The United States
presents in its history a phenomenon that has no parallel—that of
a people who initiated the statistics of their country on the very
day that they formed their government, and who regulated, in the
same instrument, the census of their citizens, their civil and political rights, and the destiny of the country."

However, by 1790, participation in a census was probably not a
new experience to many citizens of the new nation. There had
been enumerations in almost every colony outside the south and
in some southern ones. In several colonies there had been more
than one. Where actual counts had not been made, the colonists
had seen their names entered on tax or militia lists. From such
lists, from the earliest days of colonial settlement, the population
had often been estimated.

Several ratios had almost become standardized. It is known, for
example, that toward the middle of the eighteenth century, the
ratio of militia to population in all of colonial America was 1:5⅓.
The ratio varied from colony to colony and from one decade to
another.

From the settlement of Jamestown, Virginia, in 1607 to the first national census in 1790, there were at least thirty-eight counts of population in some American colony. This figure does not include estimates made from lists, with one notable exception. It also does not include censuses limited to some of the larger cities, such as Boston, Philadelphia, or New York, that were made from time to time.

The number of censuses taken in each colony from the time of its founding varied widely. By 1790, there had been eleven enumerations in New York, seven in Rhode Island. New Hampshire and Connecticut each had conducted four counts. In the seventeenth century, the population had been estimated for the most part. In the eighteenth, genuine enumerations were undertaken.

The first census of a reasonably large population in the New World was carried out in New York in 1698. There were 18,067

Early Estimates and Censuses of the Colonial Population

Colony	Year of first estimate and population		Year of first census and population	
Rhode Island	1658	1,200	1708	7,181
Massachusetts[a]	1632	2,300	1764	269,711
Connecticut	1643	5,500	1756	130,612
New Hampshire	1641	1,000	1767	52,700
New York	1664[b]	7,000	1698	18,067
New Jersey	1702	15,000	1726	32,442
Pennsylvania and Delaware	1681	500[c]	None	
Maryland	1660	8,000	1712	46,073
Virginia	1616	351	1635	5,119
North Carolina	1677	4,000	None	
South Carolina	1682	2,200	None	
Georgia	1752	5,000	None	

[a] Includes Maine.
[b] Year of British conquest. Includes Vermont.
[c] Before William Penn's arrival. In 1685, there were 7,200.

people in an area that included the territory of what later became the state of Vermont. In 1708, Rhode Island held its first census and counted a population of 7,181 colonists.

Of the thirty-eight censuses taken during the colonial era, twenty-seven were carried out before the Continental Congress met in Philadelphia on September 5, 1774. The others were conducted between 1774 and 1789, the so-called Continental Period. The pattern of enumeration set in the earlier period continued during the later years. Those colonies that had taken censuses earlier continued to do so. No new colonies entered the ranks of the enumerated.

Pennsylvania and Delaware in the middle area of the country and North and South Carolina and Georgia in the South never counted their people before the first federal census in 1790. New Hampshire, which had made two enumerations prior to the Continental Period, made two during this period. The pattern was much the same in the other colonies.

The table on the next page shows the distribution of colonial censuses.

The original source of all colonial census activity was the British Board of Trade. It needed the information on population for efficient administration. It is a historical curiosity that this should be the source; Great Britain, the mother country, had not yet enumerated her own population.

Despite the common origin, at no time during the colonial period was there a joint census in more than one colony, much less in all of colonial America. There was, also, no uniformity in the census taking. At certain times only the white people were counted. But the Maryland census of 1712 recorded a total population of 46,073 that was said to include 8,330 Negroes. In 1730, Rhode Island's population of 17,935 included 985 enumerated Indians. The Massachusetts census of 1764 included both Negroes and Indians, as did the census of Rhode Island ten years later.

The lack of uniformity went further. Some enumerations were simple counts of people. At other times, whites, blacks, and Indians were not only enumerated individually but were also classified

Censuses in the American Colonies Before 1790

Colony	Total number	1600–1699	The 18th century		
			Total	1700–1773	1774–1789: Continental period
All colonies	38	2	36	25	11
New England					
Rhode Island	7	—	7	4	3
Massachusetts	2	—	2	1	1
Connecticut	4	—	4	2	2
New Hampshire	4	—	4	2	2
Maine[a]	2	—	2	1	1
Vermont[b]	1	—	1	1	—
Middle colonies					
New York	11	1	10	9	1
New Jersey	3	—	3	3	—
Delaware	—	—	—	—	—
Pennsylvania	—	—	—	—	—
Southern colonies					
Maryland	2	—	2	2	—
Virginia	2	1	1	—	1
North Carolina	—	—	—	—	—
South Carolina	—	—	—	—	—
Georgia[c]	—	—	—	—	—

[a] Part of the census of Massachusetts.
[b] Part of the census of New York.
[c] The only colony founded in the eighteenth century; founded in 1732.

by age. In rare instances, the number of families and houses were recorded.

When the Continental Congress met in 1774, the idea that population should be the basis for sharing obligations as well as rights was widely recognized. Thus, it was quite natural that Patrick Henry, delegate from Virginia, should propose that voting strength in the new Congress should be based on the number of white inhabitants in each colony. Other delegates proposed as a basis the value of property, as well as the size of the population.

All such proposals were doomed to defeat, however, because there were no uniform population figures for all colonies. The issue was settled by giving each colony one vote.

When the shots rang out at Lexington, Massachusetts, on that historic day in April, 1775, the American colonies had about 2,500,000 people, of whom about one in five was black. This estimate does not include the Indians, who were not to be part of an American census for more than a century.

In the course of the Revolutionary War, the colonies acquired debts that they had pledged to repay in common. However, the question of how these still independent governments were to share the payments had never been decided. As early as 1775 a proposal had been made that population, including *all* black inhabitants, be the basis of sharing the repayment of the debt. Each colony was to determine its population *in some confidential way* and forward the results to the Continental Congress.

Censuses were carried out in Rhode Island and Massachusetts in 1776. Most other colonies failed to act on the proposal. Five years later, in 1781, a resolution was introduced in the Congress that called for a census of the *white* inhabitants. Although the resolution was defeated, some colonies carried out enumerations.

The discussion of the problem led to an historical attempt to estimate a population from tax lists.

Virginia was then known to be the most populous colony, although no enumerations of its citizens had been made since 1635. By 1782, however, most of its counties maintained rather accurate and comprehensive poll-tax lists. In that year, its leading citizen, Thomas Jefferson, a man of many talents, decided to estimate Virginia's population.

In his usual logical manner, Jefferson first listed the facts he knew. They were:

1. In Virginia, except for eight counties for which information was not available, there were:
   a. 53,289 free males, age 21 and over.
   b. 211,698 slaves, male and female, of all ages.
   c. 23,766 "tithable slaves"

2. In the eight counties not included above, there had been 3,161 men in the militia in 1779 and 1780.

Jefferson then listed the assumptions upon which he based his estimate:

1. The number of people under 16 years of age was equal to the number 16 years and over.
2. The number of males from 16–20 years of age were equal to the number of unmarried men in the militia, or the men between 16–50 years of age; that this was one-third of all men in the militia, or that it was about one-fourth of all men 16 years and over.
3. The number of males was equal to the number of females.
4. In the eight counties, the number known to be in the militia in 1780 was equal to the number of free males 16 years and over in 1782.
5. The ratio of free men to slaves was the same in the eight counties as it was in the rest of Virginia.

After making his calculations, Jefferson submitted the following estimates of Virginia's population.

The Population of Virginia in 1782

Population	The state	Counties included in tax lists	Other eight counties
Total population	567,614	543,438	24,176
Free population	296,852	284,208	12,644
Males	148,426	142,104	6,322
Under 16 years	74,213	71,052	3,161
16 years and over	74,213	71,052	3,161
16 to 20 years	18,553	17,763	790
21 years and over	55,660	53,289	2,371
Females	148,426	142,104	6,322
Slave population	270,762	259,230[a]	11,532

[a] Jefferson reached this total by adding the number of slaves (211,698) plus twice the number of "tithable slaves" (23,766).

The opinion of experts later was that Jefferson had underestimated Virginia's population by about 1 to 2 percent. If this was actually the case, it was a considerable accomplishment for a nonstatistician but not surprising for a man of Jefferson's genius. His estimate of the population of Virginia became the last official one prior to the census of 1790. It is interesting that as Secretary of State in Washington's cabinet, Jefferson was responsible for supervising the first census of the United States.

The failure of most colonies to count their population or to make serious estimates caused the debt settlement problem to drag on and on. It became increasingly clear that a genuine census would be carried out only by some central authority. It was almost inevitable that the Constitutional Convention would make some provision in the Constitution for a federal census to be taken at regular intervals.

The people of colonial America were never united in any common census undertaking; many were never counted at all. This gap in information about such a vital period in a people's history was an open invitation to scholars to fill the empty spaces. This challenge was accepted by many scholars; research began even before independence. After independence, the first of America's great historians, George Bancroft, presented his estimates of the colonial population in the first volume of his *History of the United States* that appeared in the 1830's.

Until recent years, estimates of the population of the American colonies were based mainly upon the work of the early colonial historians. Present-day estimates, however, have resulted from far more thorough scholarship. They are based, in the main, upon the original reports to the British Board of Trade, tax and militia lists of the times. The reports of the colonial governors to the Lords Commissioners of Trade and Plantations in the mother country have been studied. As a result, earlier estimates have been revised.

The question of the "true" size of colonial America must forever remain an open one. Other scholars will undoubtedly discover other documents. But such discoveries are not likely to result in significant changes in what is known today about the population before 1790.

On two important occasions in its history, the Bureau of the Census has published its estimates of the colonial population. The first, appearing in 1909, followed the twelfth census of 1900. In its way, it was a commemoration of the arrival of the twentieth century. The most recent was completed in the 1960's. The estimates relating to the American colonies were published as part of a statistical history of the United States. Each was based upon the soundest contemporary scholarship and is accepted as the best of its time. Both are shown on the next page to indicate the changes that were made as the result of half a century of research.

Several interesting observations may be made on the basis of the data in the table. Neither the series of estimates from 1900 nor the later one includes the Indian population. The size of this population at the time of the birth of the country will forever remain the subject of speculation. However, on the basis of the available evidence, in the early seventeenth century there were perhaps somewhat more than 100,000 Indians living within the territory of the original colonies. In later years, local efforts were made, from time to time, to enumerate them. Needless to say, the enumerations were of "pacified" Indians. As the white and Negro population increased over the years, the Indian diminished for a long time.

The colonial people, in this table, are divided into "white" and "Negro"; in the later census years, after independence, the two basic groups became "white" and "nonwhite." In the colonial period, the black population was overwhelmingly a slave population. Many of the first arrivals, in the early years of the seventeenth century, came as domestic servants. However, the slave trade soon became a source of enormous profits to the English rulers and was, therefore, encouraged. Toward the end of the colonial period, imported slaves may have exceeded 10,000 per year. However, by that time, the natural increase in the Negro population probably exceeded that number considerably.

The American Colonial Population, 1610–1780
(Based upon estimates made by the United States Bureau of the Census)

| Year | Estimates made in 1900 | Population | | | Percent increase during decade | | Negro population as percent of total |
		Total	White	Negro	White	Negro	
1610	210[a]	350[a]	350[a]	—	[b]	[b]	—
1620	2,499	2,302[c]	2,282	20	[b]	[b]	0.9
1630	5,700	4,646[d]	4,586	60[e]	[b]	[b]	1.3
1640	27,947	26,634	26,037	597	[b]	[b]	2.2
1650	51,700	50,368	48,768	1,600	87.3	168.0	3.2
1660	84,800	75,058	72,138	2,920	47.9	82.5	3.9
1670	114,500	111,935	107,400	4,535	48.9	55.3	4.1
1680	155,600	151,507	144,536	6,971	34.6	53.7	4.6
1690	213,500	210,372	193,643	16,729	34.0	140.0	8.0
1700	275,000	250,888	223,071	27,817	15.2	66.3	11.1
1710	357,500	331,711	286,845	44,866	28.6	61.3	13.5
1720	474,388	466,185	397,346	68,839	38.5	53.4	14.8
1730	654,950	629,445	538,424	91,021	35.5	32.2	14.5
1740	889,000	905,563	755,539	150,024	40.3	64.8	16.6
1750	1,207,000	1,170,760	934,340	236,420	23.7	57.6	20.2
1760	1,610,000	1,593,625	1,267,819	325,806	35.7	37.8	20.4
1770	2,205,000	2,148,076	1,688,254	459,822	33.2	41.1	21.4
1780	2,781,000	2,780,369	2,204,949	575,420	30.6	25.1	20.7

[a] The Virginia colonists.

[b] Calculations were not made until the numbers became fairly large.

[c] There were 2,200 in Virginia, including 20 Negroes, and 102 in Plymouth Colony.

[d] There were 2,500 in Virginia; 500 in New Hampshire; 400 in the later state of Maine; 390 in Plymouth, which did not become part of Massachusetts until 1691; 506 in Massachusetts; 350 in New York.

[e] There were 50 Negroes in Virginia and 10 in New York.

During the years of the eighteenth century prior to the first census in 1790, the increase in the Negro population was about twice that of the white. The latter increased about tenfold from 1700 to 1780. In the same period the Negro population rose from about 27,800 to 575,400, a twentyfold increase.

Over the years, the black people became a larger and larger proportion of the population as a whole. By 1770, it is estimated that they represented 21.4 percent of the colonial people. *This was the highest proportion ever reached in the history of the country.* From then on, as a proportion of the total population, the Negro people continued to decline.

The estimates of the black population are based upon much less solid evidence than those for the white people. Only in a few cases are they based upon actual counts. And when they are, the counts were much more casual. Errors in counting slaves were not considered to be especially significant. Many of the estimates are based upon records that remain of the slave trade. In a pattern that was to be repeated throughout American history, it is generally accepted that the estimates of the Negro population during the colonial period are too low.

Any shortcomings of colonial census taking are not surprising. Aside from the physical problems, the relationship between the colonies and the mother country made complete and accurate enumerations difficult. The censuses were the responsibility of the colonial governors. These men did not owe their appointment to their competence as administrators. The counting itself was done by justices of the peace, county officers, or sheriffs and their deputies—most often the latter. They received no extra pay for this unpleasant duty that involved a good deal of travel to ask unwelcome questions of independent colonists.

There are many surviving records of complaints about this lack of compensation. The colonial Governor Clinton of New York was responsible for the census of 1749. In making out his report, he wrote that the results might not be accurate because "the officers received no pay for this service, and it was performed reluctantly and carelessly."

With the years, the grievances of the colonists against England grew in number and intensity, leading, finally, to widespread sentiment for independence. Naturally, there was resistance to providing any information to the English rulers. Such feelings were especially strong in Connecticut and Massachusetts. The people opposed any enumeration on the grounds that it was of no use to them but might be useful to the mother country. Massachusetts, with a sophisticated population center such as Boston, made many contributions to census taking and vital statistics in the years following independence. But, in the colonial period, it did not conduct its first enumeration until 1764.

Sometimes, colonial governors evaded the instructions from the home country to carry out enumerations. They did not want to annoy the independent colonists with questions. On the other hand, they sought to avoid trouble with the English ministers. They therefore constructed estimates of the population from the tax lists, called them "censuses," and sent the numbers to England.

The attitudes of many colonists against census taking were often reinforced by religious superstitions against being counted. The biblical story of King David's census made a strong impression upon an intensely religious people in many colonies. Governor Hunter of New York blamed any imperfections of a census taken in his colony in 1712 upon superstition. In a report he noted that earlier count of the people had been followed by sickness in the colony.

Somewhat later, a historian wrote that "Governor Burnett, of New Jersey, in a communication to the British Board [of Trade] in 1726, alluding to an enumeration made in New York three years before, said, 'I would have then ordered the like accounts to be taken in New Jersey, but was advised that it might make the people uneasy . . . and that they would take it for a repetition of the same sin that David committed in numbering the people, and might bring on the same judgments.' This notion put me off at the time, but, since your lordships require it, I will give the orders to the sheriffs that it may be done as soon as may be."

Taking a colonial census also meant that great physical obstacles had to be overcome. Many of these remained important considerations for decades after independence. The territory was vast; the people were widely dispersed over it. The estimated population, excluding Indians, in all colonies was less than one million until the 1740's. Roads and communications were primitive. The people, especially those outside the few towns and cities, were fiercely independent. Sheriffs were not eager to ride out to ask what might be regarded as foolish questions. And, then, and for some time to come, there frequently were hostile Indians to contend with.

Despite these considerations, the American colonial period provided an excellent training ground for census taking. It is true that it came to a close with great empty spaces in knowledge of the population. But there were also several examples of advanced, carefully planned enumerations of populations. More important than any particular enumeration was the fact that issues of future urgency to the country were argued and then tested in living experiences. When these issues were later debated in connection with the writing of the Constitution, educated and informed men knew how they had worked out in practice.

The fundamental principle of basing representation in a law-making body upon population had already been accepted in more than one colony. New York had for many years distributed the seats in its legislature on the basis of periodic censuses. The question as to whether a census should be a simple count of people or should also classify them by certain characteristics such as sex and age had been debated. Several colonial censuses were more than simple counts. And the questions asked in the census of Rhode Island in 1774 were almost identical with those in the first federal census of the American people in 1790.

Even the great question—"Who are people?"—had been thoroughly discussed before the Constitutional Convention. The separation of "Indians taxed" from "Indians not taxed" was not a new idea when it was written into the Constitution. However, the great debate was not about the Indians. The far more important issue was how to count the Negro people.

It was perfectly clear that for purposes of representation in a law-making body, it would be a great advantage to states with large slave populations to call slaves "people." However, for the purpose of sharing taxation on the basis of population, it would be best for them to call slaves "property." Although the issue had been hotly debated, it had not been settled. But the delegates to the Constitutional Convention did not have to begin their discussion of the question as if it were totally new to them.

Most of the outstanding men who met in convention in 1787 to write the basic law of the land had some knowledge of world history. They had the writings of many men and the practices of many countries from which to learn. But on the importance of a census of population as an instrument of democratic government, they had their own rich, native experiences upon which to draw.

Chapter 2

THE ROAD TO ARTICLE 1, SECTION 2

In 1787, when the Constitutional Convention met in Philadelphia, a stagecoach traveling on a well-maintained road, such as the one between that city and New York, could cover forty miles a day without a change of horses. A person could travel from Boston to Providence in one day for a cost of one dollar.

Since stagecoaches could not carry many passengers, more people traveled by ship. This means of transportation had another advantage—meals were usually available on board. However, travelers often claimed that the ships took longer than they should to complete a voyage so that more meals would be sold at high prices.

Travel was not too common. The country was spacious, with an area of more than 800,000 square miles. But only 30 percent of it, or about 240,000 square miles, was settled. At the time of independence, there were 4.5 people per square mile. An area that contained as few as two people per square mile was considered "inhabited." Many state boundaries were still unstable, with only those of New Hampshire, Rhode Island, New Jersey, Pennsylvania, Delaware, and Maryland fairly fixed. New York still included Vermont, which became the fourteenth state in 1791, before completion of the first census.

The United States was not yet a country in which large numbers of people were concentrated in many great cities. Only five cities had populations of more than 10,000. As one would expect, these were great port cities.

At the time of the Constitutional Convention, Philadelphia, with about 40,000 people, was the largest city. It had replaced Boston for that distinction in the middle of the eighteenth century. New York would not occupy that place until 1810. Charleston and Baltimore, with about 16,000 and 13,000 people, were the other two large cities of the new nation.

The country had many newspapers, almost all of small circulation by present-day standards. Philadelphia had four daily papers, one semiweekly, four weeklies, and three monthlies. One of the weeklies later became the *Saturday Evening Post*. For a time, newspapers could be sent by mail postage-free. The newspapers carried little "news" as it is thought of today. They were mainly filled with advertising, notices of sales and auctions, information about the arrival and departure of ships, announcements of government appointments at all levels, and some "real news."

The fact that there were many newspapers may be a clue to the literacy of the people. More exact information about the proportion of people who could read and write would not be available until 1870. In that year, the first census question about literacy was asked. Then, less than a decade after the Civil War, 20 percent of the population was counted as illiterate.

There was no free public school system as yet. Outside of large towns, there were very few schools at all. The stories about the many miles Abe Lincoln walked to school many years later are known to every child.

The average person was a farmer. Others were engaged in fishing or whaling, in trade or commerce. There was very little industry. The people who worked for salaries or wages earned very little by present standards. As an example, Thomas Jefferson, as Secretary of State in President Washington's cabinet, earned $3,500 per year. The chief clerk in his office was paid $800 per year, and the three assistants, who completed the entire staff of the department, each earned $500 per year.

By 1787, perhaps as many as half of the three-quarters of a million slaves in the United States had been born in this country. The actual number of slaves imported into the colonies will never be known. The records that were kept were good, but they were good as records of *property* not of *people*. The slave trade was profitable. When some colonies tried to discourage it by setting high duties on the importation of slaves, the British disapproved. In several colonies, high duties were set on the transfer of slaves from one colony to another.

Since the first blacks were brought into Virginia in 1619, slavery had undergone several transformations within the country at the time of the writing of the Constitution. One of the earliest organized moves against the institution of slavery was a petition by the Quakers of Germantown, Pennsylvania, in 1688 to abolish it. Later, some Puritan groups joined in the protest. But the opposition was exceptional. By the year 1700 slavery was a common and accepted practice in the colonies.

However, slavery did not sit easy on the conscience of many people. In 1732, when the colony of Georgia was founded, the last before independence, it had laws against slavery. But after a period of social contact with its southern neighbors and because of the economic needs of its type of agriculture, Georgia legalized slavery. By the middle of the eighteenth century, slavery was recognized throughout the colonies.

In most colonies, a man had a legal right to set his slaves free. However, two factors worked against the frequent exercise of this right. In the first place, it was regarded as setting a bad example to have free blacks living within the same area as slaves. Secondly, following from this, the laws and regulations dealing with the freeing of slaves were made extremely complicated. As a result, only the most principled and conscientious people went to the trouble of doing so.

In the years before the adoption of the Constitution, some states abolished slavery within their territory. By 1783, Pennsylvania, Massachusetts, New Hampshire, and the territory that later became Vermont had done so. By the following year, Connecticut and Rhode Island had followed suit. It is well to note that New York was not among these states. In that state, the ownership of slaves was surprisingly high; one out of every seven white families owned slaves. In South Carolina, the proportion was one out of three.

As the first census approached, slavery as an institution had existed in America for 170 years. Despite the position of New York, as well as New Jersey, it was not hard to predict that the time was not far away when slavery would create a difference between North and South.

The pattern of relations with the Indians had also been established by 1787. It is likely that east of the Allegheny Mountains, within the area of the original thirteen states, fewer than 10,000 Indians remained. In situations where it was less troublesome, Indian land had been acquired by purchase. But, for the most part, Indians had simply been driven from the land.

The Indian population had suffered a sharp reduction over the years. Many had been driven westward, into the new territories. Thousands were killed in battle. Still others died from diseases and vices that had come about from contact with the white man. Within the original colonies, there were areas where Indians were kept as slaves. During this time there also appeared the attitude that was to influence American thinking about the Indian almost up to the twentieth century. This was that the Indian was doomed to extinction; that nothing could keep him from dying out.

As W. S. Rossiter of the Bureau of the Census wrote in 1909 in *A Century of Population Growth*, "By 1790 the Indian had ceased to be a factor of any consequence in the affairs of the states enumerated at the First Census. The Indians living in the area enumerated consisted of a few scattered remnants of once powerful tribes."

The Constitution, when drafted, provided for the enumeration of Indians "taxed." This was interpreted to mean those living as free citizens outside reservations or other places set aside for them. It is doubtful that any such Indians were included in the first census of the United States.

These factors—transportation, newspapers, literacy, the kind of work people do, the presence and the attitude toward minorities —have been discussed because they are important factors in the success of a census. But they are also meant to convey the "look and feel" of the country at a time when great discussions were under way that would determine its future.

Some states were large and populous and their future was clearly one of great expansion. Other states would obviously remain small in territory and in number of people. In the Southern states, slavery had come to be accepted as a "permanent" institution. The Northern ones, including New York and New Jersey, would undoubtedly expand their economies without the need for human slavery. And at the western borders, there was a vast territory, still practically unpopulated except by Indians. This vast expanse could possibly, in the not too distant future, exceed in size, population, and importance the original colonies. All these elements—large and small, slave and nonslave, and the great unknown—were all at work shaping men's attitudes as to how the country was to be governed. A key question was on what basis the number of representatives who would make the laws should be distributed.

Population had been used as a basis for representation in some colonies. Also, it seemed to many to be the only logical and sensible method of apportionment. However, there was no certainty that this principle would be accepted when the states came together under the Articles of Confederation. The obstacles to be overcome were clear. The smaller states feared that they would be dominated by the larger. The states with large slave populations would want to have them counted in determining representation but not in distributing taxes.

The first draft of the Articles of Confederation presented to the Continental Congress contained a provision for a triennial census. The findings of the census were to become the basis for sharing not only the costs of the war but also the general expenses of government. But the proposal was rejected. When the Articles of Confederation were finally adopted, Article VIII stated that the costs of the war were to be paid from a common treasury "which shall be supplied by several in proportion to the value of all land within each state."

Article IX of the same document provided that a "Committee of the States" could "build and equip a navy" and "agree upon the number of land forces, and make requisitions from each state for its quota, in proportion to the number of white inhabitants in such state."

Many historians believe that the Congress expected that a census would determine "the value of all land" as well as "the number of white inhabitants." However, there was no mention of a census in the Articles of Confederation, and no census was ever taken under it. "The value of all land" was determined by the states themselves and was freely manipulated by them. There was never any independent check. As a result, years after the end of the war, the outstanding debts remained unpaid because there was no fair way of sharing them.

A determined effort was made in 1783 to amend the Articles of Confederation. This was at a time when Congress sought to levy some heavy taxes upon the states. For a period of twenty-five years the states were to contribute a total of $1,500,000 each year. And the basis for determining each state's share would be population rather than land values. The amendment that was introduced proposed that each state contribute "in proportion to the whole number of white and other free citizens and inhabitants of every age, sex, and condition, including those bound to servitude for a term of years, and three-fifths of all other persons not comprehended in the foregoing description, except Indians not paying taxes, in each State."

The amendment, which also called for a census every three years, was never ratified by the states; the Articles of Confederation remained unchanged. However, the proposal itself became historic. It was later referred to in the Constitutional Convention. A study of the wording reveals that it contains all the basic elements that later became Article I, Section 2, of the Constitution.

When the Constitutional Convention met in Philadelphia in May, 1787, the shortcomings of the Articles of Confederation were obvious to many people. Among other failures it was clear that land value was not a basis upon which to share taxes. Although the delegates were called together to patch up the old Articles, it quickly became clear that an entirely new document would be drafted by the Constitutional Convention.

Once the principle was accepted that there would be a legislative body, or Congress, with two houses, a great debate began as to how their membership would be selected. It was apparent very early that the larger states would seek representation that would be in keeping with their populations. One of the earliest resolutions presented to the Convention stated "that the representation should be proportional to population and that five slaves should be counted as three free men."

This proposal was adopted with the understanding that it applied only to the lower house of Congress, or House of Representatives. But, in the convention, with all delegates sitting as a Committee of the Whole, a proposal was introduced that the same principle—representation proportional to population—apply to the upper house, or Senate, as well. It was approved by a six to five vote!

This, of course, did not end the matter. Within the Convention the issue remained a bitter one, so bitter that it almost tore the Convention apart. Professor Max Farrand, perhaps the leading historian of the Convention, later wrote, "When the Convention finally got at the question of proportional representation, nearly three weeks were spent in reaching a conclusion. More than once any satisfactory solution of the difficulty seemed impossible, and

the Convention was on the point of breaking up. Gouverneur
Morris afterwards said that 'The fate of America was suspended
by a hair.' "

John Rutledge, delegate to the Convention from South Carolina, said later that they were "the most fundamental points, the
rules of suffrage in the two branches."

Finally, it was proposed that a committee of one representative
from each state be appointed to work out some compromise.
Probably with relief and hope, the Convention adopted the proposal.

The Compromise Committee reported back with the following
recommendations:

1. In the lower house of Congress there should be one representative for each 40,000 population, counting three-fifths of the
slaves.

2. In the upper house each state should have an equal vote.

With the general principles accepted, the Convention appointed a Committee of Five to fix the number of representatives
from each state that would sit in the lower house of Congress
when it first met; also, to decide upon a method by which to
change the number of representatives in the future.

The committee, after deliberations, proposed that the lower
house consist of fifty-six members. It further proposed that future
representation be based upon *wealth and the number of inhabitants.*

A fifty-six member House of Representatives was unacceptable
to the Convention, for reasons to be discussed. After rejecting the
proposal, it appointed a new committee that returned with a rec-
ommendation for a sixty-five member lower house.

At this point, Edmund Randolph of Virginia rose in the Convention and proposed that a census, taken at regular, stated intervals, should be adopted as the basis for determining changes in
population and wealth. Representation from the states in the
lower house would be adjusted according to the census results.

Hugh Williamson of North Carolina then offered an amendment to Randolph's proposal. It stated that the census should be taken of the free, white inhabitants and three-fifths "of those of other descriptions." Randolph accepted the amendment to his proposal.

It seemed as if the Convention was about to settle this thorny issue. However, great maneuvering now began for advantage before final adoption. Georgia and South Carolina made a last, desperate attempt to gain full recognition for and increased representation from their large slave populations. They proposed that the latter be counted equally with whites. The Convention defeated this easily.

When the original resolution was adopted, somewhere along the way it had dropped the word "wealth" as a basis for determining representation. But the issue was far from settled. When some suggested including "wealth," other delegates responded that the number of people was an excellent measure of wealth. Also, people were more easily counted.

It was finally decided that a vote should be taken on the question of whether population, wealth, or both should decide the number of representatives each state would have in the lower house. In a rare unanimous vote, the delegates decided that a census would be the basis for deciding representation.

Two important votes in committee then followed quickly. In the first, by six states to four, it was decided that the census should be of "free, white inhabitants." To make its intention doubly clear, the committee voted by the same margin, six to four, to *reject* the section that would include "three-fifths of the inhabitants of other descriptions."

When this was reported to the full Convention, the delegates rejected the entire resolution!

After this agony in the midst of a hot Philadelphia summer, it was as if the Convention had not advanced an inch.

The following morning, Gouverneur Morris of Pennsylvania offered the following proposal: That a clause be added to the original resolution to state that taxation should be in proportion to representation. It was proposed from the floor of the Convention that the wording be amended to read "direct taxation." A unanimous vote of acceptance quickly followed.

That same day, the final resolution was put together, including the various amendments that had been accepted. It read:

". . . representation ought to be proportional according to direct Taxation and in order to ascertain the alteration . . . which may be required from time to time . . . that a Census be taken within six years . . . and once within the term of every Ten years afterwards of all the inhabitants of the United States in the manner and according to the ratio recommended by Congress in their resolution of April 18, 1783."

The "ratio" was, of course, the three-fifths ratio referred to earlier for counting the slave population.

On July 16, the entire compromise was adopted by the delegates. Its important features were:

1. a. The lower house would have a certain number of representatives from each state. The initial total would be sixty-five members. In the future, seats in the House of Representatives would be based upon population, determined by a census taken at fixed intervals. Slaves would be included in the census count on the three-fifths basis.

   b. Direct taxation would be in proportion to representation; indirectly, in proportion to population.

2. There would be an upper house, or Senate, in which each state would be equally represented.

This, according to Professor Max Farrand, was the "Great Compromise" of the Convention and, finally, of the Constitution. Most important was agreement upon equal representation in the Senate after proportional representation for the lower house.

The states of Connecticut, Delaware, Maryland, New Jersey, and North Carolina voted for the compromise. Georgia, Pennsylvania, South Carolina, and Virginia rejected it. The Massachusetts delegation was split. And New York did not vote; its delegates did not like the way things were going and had left for home.

There were many antagonistic interests represented at the Convention. However, it is Professor Farrand's view that the fundamental conflict was not between the slave and the free states. Slavery had not yet become either an important or a strong moral issue. He believes that the strong and growing financial interests in the Atlantic Coast states wanted to retain control of the legislative process. They feared the future growth of the states from the western territories. The provision that there be equal representation in the Senate was to the advantage of these interests.

The decisions of the Constitutional Convention were referred to its Committee of Detail to work out the exact wording. What finally came out of this committee became Article I, Section 2, of the Constitution of the United States. It reads as follows:

"Representatives and direct Taxes shall be apportioned among the several States which may be included within this Union, according to their respective Numbers, which shall be determined by adding to the whole Number of free Persons, including those bound to Service for a Term of Years, and excluding Indians not taxed, three fifths of all other Persons. [This provision, which refers to the counting of the slaves, was eliminated when the Fourteenth Amendment to the Constitution was adopted after the Civil War.] The actual Enumeration shall be made within three Years after the first Meeting of the Congress of the United States, and within every subsequent Term of ten Years, in such Manner as they shall by Law direct. The Number of Representatives shall not exceed one for every thirty Thousand, but each State shall have at Least one Representative; and until such enumeration shall be made, the State of New Hampshire shall be entitled to choose three, Massachusetts eight, Rhode Island and Providence Plantations one, Connecticut five, New York six, New Jersey four, Pennsylvania eight, Delaware one, Maryland six, Virginia ten, North Carolina five, South Caroline five, and Georgia three."

The Convention had available to it estimates of the white and slave populations in the various states. Mainly on the basis of these estimates the Convention decided how many representatives each state should have until the first census was taken. The table shows the estimates, with calculations added by the author.

Population Estimates Used by the Constitutional Convention to Determine the Number of Representatives in the Lower House of Congress from Each State before the First Census

State	Population used in apportionment		Mathematical entitlement: Percent applied to 65 Representatives	Number of Representatives assigned by the Constitution
	Number	Percent of total		
With no Negro slaves included:				
Connecticut	202,000	7.9	5.1	5
Delaware	37,000	1.4	0.9	1
Massachusetts	360,000	14.0	9.1	8
New Hampshire	102,000	4.0	2.6	3
New Jersey	138,000	5.4	3.5	4
New York	238,000	9.2	6.0	6
Pennsylvania	360,000	14.0	9.1	8
Rhode Island	58,000	2.2	1.4	1
Including ⅗ of Negro slaves (total number in parentheses):				
Georgia (20,000)	90,000	3.5	2.3	3
Maryland (80,000)	218,000	8.5	5.5	6
North Carolina (60,000)	200,000	7.8	5.1	5
South Carolina (80,000)	150,000	5.8	3.8	5
Virginia (280,000)	420,000	16.3	10.6	10
Total used in apportionment	2,573,000	100.0	65.0	65
Negroes omitted (⅖)	208,000			
Actual estimated population	2,781,000			

The third column of the table shows how many representatives each state would have received if the division had been based strictly on the logic of mathematics. Massachusetts, for example, with 14 percent of the total population used in the calculations, should have received nine representatives in a house of sixty-five members ($14.0 \times 65 = 9.1$). However, as the fourth column of the table shows, it received only eight. The same held true for Pennsylvania. Virginia, which should have been entitled to eleven representatives, received only ten.

It is obvious that, while mathematics played a part, it was not the source of all decisions. Behind the scenes of the Convention, there was a good deal of hard bargaining, or "horse trading." The larger states made concessions so that the smaller would not rebel against the principle of basing representation upon population.

The table also illustrates some problems that were still the subject of debate well into the twentieth century. For example, New Jersey, with 3.5 percent of the population, received four representatives; Rhode Island, with 1.4 percent, received only one. Thus, the former with less than two and one-half times the actual population of the latter, received four times as many representatives. The question of what to do about "major fractions" such as .5 was discussed well into the future.

The Convention adopted the Constitution and adjourned on September 17, 1787. In a way, the historic document was an accident. The delegates had come together at Philadelphia for the purpose of amending the Articles of Confederation. Many objections arose because of a feeling that the delegates had gone beyond their authority in drafting a new document. There were, in addition, objections to specific sections of the Constitution, as could be judged from the close vote on adoption. It remained to be seen how strong these objections were as the Constitution now went to the states for ratification.

Many voices were now heard throughout the country to urge acceptance or rejection. In New York, where opinion was sharply divided, on October 27, 1787, there appeared in the press the first

issue of *The Federalist*. Each issue was signed *Publius*, but it is
known that the authors were Alexander Hamilton, James Madison, and John Jay. In calm and reasoned tones, *The Federalist*
papers examined the important sections of the proposed Constitution and showed how they would work for the national interest.

Some historians believe that *The Federalist* papers had only a
minor influence upon the course of ratification. However, because
of their distinguished authorship, they indicated the thinking of
the time, as well as the arguments used to influence opinion. In
addition, since Madison has often been called "the father of the
Constitution," they are documents that reveal some of the intentions of the men who framed the Constitution.

The Federalist No. 54 discussed the constitutional provision
that bases representation in the lower house of Congress upon
population. The author, either Hamilton or Madison, began by
stating, "It is not contended that the number of people in each
State ought not to be the standard for regulating the proportion of
those who are to represent the people of each State. The establishment of the same rule for the appointment of taxes will probably be as little contested; though the rule itself, in this case, is by
no means founded on the same principle."

Then, in the manner of a classic debate, the author presented
two extreme views.

Some people, *The Federalist* contended, state, "Slaves are considered as property, not as persons." It followed that they "ought
therefore to be comprehended in estimates of taxation which are
founded on property, and to be excluded from representation
which is regulated by a census of persons."

The above was *The Federalist's* statement of the anti-slavery
position. Why, it asked, should the southern states increase their
representation in Congress as a result of "the barbarous policy of
considering as property a part of their human brethren . . ."

The Southern point of view was then presented. In effect, the
argument went, all states will make their own laws as to who can
and who cannot vote. But the people excluded from voting will

still be counted in the census and the state's representation will be based upon their number, as well. How much different is this, argued the imaginary Southerner, from counting slaves as whole persons for purposes of representation?

However, the argument continued, "Let the case of the slaves be considered, as it is in truth, a peculiar one. Let the compromising expedient of the Constitution be mutually adopted, which regards them as inhabitants, but as debased by a servitude below the equal level of free inhabitants; which regards the *slave* as divested of two-fifths of the *man*."

In conclusion, *The Federalist No. 54* explained the ingenious balance at the heart of Article I, Section 2, that assured an accurate census. It stated:

"In one respect, the establishment of a common measure for representation and taxation will have a very salutary effect. As the accuracy of the census to be obtained by the Congress will necessarily depend, in a considerable degree, on the disposition, if not on the cooperation of the States, it is of great importance that the States should feel as little bias as possible to swell or to reduce the amount of their numbers. Were their share of representation alone to be governed by this rule, they would have an interest in exaggerating their inhabitants. Were the rule to decide their share of taxation alone, a contrary temptation would prevail. By extending the rule to both objects, the States will have opposite interests, which will control and balance each other, and produce the requisite impartiality."

A common fear at the time had to do with the size of the House of Representatives. A small body, it was said, would not represent all possible views; also, it would tend to become aristocratic. During the Convention, it was seen that the delegates rejected their own committee's proposal that the lower house contain fifty-six members; they forced an increase to sixty-five. But, people asked, was sixty-five enough? What if the population increased?

The Federalist No. 55 explored this problem. Also, since the country had just fought for and won its independence, the author (either Madison or Hamilton) could not resist some boastful forecasting. He wrote:

"The number of which this branch of the legislature is to consist, at the outset of the government, will be sixty-five. Within three years a census is to be taken, when the number may be augmented to one for every thirty thousand inhabitants; and within every successive period of ten years the census is to be renewed, and augmentations may continue to be made under the above limitations. It will not be thought an extravagant conjecture that the first census will . . . raise the number of representatives to at least one hundred. . . . At the expiration of twenty-five years, according to the computed rate of increase, the number of representatives will amount to two hundred; and of fifty years, to four hundred. This is a number which, I presume, will put an end to all fears arising from the smallness of the body."

"The foresight of the Convention has accordingly taken care that the progress of population may be accompanied with a proper increase of the representative branch of the government."

These issues were so important that *The Federalist No. 58* dealt with them again. The provision for a regular census was again used as an assurance to calm common concerns.

New York, by a vote of 30–27, became the eleventh state to ratify the Constitution. What is significant in this account is that the ten-year census guaranteed by Article I, Section 2, became a powerful argument for ratification of the Constitution.

Chapter 3

THE FIRST CENSUS:
TO ASK MORE OR LESS

Article I, Section 2, of the Constitution requires only a count of the free inhabitants, slaves, and whatever Indians paying taxes may be found in the country. It makes no provision for asking people their sex, age, or even exact place of residence within a state. The article certainly never foresaw that, under its cover, people would be asked the number of rooms in their home and whether they owned a color television set. Yet, from the earliest debate in Congress until the decisions about the contents of the census of 1970, angry words have been exchanged between those who would ask more and those who sought less.

In view of the constitutional question, it is interesting that the first spokesman in Congress for a broad census was James Madison, who had played such an important part in framing the Constitution. With remarkable foresight, he said that if the proper questions were asked, the census results could be used to guide legislation. At the time, his opinions were interpreted to mean that "if this bill [the census act] was extended so as to embrace some other objects besides the bare enumeration of the inhabitants, it would enable them [members of Congress] to adapt the public measures to the particular circumstances of the community." James Madison could have been talking about antipoverty legislation of the 1960's.

Madison reminded Congress that governments had always sought such information but had never been able to obtain it. Now, he said, through the census, it could become available. "If the plan was pursued," his statement in the *Annals of Congress* continues, "it would give them an opportunity of marking the progress of the society and distinguishing the growth of every interest."

There would be other advantages in a detailed census inquiry, he continued. It would provide a check on the correctness of the entries if the age question, for example, were made up of several classes. Then, the parts would have to add up to the whole. It is a clue to Madison's genius 'that today questionnaires frequently are designed to provide checks on the inner consistency of questions.

There were, of course, objections to Madison's proposals. One stated that, in asking people too many questions, it would cause them to suspect that the government wanted "to learn their ability to bear the burden of direct or other taxes."

The exact details of Madison's proposals are unknown. However, reports of the time lead to the belief that the first census legislation passed by Congress included many of his ideas. As passed by the House of Representatives, the first census act provided for the collection of the following information:

1. Free white males under 16
2. Free white males above 16
3. White females
4. Free blacks
5. Slaves
6. "The number of persons employed in the various arts and and professions carried on in the United States."

Question 6 was a Madison proposal.

The deliberations of the Senate were secret at that time, so that there is no record of the debate on the bill. However, as it passed the Senate on February 22, 1790, and was signed by President Washington on March 1, it did not contain Question 6. The act was constructed so that the following columns were provided:

Names of heads of families	Free white males of 16 years and upwards, including heads of families	Free white males under 16 years	Free white females, including heads of families	All other free persons	Slaves

The questions as worded in the final act are technically superior to the ones that appeared earlier. The first version divided free white males into "under 16" and "above 16." How would an enumeration treat someone who was "exactly 16." The final version corrected this omission.

Also, question 4 had asked for a count of "free blacks," but as it emerged from Congress, the act sought a count of "all other free persons." Presumably, if an enumerator found that rarity—a taxpaying Indian—he would include him in this column. On the earlier form there was no room for him even if he were found to exist.

With President Washington's signature on the first Census Act, a precedent of great significance was established. Whatever the wording of Article I, Section 2, the census would not have to be limited to a simple count of inhabitants.

As passed by Congress, the act defined the nature of the enumeration in other ways. The United States marshal was named as the official census agent, an assignment that would be his for almost a hundred years. He was authorized to hire as many deputies or assistants as he might need and to assign them to enumeration districts as he saw fit, but the districts should be "plainly and distinctly bounded by water courses, mountains, or public roads."

Every person over the age of sixteen was required by law to answer the deputy marshal's questions. Refusal to cooperate could bring a fine of $20, a substantial amount of money in those days.

The enumeration was to begin on the first Monday of August, 1790, and the entire population enumerated within nine calendar months. Special legislation was passed to extend the completion time in Rhode Island, which did not ratify the Constitution until 1790, and in Vermont, which became the fourteenth state in the Union while the census was in progress.

In a census that is to be used to apportion a legislature, such as the American one, the people are usually counted on a basis known as *de jure*. This simply means "where they rightfully belong." Thus, the many American people who might be visiting Disneyland or Madison Square Garden in New York City at census time would be counted according to the state in which they made their home. In this way, California's and New York's populations would not be inflated and the home state's representation in Congress would not suffer.

Another type of census count is that made *de facto*, or one based on where people happen to be at census time.

In the census of 1790, most people were to be counted as part of their family at their "usual place of abode" on that first Monday in August. Others "without a settled place of residence" were to be counted wherever they happened to be. Lastly, "every person occasionally absent" was to be counted as belonging in the place where "he usually resides in the United States."

Thus, in theory, the census was a hybrid of *de jure* and *de facto*. However, in reality, since society was not very mobile then, by far the most people were counted where they usually or "rightfully" belonged.

Congress made no provision for a standard census schedule or even for the funds with which to have one printed. This step was not to be taken until 1830. For the first census, each deputy marshal ruled up his own forms. Most placed the six items of information that were to be obtained at the head of the columns; they entered the responses on horizontal lines. Since even the size of paper then in common use was not standardized, as it is today, the final census returns consisted of a mixture of various sizes of paper drawn up in every conceivable way.

Congress was frugal in other ways. Perhaps in a country that had just emerged from a war and that was burdened with many debts, this was not only necessary but also wise. However, it made absolutely certain that the first census of the country would not be a means of enriching anyone. There were three basic pay scales for the assistant marshals, based upon the density of the districts in which they worked. The rates were as follows:

1. $1 for each 300 persons enumerated in cities and towns with more than 5,000 inhabitants.
2. $1 for each 150 persons enumerated in county districts.
3. $1 for each 50 persons enumerated in areas where the population was widely scattered. This pay scale had to be approved by the district judge.

At the end of his enumeration, the deputy marshal was to make a summary of his count. For each copy of the summary, of which there were usually two or three, he was paid two dollars.

Even for the time, the rate of pay was low. In several places, it was difficult to hire assistant marshals. In South Carolina this difficulty delayed completion of the census within the legal deadline. The members of the House from that state requested an extension of time and an increase in the pay of the deputies. They were granted an extension of time until March 1, 1792, but the increase in pay was denied.

The marshals themselves, important officeholders at that time, were not treated with greater openhandedness. Their pay scale was fixed by Congress as follows:

Area	Total compensation
Delaware, Rhode Island	$100
Connecticut, Maine, New Hampshire, New Jersey, Vermont	200
Georgia, Kentucky	250
Maryland, Massachusetts, New York, Pennsylvania, South Carolina	300
North Carolina	350
Virginia	500

Even though these were "extra" earnings for the marshals, it should be remembered that it was for nine months of difficult work during which they had responsibility for a greatly enlarged staff.

The assistant marshals, after taking their oath of office and ruling up their enumeration sheets, set out to count the population.

In large cities and towns, and especially where there was a history of colonial census taking, problems were few. But problem areas existed. In some places there were strong superstitions against being counted. In others, the population believed that increased taxation would follow the enumeration. In South Carolina, several people were brought to court and fined for failure to co-operate with the deputies. And, in the remote areas of the interior, people were suspicious and hostile Indians a continuing concern for a lone deputy riding a wilderness trail. If a family here and there was not enumerated, it was hardly surprising.

After completing his enumeration, each deputy marshal was required to prepare the summary of his count. These were to be sent to the marshal. However, before doing this, he had to post two copies of his summary "at two of the most public places" in his district for inspection.

The marshals, after receiving the original enumeration sheets from their deputies, were obliged to file them in the district court. The summaries that they had prepared from their own deputies' totals they had to send directly to the President. In actual practice, they went to the Secretary of State, Thomas Jefferson.

The total cost of the first census of the United States was $44,377.28. While this was a great deal of money for the infant nation, it represented an expenditure of about 1.1 cent per person enumerated. At this rate, the census of 1970 would cost slightly in excess of $2,000,000. In actual fact, it will probably cost about a hundred times this amount.

To those familiar with his varied interests, it may be surprising that Thomas Jefferson did not play a more active role in the first census. This inventive genius, with his highly developed sense of order, would have seen the desirability of a uniform census schedule. However, George Washington had been inaugurated barely one year earlier, on April 3, 1789. Jefferson was his secretary of state in a government whose structure was far from complete when the Census Act was passed. Jefferson, with a staff of only four people, was probably taken up with the major responsibility of his office—the conduct of foreign affairs. Ministers from foreign governments had to be received, American ones selected and then instructed; treaties had to be negotiated.

As part of his official responsibilities, Jefferson forwarded copies of the Census Act to the governors of the states. Unless the records have been lost, he did not directly instruct the marshals as to their duties. This act was probably performed by the governors of the states. To each governor, Jefferson sent the following letter:

> OFFICE OF THE SECRETARY OF STATE
> *Mar 31st, 1790*
>
> Sir:
>
> *I have the honor to send you, herewith enclosed, two copies duly authenticated, of the Act providing for the enumeration of the Inhabitants of the United States; also of the Act to establish an uniform rule of naturalization; also of the Act making appropriations for the support of the Government for the year 1790 and of being, with sentiments of the most perfect respect.*
>
> *Your Excellency's most obed't & most h'ble servant,*
> *Th. Jefferson*

Jefferson did take one important action that went beyond his official responsibilities. The Census Act of 1790 made no provision for any enumeration of either the Southwest or Northwest territories. The former included the soon to be state of Tennessee. The Northwest Territory would eventually become the midwestern states of Illinois, Indiana, Michigan, Ohio, and Wisconsin. The governor of this enormous area was, in 1790, fully occupied in Indian warfare. Consequently, census activities were hardly likely to be looked upon with favor. However, it occurred to Jefferson that there was no reason why the people in the Southwest Territory should not be enumerated.

On March 12, 1791, Thomas Jefferson wrote to Governor Blount of the Southwest Territory. After telling him about the provisions of the Census Act, Jefferson reminded the governor that there would not be another census for ten years. Therefore, he asked, would it not be desirable if the people in his territory were enumerated at the same time as the people in the states? He suggested that Governor Blount use the same classifications as would be used elsewhere. And, lest there be any doubt, he pointed out that Congress had appropriated no money for the undertaking. However, he made a suggestion to Governor Blount. "As, however, you have Sheriffs who will be traversing their Districts for other purposes, it is referred to you whether the taking of the census on the general plan, could not be added to their other duties, and as it would give scarcely any additional trouble, whether it would require any additional reward, or more than some incidental accommodation or advantage, which, perhaps, it might be in your power to throw in their way. . . ."

The enumeration of the city of Boston began on August 2, 1790, and, twenty days later, its 18,038 inhabitants had been counted. Needless to say, the enumeration did not proceed as quickly or as smoothly everywhere in the country. However, as the historic year 1790 drew to a close, the census results from several cities, and even some states, had appeared in local newspapers. At the end of the nine-month period specified in the census law, the enumeration had been completed throughout the United States, excepting South Carolina, due to difficulties cited earlier, and Vermont, where the census started at a later date.

In his third annual message to Congress on October 25, 1791, President Washington reported "the completion of the census of the inhabitants, for which provision was made by law." On October 27, he sent the results of the count to Congress, noting the absence of information for South Carolina. By March 3, 1792, Congress received the complete results of the enumeration of the country.

It is well to note that Washington, in his message to Congress, called the count a "census." Earlier historians had questioned the use of the word since it is not contained in the Census Act as passed by Congress.

The census revealed a population of just under 4,000,000 people, distributed by states and census classifications as follows:

The Population of the United States in 1790 (The Results of the First Census)

District	Total	Free white males of 16 years and upward, including heads of families	Free white males under 16 years	Free white females, including heads of families	All other free persons	Slaves
Vermont	85,539 [a]	22,435	22,328	40,505	255	16 [b]
New Hampshire	141,885	36,086	34,851	70,160	630	158
Maine	96,540	24,384	24,748	46,870	538	—
Massachusetts	378,787	95,453	87,289	190,582	5,463	—
Rhode Island	68,825	16,019	15,799	32,652	3,407	948
Connecticut	237,946	60,523	54,403	117,448	2,808	2,764
New York	340,120	83,700	78,122	152,320	4,654	21,324
New Jersey	184,139	45,251	41,416	83,287	2,762	11,423
Pennsylvania	434,373	110,788	106,948	206,363	6,537	3,737
Delaware	59,096 [c]	11,783	12,143	22,384	3,899	8,887
Maryland	319,728	55,915	51,339	101,395	8,043	103,036
Virginia	747,610	110,936	116,135	215,046	12,866	292,627
Kentucky	73,677	15,154	17,057	28,922	114	12,430
North Carolina	393,751	69,988	77,506	140,710	4,975	100,572
South Carolina	249,073	35,576	37,722	66,880	1,801	107,094
Georgia	82,548	13,103	14,044	25,739	398	29,264
Total, exclusive of Southwest and Northwest Territories	3,893,637 [c]	807,094	791,850	1,541,263	59,150	694,280
Southwest Territory	35,691	6,271 [d]	10,277 [d]	15,365	361	3,417

[a] This total was later reduced by 114 because of errors in addition in several reports from the towns.
[b] There was an original reporting error that was not corrected for decades until the original reports were checked. There were never any slaves in Vermont.
[c] This was originally reported as 59,094 because of an error in addition. It also made the total incorrect.
[d] In the Southwest Territory, the age groups were: "21 years and upward" and "Under 21 years."

The census summaries that the marshals sent to the President and that became the responsibility of Jefferson were as varied in their design as were the sheets ruled up by the deputy marshals. New York, Vermont, Massachusetts, Rhode Island, and part of New Jersey included detailed counts for their towns and cities. Other marshals showed only the county totals within their states; occasionally, they listed totals for some of the larger towns and cities. On several summaries there were errors in addition.

Some marshals forwarded unexpected "bonuses" in the form of important additional information. The marshal for Massachusetts included in his summary the number of dwelling places in the towns and cities. The one for New York forwarded not only the totals of the excess of males over females in the white population but also showed free blacks by age groups. And Clement Biddle, the marshal for Pennsylvania, in 1791 published a directory for the city of Philadelphia that included the names and occupations of most of the inhabitants. It is generally assumed that he gathered the information during the census.

The census findings were printed officially in a small volume of fifty-six *octavo* pages. A summary of the total population of the United States, by district, had been prepared in Jefferson's office. In addition to this, the publication included only reproductions of the original returns prepared by the marshals. The actual printing was done by various private printers, first in Philadelphia and later in Washington.

The printed edition contained no analysis of the results; this would not come until the seventh census in 1850. However, several individuals wrote comments about the census or tried to interpret its results. One of the earliest interpretations was contained in a work called *Views of the United States,* published in 1794 by Mr. Tench Coxe, an assistant to Alexander Hamilton, who was then Secretary of the Treasury. Since the eighteenth century, the first census has been studied and analyzed by many experts in universities and in the Bureau of the Census.

Some interesting information about the young country comes to

light from a study of even the meager census data. Of the 3,890,-
000 people, excluding those in the Southwest Territory, 3,140,000,
just under 81 percent, were white. The remainder, about 753,000,
just under one person out of five, were black, since most authorities agree that probably few, if any, "Indians paying taxes" were
included in the first census. About 92 percent of the black people
were slaves. The census disclosed that about 250 families had 100
or more slaves.

The separation by Congress of "free white males" into those
under 16 years of age and those older was not accidental. The
807,000 free white males who were 16 years of age and over at
census time formed the primary manpower pool—military and
industrial—of the young nation. This was an extremely important
statistic for a proud people with plans for the future.

The original, hand-ruled, enumerators' schedules for the first
census have been lost for several of the states. Those for New
Jersey, Delaware, Georgia, Kentucky, and the Southwest Territory disappeared many years ago, and, despite every effort to
locate them, no trace has ever been found. The schedules for Virginia were probably destroyed when the British burned Washington, D.C., during the War of 1812. The schedules that remain
include about three-fourths of the white population at the time of
the census of 1790.

An interesting analysis has been made of the names appearing
on the schedules. *For the entire white population,* there were only
27,337 *basic* family names! And if names such as White and
Whyte are counted separately, there were perhaps no more than
35,000 *distinct* family names in this population. Most of the names
were English and Scotch, with many Dutch names in New York
State.

The clustering of the names meant that enumerators often had
to add characteristics to identify the people whom they had enumerated. The census sheets include many entries of the kind:
"Anna Woodhull (widow of Aaron)."

Very few men had middle names. It has been pointed out that

only three signers of the Declaration of Independence had middle names: Robert Treat Paine, Richard Henry Lee, and Francis Lightfoot Lee. Enumerators often added further identifying information to a man's name, such as his village of birth, as: "Robert Lowell (of Wessex)."

From the census data, it was possible to determine that the average family size at that time was 5.7 persons. It took about a hundred years for the average size of the American family to fall by one person.

The public announcement of the population of the country set off a shock wave of disappointment. Most people, including well-informed ones, had anticipated a population well above 4,000,000. Official expectations are indicated in a personal letter written by Thomas Jefferson as late as January, 1791. He wrote, "The census has made considerable progress, but will not be completed till midsummer. It is judged at present that our numbers will be between four and five millions. Virginia, it is supposed, will be between 7 and 800,000." Virginia was, of course, Jefferson's native state; therefore his interest in it.

By midsummer, however, after the returns had been counted, he wrote to William Carmichael, "I enclose you a copy of our census, which so far as it is written in black ink, is founded on actual returns, what is in red ink being conjectured, but very near the truth. Making very small allowance for omissions, which we know to have been very great, we may safely say we are above four millions."

Secretary Jefferson was concerned about the effect of the size of the population upon foreign opinion. He sent America's ministers abroad copies of the census results, with explanations as to why, in his opinion, the totals were seriously in error.

But, more than anything, a letter sent July, 1791, from George Washington to Gouverneur Morris, former delegate to the Constitutional Convention and soon to become Minister to France, states the attitude toward the census best. He wrote:

"In one of my letters to you, the account of the number of inhabitants which would probably be found in the United States on enumeration was too large. The estimate was then founded on the ideas held out by the gentlemen in Congress of the population of the several states, each of whom . . . looking through a magnifier, would speak of the greatest extent to which there was any probability of their numbers reaching. Returns of the census have already been made from several of the states, and a tolerably just estimate has now been formed in others, by which it appears that we shall hardly reach four millions; but this you are to take along with it, that the real number will greatly exceed the official return, because, from religious scruples, some would not give in their lists; from apprehension that it was intended as the foundation of a tax, others concealed or diminished theirs; and from the indolence of the mass and want of activity in many of the deputy enumerators, numbers are omitted. The authenticated number will, however, be far greater, I believe, than has ever been allowed in Europe, and will have no small influence in enabling them to form a more just opinion of our present growing importance than have yet been entertained there."

Were the census results really so inaccurate? Probably not. Many census historians believe, as Washington hinted in his letter, that the disappointment was due to the exaggerated hopes born of a newly won independence, as well as to the unrealistic estimates of the colonial population.

Whatever the feelings of the people and their government about the enumeration, the official census returns now had to serve the purpose for which they were collected: to apportion the House of Representatives among the states. This would be the first use of Article I, Section 2. It should not be surprising, therefore, that a fight broke out over the interpretation of some of its provisions. The heart of the dispute was the clause that stated:

"The Number of Representatives shall not exceed one for every thirty thousand."

Its interpretation was debated in the House and Senate for five months. The basic positions can be summarized as follows:

The clause meant that there should not be more than one representative for each 30,000 population:

1. *In each state.*
2. *In all the states.*

The first position would have resulted in a House of 112 members; this was favored by the House itself.

The second position would have resulted in a House of 120 members; this was favored by the Senate.

After long debate, the House passed and sent to the Senate a bill that called for 112 members. The Senate returned it to the House after adding eight seats *for large fractional remainders.*

The Senate's bill finally passed—but President Washington vetoed it on April 5, 1792, on the advice of Thomas Jefferson. He wrote to Washington, stating that the bill as passed was unconstitutional. "Fractions must be neglected," Jefferson stated, "because the Constitution . . . has left them unprovided for." A revised bill was passed by Congress on April 14, 1792.

Jefferson's opinion and Washington's veto set a very important precedent. Their method was used to apportion Congress for the next fifty years until it came under attack by another historic personality, Daniel Webster. The method came to be known as "the Jefferson method" or "the method of rejected fractions."

There were some interesting postscripts to the census. In 1791, Sir John Sinclair, a former president of the Board of Agriculture in Great Britain, began to put together a statistical summary of Scotland. He hoped that it would become a kind of *Domesday Book* for that land. After the enterprise was under way, President Washington was asked for his opinion about it. On March 15, 1793, just one year after the completion of the battle for apportionment, Washington wrote to Sir John:

*"I cannot but express myself highly pleased with the under-
taking in which you are engaged (that of drawing up the
Statistical Account of Scotland), and give my best wishes
for its success. I am full persuaded, that when enlightened
men, will take the trouble to examine so minutely into the
state of society, as your inquires seem to go, it must result in
greatly ameliorating the condition of the people, promoting
the interests of civil society, and happiness of mankind at
large. These are objects truly worthy the attention of a great
mind and every friend to the human race, must readily lend
his aid towards their accomplishment."*

Also in 1793, J. Phillips, Printer, of Lombard Street, London,
England, reprinted the entire volume of the American census results, as if to show the mother country how its sprawling infant
had grown.

In evaluating the first census, one fact stands out above all
others. As in the Sudan more than a century and a half later, the
census had a unifying effect upon the country. The citizen saw
federal officers engaged in a federal enterprise. For many, this
probably was the first exposure to such national activities during
the brief life of the republic.

Whatever its accuracy, there are no records that the census was
not fairly taken. Inaccuracies were due to inexperience and factors beyond the control of census officials. The subsequent apportionment of the House of Representatives reflected, as nearly as
possible, the distribution of the population. In addition to its acknowledged place in history, the American census of 1790 must be
evaluated as a highly successful enterprise.

Chapter 4

THE CENSUS BEFORE THE CIVIL WAR

In the years between the first census and the Civil War, the American people saw their territory and population expand enormously. The country was still agricultural and youthful in its outlook. After the war, things were never quite the same. The United States began the quick transition from an agricultural to an industrial nation. In fewer than the seventy-odd years from its birth to the Civil War, it stood in the front rank of the world's greatest powers.

The census reflects these changes and was, in turn, affected by many of the events. The Civil War, for example, marked the end of a major census classification—that of the black slave. The Fourteenth Amendment to the Constitution restored the missing two-fifths to the black person. Never again would only three-fifths of him be counted for purposes of representation in Congress. The whole conception of the census and the enumerating process went through important changes on the way to the modern census.

From 1790 to 1860, between the first and the eighth censuses, the territory of the United States increased 3.6 times. The settled area, that containing at least two persons per square mile, increased fivefold. However, the population increased eightfold, from a little less than 4,000,000 in 1790 to more than 31,000,000 in 1860.

Changes in Territory and Population of the United States Between
the First and Eighth Censuses, 1790–1860

Census year	Area in thousands of square miles			Population in millions of people
	Total	Covered by enumeration	Settled[a]	
1790	820.4	417.2	238.9	3.93
1800	820.4	434.7	305.7	5.31
1810	1,699.8	556.0	407.9	7.24
1820	1,754.6	688.7	508.7	9.64
1830	1,754.6	877.2	632.7	12.87
1840	2,943.1	1,183.9	807.3	17.07
1850	2,974.2	1,519.2	979.2	23.19
1860	2,974.2	1,951.5	1,194.8	31.44
Number of times it increased from 1790–1860	3.6	4.7	5.0	8.0

[a] Inhabited by at least two persons per square mile.

When Kansas was admitted to the Union in January, 1861, it
became the thirty-fourth state. In 1810, Washington, D.C., had
been enumerated separately for the first time. The national increase in population was due to the numbers in the newer states,
as well as to the growth in the original members of the Union. Of
the latter, Pennsylvania's population had increased seven times.
But only New York had grown more rapidly than the nation itself.
In the seventy-year period, its population had increased 11.4
times.

The increase in the nation's population from census to census
during this era proceeded with amazing regularity. The average
increase for each ten-year cycle was 34.6 percent. And not a single
increase differed from the average by as much as 2 percent! The
smallest increase, from 1830 to 1840, was 32.7 percent; the greatest,
from 1800 to 1810, was 36.4 percent, as shown on pages 210–211.

This extraordinary regularity made it possible for Elkanah Watson, a pioneer in agricultural organization, to make one of the
most accurate long-range forecasts of population growth ever re-

corded. In 1815, he forecast the population for each census until 1860 with little or no error. Since most population forecasts are based on the trends of the past, the increase in population from 1790 to 1800, 35.1 percent, was enough of a basis for an accurate forecast.

Watson should have stopped at the Civil War. Instead, he made predictions even for early twentieth century censuses. When the rate of population increase declined after the Civil War, Watson's forecasts became more and more unreal. By 1900, his forecast was ahead of the actual population by about 33 percent, or 25,000,000 people.

The smoothness of the pre-Civil War growth was responsible for a much more historic forecast. After studying the results of the census of 1860, President Abraham Lincoln, in a message to Congress, predicted that the American population in 1925 would be 215 million! This was an overstatement of a mere 100 million people. It was based on the 31.44 million population recorded by the

Changes in the Population of the United States

Census year	Total population		White population	
	Number in millions of people	Percent change from census to census	Number in millions of people	Percent change from census to census
1790	3.93	—	3.17	—
1800	5.31	35.1	4.31	35.7
1810	7.24	36.4	5.86	36.1
1820	9.64	33.1	7.86	34.1
1830	12.87	33.5	10.54	34.0
1840	17.07	32.7	14.20	34.7
1850	23.19	35.9	19.55	37.7
1860	31.44	35.6	26.92	37.7

1860 census, and if one adds one-third of the total every ten years, the estimated total in 1925 is about 215 million.

The Civil War was an important dividing line in the country's rate of growth. In the decade from 1860 to 1870, the population grew by only 26.7 percent. The rates of increase in the decades from the nation's birth until the Civil War were never again equaled.

With the exception of one decade, the white population always increased more rapidly than the black. From 1800 to 1810, the black population increased 37.5 percent; the white, 36.1 percent. But this was the result of special historic circumstances. The importation of slaves was prohibited by law after January 1, 1808. To beat the deadline, there were heavy imports of slaves before that date. After 1810, each census recorded a greater increase for the white population.

The white population grew 8.5 times during the seventy-year period; the black increased a little less than sixfold. Since 90 per-

Between the First and Eighth Censuses, 1790–1860

Negro population					
Total		Slave		Free	
Number in millions of people	Percent change from census to census	Number in millions of people	Percent change from census to census	Number in millions of people	Percent change from census to census
.76	—	.70	—	.06	—
1.00	32.3	.89	28.1	.11	82.1
1.38	37.5	1.19	33.3	.19	71.9
1.77	28.6	1.54	29.1	.23	25.3
2.33	31.4	2.01	30.6	.32	36.8
2.87	23.4	2.49	23.8	.39	20.9
3.64	26.6	3.20	28.8	.43	12.5
4.44	22.1	3.95	23.4	.49	12.3

cent or more of the blacks were slaves, it was the increase in the number of slaves that determined the increase in the Negro population. The number of "free colored," almost entirely black, grew eightfold, from about 60,000 in 1790 to 490,000 in 1860. The increase was mainly the result of the freeing of slaves in the northern states as well as the increase resulting from the many who escaped Southern slavery by way of the "underground railroad." Others won freedom after military service; a few bought their freedom. By and large, they worked as skilled craftsmen after obtaining freedom. Others had served out fixed terms of service as indentured servants.

For reasons discussed later, the counting of the black population, slave or free, was always much less accurate than that of the white population. Estimates are, therefore, subject to much wider error.

In 1820, for the first time, the black population was enumerated by age group. The slaves and "free colored," both men and women, were counted by age, as follows:

1. Under 14 years
2. 14 and under 26 years
3. 26 and under 45 years
4. 45 years and older

These groupings were used for exactly one census. In 1830, they broadened to six age classes:

1. Under 10 years
2. 10 and under 24 years
3. 24 and under 36 years
4. 36 and under 55 years
5. 55 and under 100 years
6. 100 years and older

The same age classes were used in the census of 1840. In 1850, when the entire basis of the census changed, all people were enumerated according to their exact age.

In the early censuses the age groups, for whites as well as blacks, were frequently changed. When exact ages were finally recorded for everyone, it was impossible to construct a consistent age picture of the people from the time of the birth of the republic. Modern demographers and statisticians have created such age distributions. However, in the United States the problem was enormously complicated by the fact that much of the growth in population came from immigration, as well as from natural increase.

The census results reflected the growing division of the country into free and slaveholding areas. In 1790, about one-sixth of the families in the United States owned slaves. The average slaveholding family had about seven slaves. In the last census before the Civil War, less than one-tenth of the families were slaveholding, but they kept an average of about ten slaves. In 1850, 1,733 families had 100 or more slaves, almost all from southern states.

In the Northern states, each census recorded fewer and fewer slaves. There were about 10,000 slaves in New York State in 1820. Ten years later, enumerators reported only 75. By 1850, no slaves were reported in the North. In the census that year, 2,300 slaves were reported in Delaware, the northernmost state to have any. On the eve of the Civil War, the division between north and south was deeply engraved in the census records.

As the population grew, so did the number of census questions. Very few voices were raised to question the authority of the government to find out more during a census than the mere size of the population. The number of inquiries had increased so much with each census that Congress, in the Census Act of 1850, felt compelled to state ". . . it being provided that the number of said inquiries, exclusive of the enumeration, shall not exceed one hundred." Of course, the vast outpouring of questions included censuses of industry and agriculture, as well as population.

The cost of counting the people had also risen. The population enumeration of 1850 was the first million dollar census in the nation's history. It also cost much more to count each person. In 1790, each individual had been enumerated at a cost of about 1.1 cents. By 1860, 6.3 cents was spent for each individual included in the census count.

One new element of cost was the census schedule itself. The first three enumerations used makeshift schedules drawn up by the individual deputy marshals according to their private mathematical and artistic impulses. In 1830, a uniform printed schedule was introduced. It was about 15 × 18 inches in size, rather large and bulky. There was space for the enumeration of twenty-eight families on each sheet. The age classifications for the white population had been extended as follows:

1. Under 5 years	8. 50 and under 60 years
2. 5 and under 10 years	9. 60 and under 70 years
3. 10 and under 15 years	10. 70 and under 80 years
4. 15 and under 20 years	11. 80 and under 90 years
5. 20 and under 30 years	12. 90 and under 100 years
6. 30 and under 40 years	13. 100 years and older
7. 40 and under 50 years	

Since the population exceeded the 10,000,000 mark for the first time in the country's history, the uniform-size schedule made the task of tabulating the results considerably easier.

In the period during which the population increased about eightfold, the number of representatives in the lower house of Congress rose from 105 after the census of 1790 to 241 after 1860. Many people believed that the House was growing too large for serious debate. However, in 1790 a representative spoke for 33,-000, people; by 1860, each member of the lower house represented about 127,400 people.

The controversy over how to apportion the House had been settled in 1790 by Jefferson's "method of rejected fractions." About forty years later it broke out again. The attack upon Jefferson's interpretation was led in Congress by the great orator from New Hampshire, Daniel Webster. Webster's argument was that the method not only discriminated against the small states but was unconstitutional, as well.

To understand the controversy, one must realize that Article I, Section 2, contains three basic sections for deciding the number of representatives from each state. They are:

1. The number of representatives shall not exceed one for every thirty thousand population.

2. Representatives shall be apportioned among the several states according to their respective numbers.

3. Each state shall have at least one representative.

Jefferson's interpretation rested mainly on the first section. In his view, the Constitution provided for "one" representative for a round number. It said nothing about fractions, and they were, therefore, to be rejected.

Webster now argued that Jefferson's method was unconstitutional because it ignored the second section "according to their respective numbers." In addition, he claimed, it always worked out to the disadvantage of the small states. Just how this came about can be seen from the following imaginary situation:

Representatives are to be assigned after the census of 1790 to two states. It is to be made on the basis of one representative for each 33,000 people.

1. State A has a population of 350,000. Under Jefferson's method it receives ten representatives. Thus, 20,000 people are "unrepresented." They are 5.7 percent of the state's total population.

2. State B has a population of 50,000 and receives one representative. As in State A, 20,000 people are "unrepresented." *But they compose 40 percent of the state's population.*

State A has seven times as many people as State B—but ten times as many representatives.

Webster proposed that a state receive one representative for a "major fraction," defined as being any fraction greater than one-half. By this method, State A would have received eleven representatives; State B, two. In Websters view, this reflected the relationship of populations more accurately.

It is interesting to note that Jefferson came from Virginia, then the largest state. Webster, a New Hampshire man, came from one of the smallest.

Webster raised the issue in 1830, but there was no change in the method. However, in 1842, after the sixth census, an apportionment law was passed granting "one additional representative for each state having a fraction greater than one moiety of the said ratio," that is, a fraction greater than one-half.

The controversy, however, was far from settled.

After the census of 1850, Congress tried another approach. It specified that there were to be 233 members of the House of Representatives. It then ordered the Secretary of the Interior, to whom responsibility for the census had been transferred, to assign the members by the following method:

1. The population of the country, as shown by the census, was to be divided by 233.
2. The population of each state was to be divided by the quotient.
3. Each unit was to be assigned one representative, *with enough seats left over to take care of large fractions.*

After performing Step 1, it was found that each representative would speak for 93,420 people.

Under Step 2, if a state had a population of 237,000, its representation would be determined as follows:

$$\frac{237,000}{93,420} = 2.54$$

The state was immediately assigned two representatives. Since the remainder was a "major fraction," greater than one-half, it became *eligible* for a third seat.

Even now the problem was not solved. Jefferson had stressed the first part of Article I, Section 2. Webster had shown that the second part could not be ignored. *But neither man had considered the third part.* This said simply, "Each State should have at least one Representative." Everyone had always taken it for granted since no state had ever been deprived of at least one seat in the House. But, in the continuing drama of apportioning the House, it would soon occupy the center of the stage. Over the years the story had become like a television serial that closes with, "See next episode."

With the Civil War another aspect of census taking ended. This was the direct involvement of many of the early presidents in the affairs of the census. Several whose terms of office included preparations for a census or reporting its results became almost direct participants. Washington received the reports of the marshals in the first census. He showed an intense interest in the results.

Madison's influence upon the census was historic in taking it beyond the mere counting of the population. Jefferson's influence extended beyond his governmental offices, as will be seen in his role as President of the American Philosophical Society. Later, Martin Van Buren's acceptance of honorary membership in the American Statistical Association linked him with that organization's close ties with the census. And Abraham Lincoln's study of the results of the census of 1860 may have led him to establish what may be the world's record for inaccurate population forecasts.

No president's passion for the enumeration, however, approached that of John Quincy Adams. During his presidency, from 1825 to 1829, there was no census. And this may well have been one of the great regrets of his life. But, as Secretary of State in the cabinet of President James Monroe, he was in charge of the fourth census in 1820.

President Adams's thoughts and ideas survived in his *Memoirs,* a rich record of his life and times. Throughout it appear many references to his involvement with the census. The self-portrait that comes out of the record is that of a man who did everything but count the people himself. Leonard D. White says in *The Jeffersonians* that the fourth census was, for Adams, in his own words, "one of the most urgent objects of attention."

"The orderly and systematic mind of John Quincy Adams," in White's discription, began, at first, to make the necessary preparations for the census of 1820. He searched for a copy of the instructions to the deputy marshals in the previous census. There was not a single copy to be found in the State Department! By chance, Adams learned that instructions had been printed in the *National Intelligencer,* a newspaper of that time. When he found a copy, he discovered that the instructions of 1810 were a direct copy of those of 1800. They were now useless.

Patiently, Adams wrote his own instructions, stating that "each census ought to be an improvement upon the last preceeding it." He designed the schedules and thought of new questions to ask. Even the pay of the assistant marshals concerned him, especially since additional questions would make more work for them. Apart from concern for their efforts, Adams wrote that "this will probably produce obstacles to the execution of the law."

As a result of his experiences with the census of 1820, Adams resolved that future secretaries of state would not face the same problems. He ordered records to be kept of any correspondence that had anything to do with the census. Also, a memorandum book was maintained in which any "incident of importance in the progress of the enumeration" was to be noted.

President Adams's fourth annual message to Congress on December 28, 1828, dealt with the forthcoming fifth census. This was earlier than Congress ever acted on census matters but characteristic of Adams. Among other things, he proposed that the critical date for the census be changed from August 1 to June 1. He suggested that the number of age classifications be increased. And, in keeping with ideas born during the census of 1820, he asked that the pay of the marshals be increased.

Congress finally acted on census matters on March 23, 1830, after Adams was out of office. They agreed to his first two requests. But the pay of the marshals, increased in minor detail, remained as low as ever.

On January 10, 1800, a resolution adopted by the American Philosophical Society, whose president was Thomas Jefferson, reached the United States Senate. In Jefferson's words, it asked Congress to expand the census "in order to ascertain more completely the causes which influence life and health, and to furnish a curious and useful document of society in these States, and of the conditions and vocations of our fellow citizens."

The resolution proposed additional age classifications, as well as questions on occupation. The society suggested nine occupational groups, including one for "Persons of no particular calling, living on their income."

Great stress was laid on obtaining birth and death statistics. Such records, except those kept by churches, were almost completely lacking in the United States. From such information, the society stated, one could determine "the ordinary duration of life in these States, the chances of life for every epoch thereof, and the ratio of the increase of their population, firmly believing that the result will be sensibly different from what is presented by the tables of other countries by which we are from necessity, in the habit of estimating the probabilities of life here."

The resolution is of great historic importance. It marks the beginning of citizen participation in the affairs of the census. From that time, this participation has only increased and broadened. Today, from planning stage, to the wording of questions, to final analysis of the returns, the decennial census is one of the best examples of partnership between citizens and their government.

In 1839, the American Statistical Association (ASA) was founded at Boston, Massachusetts. President Martin Van Buren accepted honorary membership. At the time, the ASA had less than a dozen members, most of whom were important men in fields other than statistics. But, almost from the day of its founding, the association became involved in the affairs of the census, a relationship that deepened with time.

The start of the relationship was not a promising one. One of

the earliest acts of the ASA was a sharp attack upon the failures of
the census of 1840, delivered by Dr. Edward Jarvis, who became
the association's president in 1852. Later, the accuracy of his criticism was acknowledged. However, the ASA was not content
merely to play the part of critic. James D. B. DeBow, a corresponding member of the ASA, helped plan the census of 1850 and
became the first to hold the title of Superintendent of the Census
in carrying it out.

Lemuel Shattuck, a founding member of the American Statistical Association, was one of the earliest, really distinguished
American statisticians. He modernized the registration of births
and deaths in Massachusetts, his native state. Because of the
faults of the census of 1840, Shattuck organized and carried
through a pioneer census of the city of Boston in 1845. This extremely successful census became a model for the American census of 1850, the best up to that time. For this census, he drafted
five of the six schedules and wrote the instructions for the enumerators.

These three pioneers—DeBow, Jarvis, and Shattuck—established the precedent of association between the ASA and the census organization. Its members have served in many ways. Several
of its officers became superintendents of the census. Very early,
the ASA took the lead in the successful campaign for the creation
of a permanent census office. Today, it seeks recognition of the
need for a five-year census. However, throughout its history, its
most important contribution has been in supplying ideas and serving as friendly and constructive critic.

The first six enumerations, from 1790 to 1840, were, in a way, a
training ground for a modern census. The early efforts had many
errors in planning and execution. Among the many was the failure
to establish and maintain proper age classes. In 1870, these early
censuses were corrected to be uniform in their classifications by
county and color of the respondent. Later, other experts adjusted
the original material for the responses as to sex and age.

The seventh census in 1850 was a pioneer census that has been called the first adequate enumeration of the people of the United States. It was historic in another sense; it occurred several years before the calling together of the first International Statistical Congress by Adolphe Quételet of Belgium, the outstanding statistician of his time. This congress had an effect upon census taking throughout much of the world. Since it came before the congress, the census of 1850 must rank as an outstanding world effort in this area of human activity.

In 1850, for the first time in American census history, the *individual* was the object of enumeration. Before then, it had been the family, with its members enumerated as they related to the head of the household.

The content of the census schedule was not fixed by act of Congress, as in the past. It was to be drawn up by the men responsible for the conduct of the enumeration. The result was six separate schedules, including one each for agriculture and industry. One of the population schedules was for the "free" inhabitants, another for slaves. The fifth schedule would have delighted Jefferson and the members of the American Philosophical Society; it was designed to obtain a complete profile of those who had died during the year, including color, sex, age, number of days of illness and cause of death. Such information had been sought fifty years earlier but without success.

The last schedule, for social statistics, sought to obtain a description of American life and society. It contained questions about schools and colleges, libraries, newspapers and magazines, religion, crime, poverty, and wages. It was a unique and ambitious undertaking.

It was the first census conducted by the recently created Department of the Interior rather than the State Department. A new personality made his appearance—the Superintendent of the Census—who was to remain an officer of prestige and importance until the twentieth century.

New ground was broken in another respect. For the first time, census results were collected and tabulated in a central office in Washington, D.C. Also, for the first time, there was an analysis of the significance of the tremendous volume of information collected.

The only important carryover from the past was in the printing of the census findings by a private contractor. When, after the 1860 census, the results were printed in the new Government Printing Office, the American census, having just enumerated more than 31,000,000 people, attained a significant level of maturity.

Chapter 5

TOWARD A COMPUTERIZED CENSUS

In 1865, at the end of the Civil War, much of the South lay in ruins. This was true of the face of the land and many of the structures on it; it was true, also, of the social organization built upon slavery. Among factors that would affect a census, the transportation system was destroyed; railway lines and bridges had been wrecked everywhere. Even more than the physical ruin, the hostility that had grown through four years of bitter fighting was not likely to lead to the cooperation necessary for accurate enumeration. The structure of government, upon which a census relies, had been taken apart in the South. The new reconstruction governments, however willing and able, had never had any experience with census taking. Besides, they were occupied with more urgent problems.

For years after the war, thousands of former slaves wandered over the land, often far from their former homes. This was the first of the great internal migrations of the black people of the United States. Similar uprooting of blacks would take place after every war in American history. Wandering people are not likely to be counted accurately.

It is not surprising, then, that the census of 1870, the first after the Civil War, was inaccurate. In later years, the population that was, at that time, announced to be 38.5 million was adjusted to 39.8 million.

Amid the postwar chaos, there was a dramatic example of the enduring quality of the American census. In many respects severe penalties were imposed upon the South and its citizens. But when the war was over, the southern marshals and their assistants who had participated in the census of 1860 were finally paid for their work.

At the center of planning for the census of 1870 was the chairman of the House Committee on the Census, General James A. Garfield, later President of the United States. General Garfield was one of the most capable men ever to hold that important post in the House of Representatives. He made several proposals that were designed to change the nature of the census and modernize it. When a bill including these changes was submitted to Congress, it was passed by the House but rejected by the Senate.

Garfield's reforms might have passed the Senate but for one important factor. The magazine, *The Nation,* in its issue of February 14, 1870, stated that the Senate rejected the bill because it would have given to the House the power to appoint the marshals and their deputies, a power exercised up to then by the Senate.

There was another reason for the failure to consider the bill on its merits. Between the end of the war and the ninth census, Congress was occupied with the adoption of the Fourteenth and Fifteenth Amendments to the Constitution, the treatment of the Southern states for their rebellion, the military occupation of the South, and the place of the Negro in postwar society. Census problems did not seem to justify major debates.

Garfield's work was not in vain. His proposed reforms were later adopted for the census of 1880. But because of the failure of Congress to act, the first postwar census was taken under the same law that had been in effect for the censuses of 1850 and 1860. The great, historical difference was that this was the first census in American history that had no questions about slaves. With these removed, there was room for others. There was no shortage of substitutes for consideration.

The most important new question in the 1870 census was one based upon the provisions of the Fourteenth Amendment. No state could any longer deny, limit, or interfere with the right to vote of the freed slaves. If a state did, its representation in the House was to be reduced proportionately. One of the aims of the ninth census was to determine how many potential voters there were and how many had not been allowed to use that right.

The enumeration of 1870 was a peculiar mixture of old and new. The instructions to the assistant marshals stated, "Each assistant will provide himself with a secure portable inkstand, good ink, and a sufficient number of pens. All entries will be carefully dried with the blotting paper which accompanies each portfolio." These sentences could have been lifted without change from the instructions for any colonial census.

But this census was the first to make significant use of machines in tabulating census results. The machines, which did tallying, had been invented by Colonel Charles W. Seaton, then chief clerk of the census and later superintendent of the 1875 census of New York State. With the American population rapidly approaching the 40,000,000 mark, Colonel Seaton's machines were important tools.

Before the end of the century, a more impressive stride was taken toward mechanizing the tabulation of census data. Herman Hollerith, an employee of the Bureau of the Census, invented a machine that could sort and count punch cards on which information had been entered in the form of codes. Hollerith machines, as they were called, were used in the census of 1890. It is estimated that they saved the bureau $5,000,000 in tabulating costs. A little later the machines that punched the holes in the cards, as well as those that did sorting, were converted to electricity. From then on, there was increasing use of machinery up to the most advanced computers.

The advantage of machinery is not merely speed or economy. It permits more comprehensive analysis of information. For example, common census questions request information about age, occupation, and industry. To attempt to "cross-tabulate" these items, that is to tabulate by hand age by occupation within industry for a population of many millions, is to attempt the near impossible. With electrical tabulating machines, such analyses are possible. They may provide valuable information about a country's economy and its work force.

The results of the census of 1870 were presented on specially drawn maps and charts. From this beginning, the use of attractive, visual presentation of census findings would, like the use of machinery, continue to expand. At this point in American history, the steady westward shift of the population was clearly reflected in the census results. The "center of gravity" of the population had moved to a point just east of Cincinnati, Ohio, and stood ready to leap into Kentucky.

With completion of the census of 1870, the long service of the marshals and their assistants finally came to an end. Perhaps more than any other act, this indicated the changing attitudes toward the census. In truth, with 40,000,000 people to enumerate, the system of marshals had become inefficient. A marshal was an officer of the courts of the United States. He was selected for qualities that were not necessarily those needed to be an efficient supervisor of census takers.

However, a factor that had come to be more important was that he was not appointed by the Superintendent of the Census and was not really responsible to him. After the tabulation of the census, the superintendent returned to private life; the marshal remained an officer of the court. As superintendents began to come from the ranks of professionals with statistical training, including officers of the American Statistical Association, they looked forward to working with men who had more appropriate qualifications.

In 1880, for the first time in American history, civilian census supervisors were appointed who outranked the marshals. The new census law authorized the appointment of as many as 150 men to replace 75 marshals. From this time forward, all census takers were called "enumerators."

The new act officially created a census office in the Department of the Interior. The post of Superintendent of the Census, to be filled by presidential appointment, also received official blessing. But Congress was not yet ready to act on a *permanent* census office. To erase any doubt about this, it specified in the act that the *term* of the superintendent and *the office itself* should come to an end with the publication of the census results.

The census of 1880, in which 50.2 million people were enumerated, was by far the best and most thorough enumeration since 1790.

Whatever else may be remembered about the tenth census, it will be most notable for one factor important to all census work—money. Never had so many problems arisen involving money. The census law was passed in 1879. But Congress made no appropriation of money until June 16, 1880—two weeks after the census had started! Then, in January, 1881, the enumerators in New York, New Jersey, and Kentucky petitioned Congress for an increase in pay. They were receiving 10 cents for each 100 names, hardly a lordly sum even in those days.

The enumerators were not alone. Many supervisors joined them. Many Congressmen must have looked back longingly to "the good old days" of the marshals and their assistants.

The money problems did not end with these requests. In the middle of 1881, the money that Congress had appropriated ran out! The work of tabulating the census was carried out by 700 volunteers. Although the enumerators and supervisors did not get more money, Congress did provide funds later with which to pay the patriotic volunteers.

As the century moved to a close, the American census was in the forefront of world efforts in that field. However, there was a great gap in the American statistical description of its people. Almost every census included questions about the characteristics of people who had died during the year—their age, sex, color, cause of death, and similar questions. In the United States these questions almost *had* to be asked. In the registration of deaths (and births), this country lagged far behind most of the advanced countries of the world. There was no national system of registration. Only one-sixth of the people lived in areas where the registration of a death was compulsory. For the rest of the nation, the standards of colonial times still prevailed.

"Indians not taxed" became persons in the census of 1890 when, for the first time, they were enumerated. It was also the first real enumeration of Alaska. And, for the first time, what were to be the forty-eight states of the continental United States were included in a census, although the territories of Arizona, New Mexico, Oklahoma, and Utah had not yet attained statehood.

The last American census of the nineteenth century revealed a population of 63,000,000. The United States had become one of the largest nations in the world and, perhaps, the largest *counted* one. There were many interesting demographic facts about the American people at the turn of the century.

The census-to-census increases in population were at a lower rate than those before the Civil War. But, since that conflict, the population had doubled. One of the unique features of this later growth was the tremendous increase in immigration. In the decade from 1880 to 1890, of every five new Americans, more than two were white immigrants. In all, from 1880 to 1900, about 10,000,000 immigrants are estimated to have entered the country. This wave was so powerful that it changed the characteristics of the population. A high proportion of the immigrants were young white males. They caused the proportion of the nonwhite, mainly black, population to decline in relation to the total. In 1870, "nonwhites" had been 13.8 percent of the population. By the end of the century, they were only 12 percent and still declining. They were not to make up 12 percent of the total population again until the census of 1970.

The absorption of immigrants on so vast a scale is one of the most significant population facts of modern history.

After his work was done, Robert P. Porter, superintendent of the eleventh census wrote, "The Superintendent in both the last two censuses [1880 and 1890] was appointed in April of the year preceding the enumeration, but when I was appointed I had nothing but one clerk and a messenger, and a desk with some white paper on it." Article I, Section 2, provided for an enumeration of the population every ten years; it was a clear provision. Yet, as the United States entered the twentieth century with a population of 76,000,000, there was no permanent governmental agency to carry out the constitutional requirement. For every census a new structure was built. With publication of the results, it was stripped to the ground.

This utter lack of continuity, whether shown by President Adams's search for the instructions to the enumerators or by the blank paper on Superintendent Porter's desk, had important consequences. In the first place, any census was too much influenced by the character of the superintendent. If he was a good organizer, had a knowledge of statistics, and was conscientious, the census was likely to be satisfactory. If he was only a political appointee, as several were, the enumeration suffered. Generally, a good *permanent* organization can offset an unqualified director.

It was the country's good fortune that the superintendents, especially in the later years of the nineteenth century, tended to be eminent men. They accepted the appointment as an honor and a challenge, as well as a patriotic duty. But appoinment as Superintendent of the Census held no promise of a permanent government career.

The absence of permanency, although it seemed to be economical, was really extremely wasteful. Very often, as the money that Congress had appropriated ran out, census tabulations were completed by inexperienced clerks in the Department of the Interior. Far more serious was the situation described by E. Dana Durand, director of the thirteenth census. He wrote, "For the past three censuses, the population schedules have carried questions regarding the number of children born to each woman and the duration of marriage, but never has the Census Bureau had time or money to tabulate the answers."

Another great source of waste was hidden. Business and government agencies at all levels had come more and more to use and rely upon census findings. However, five or six years after a census, if a user of census statistics needed more information or expert interpretation, there was no one with whom he could correspond. The census office had posted an "Out to lunch" sign for the next five years.

The need for a permanent office had long been recognized. In 1845, after the disastrous census of 1840, which is discussed more fully in another chapter, a Congressional committee had recommended the establishment of a "Bureau of Statistics." The then Secretary of the Treasury, George Bibb, supported the proposal. The superintendent of the seventh census, James DeBow, wrote in 1850, "Unless there is machinery in advance at the seat of Government no census can ever be properly taken and published. There is a peculiar education required for these labors which neither comes from zeal or genius, but is the result only of experience."

From this time on, Congress received a steady flow of advice on the desirability of a permanent census agency. There were almost annual resolutions by the American Statistical Association and, later, by the American Economic Association.

In 1891, the Senate asked the Secretary of the Interior "to consider the expediency of the establishment of a permanent census bureau and to embody the results of his consideration with a draft of a bill." The secretary's report contains favorable testimony from business organizations, labor unions, statisticians and churchmen, heads of state agricultural and health departments—in short, from each of the growing number of groups that relied upon and used census results. The report recommended the immediate establishment of a permanent census bureau.

A bill to accomplish this was introduced in 1893, but no action was taken until 1896. A joint Congressional resolution that year asked the Secretary of Commerce and Labor to draft a plan for the bureau. Soon, however, Congress had to act on the next census, the first of the twentieth century. At this point, the intent of Congress was clearly shown in the provisions of the Census Act of 1899.

Under the terms of the act, the twelfth census was to be supervised by a *director* of the census. The *assistant director* was to be someone "who shall be a practical, experienced statistician." They were to be assisted by five *chief statisticians,* "persons of known and tried experience in statistical work." This was a direct invitation for greater professionalism.

Now that the possibility of permanent service existed, some eminent men were attracted to the census office. William R. Merriam became director of the census of 1900; later, he served as the first director of the permanent office. Dr. Frederick H. Wines was the assistant director. Walter F. Willcox, later president of the American Statistical Association, was one of the five chief statisticians.

So that no one would think that this was the permanent census office, Congress clearly stated in the Census Act of 1899 that "nothing herein contained shall be construed to establish a census bureau permanent beyond the twelfth Census."

The climax to the long campaign came on March 6, 1902. An act of Congress established a permanent Bureau of the Census. An act of 1903 transferred the bureau from the Department of the Interior to the then Department of Commerce and Labor, now the Department of Commerce.

The bureau had no duty to "promote" or "advance" anything; it was to be a fact-gathering agency. Some of its assignments may seem strange today. Among other duties, it was responsible for preparing uniform accounting methods for the cities to rescue many from a state of near chaos. The bureau also maintained its own machine shop to perfect its tabulating machines. At the beginning of the century, these were not in widespread use.

What was really expected of the bureau, however, was best expressed by the Secretary of Commerce and Labor in his annual report of 1902. In his opinion, the bureau should aim to be "the greatest statistical laboratory of the United States government, worthy to rank with the best statistical offices maintained by European governments." Today, no one doubts that it has fulfilled these hopes.

The first task of the new Bureau of the Census was to complete the tabulations of the census of 1900. It soon had to prepare for the first census of its own planning, the thirteenth census in 1910. The census "target date," or "critical moment" of midnight June 1 on which to begin the census, was judged to be unrealistic in view of the changes in American life. Wealth had increased considerably. Although the automobile was not yet a popular family vehicle, the great mobility of the American people had begun. By early summer many people might be traveling or be away at summer homes. In 1910, the "target date" was the early spring one of April 15.

Another aspect of census taking received fresh thought. As the population rose and more and more users asked for more and more census questions, the cost of meeting the requirements of Article I, Section 2, rose steeply. In 1910, for example, 70,000 enumerators were used. In the search for economy, there were experiments with self-enumeration. Census schedules were mailed to families who were expected to fill them out and return them in a specified way.

The results were poor. Some said that this was due to the fact that there was no penalty for failure to return the census schedules. However, it may be that, due to the heavy flow of immigrants still coming into the country, many people could neither read nor write English. With the best will in the world, they could not have completed the questionnaires.

The director of the bureau at that time, E. Dana Durand, still believed that the census of the future would use the Post Office. It may be interesting to note that the census of 1970 will place very great emphasis upon self-enumeration.

The large immigrant population affected the census in another way. There continued to be great interest in the national origin of the new Americans. Immigration statistics have always been difficult to collect accurately. In those years, with a flood of people coming to American ports, the job of maintaining statistics was poorly planned and performed. The census attempted to correct what others had failed to do.

A variety of questions were framed in the many attempts to find out where everyone had come from. Some asked "nationality" or "country of origin"; others inquired about "mother tongue" or "language spoken at home." All failed. The Austro-Hungarian Empire was then called "a prison-house of nations." What nationality then was a Serbian who had come from there, or a Finn or Pole who came from Czarist Russia? If a family left Poland and stopped in England for a while, as many did, before continuing to the United States, what was its "country of origin"? What was learned about a Jewish family whose "language spoken at home" was Yiddish? The people came and helped to build the country. How many came from any particular point on the globe was never determined with any accuracy. In looking back, it doesn't seem to matter very much.

The general view of the census of 1910, the first under the infant bureau, was expressed by Assistant Director W. F. Willoughby, who said that "the Thirteenth Census of population is thus much the most comprehensive census of population that has ever been taken by the United States."

The early twentieth century saw the almost complete disappearance of another feature of census life—the state census. Well into the nineteenth century, many states made their own enumerations, usually in mid-decade. They used the results most often to apportion representation in their legislatures—the same justification as for the national census. By 1914, however, although twenty-seven states had provisions in their constitutions for censuses, only ten went through the motions of taking them. As the activities of the Bureau of the Census expanded, the state census became a thing of the past. In the 1960's, only Kansas and Massachusetts were conducting mid-decade enumerations. Some states paid the bureau to carry out special censuses within their borders. Others estimated their populations, using the latest techniques developed by theoretical statisticians. Their "raw materials" were the vital statistics collected by their Departments of Health.

One of the most significant changes in American social organization was revealed by the census of 1920. For the first time, the urban population exceeded the rural. About 51 percent of the 106 million Americans were then living in an urban, or city, environment. This trend had been under way since the birth of the republic but was long hidden by addition of more and more new states. It continues to this day; by 1960, seven out of ten Americans were living in an urban area.

The definition of "urban" used by the Bureau of the Census since 1950 is a technical one. Its basic aim, however, is to include all people living in communities with populations of 2,500 or more as well as those residing in the suburban ring around large cities with populations of 50,000 or more.

The "rural" population includes those who live in all other places. They are further divided into those living in "rural farm" and "rural nonfarm" communities. Both rural groups continue to decline in the proportion of the American people who dwell there.

The urban-rural separation is unique so that very few international comparisons are possible. Each country makes its own definitions. In the Soviet Union, for example, an urban place is one where urban activities are carried on. A mining town of any size could be classed as an urban place. In some of the developing countries, "urban" may include any place where there is a regular market.

The census generally reflects the important stages in a country's development. As noted before, one rare exception in American history is the Great Depression of the 1930's. Plans for the census of 1930 were made during a period of great prosperity. Two of the questions were designed to find out how many families owned radios and what the value of their home was. At census time in April, 1930, the stock market had already been hit by the worst catastrophe in its history. But the economic effects had not yet touched the average person. And President Herbert Hoover offered the American people reassuring words.

Shortly after the enumeration was completed, many of the radios the people had said that they owned, often large consoles resembling modern television consoles, were forfeited for failure to pay the installments on them. The homes upon which the people had placed a value could be bought from the banks that had seized them for the balance of the mortgage payments. Businesses and farms were lost or abandoned by their owners. The first administration of President Franklin D. Roosevelt began, and the most urgent problem, in addition to feeding the starving, was to restore a measure of hope.

Almost nothing of all this appears in the census records.

By the next census, much of the economy had been restored. Europe was at war. The American social scene was about to be changed beyond recognition. It was clear to informed people that *this* census would be the last before American participation in a major war. The census of 1940 could not recapture the elements of the Great Depression. It could only prepare a profile of the people prior to their transformation in ways that could not then be foreseen.

In many ways, the census of 1940 was the first contemporary census. Rather than being simply a vast counting operation, it made use of advanced statistical techniques. It introduced new ideas that had been tried only on an experimental basis. Above all, the census of 1940 was the first in which sampling was used.

A sample differs from a census in that it deliberately includes only *part* of the whole. On the basis of the sample results, statisticians draw conclusions or make generalizations about the entire population from which the sample was selected. They can also calculate the size of the "error" that results from the sampling procedure. This means that if the sample shows, for example, that

3.1 percent of the male population are war veterans (a sample question in 1940), the "real" percent, if everyone had been asked the question, might have been 3 or 3.2.

Sampling procedures were used for such questions as veteran status, the possession of a Social Security number, occupation and industry, and several others. Sampling was also used in checking the completed census questionnaires and the key-punched cards that were created from them.

The *sampling ratio* was 5 percent; every twentieth person was included in the sample, and only that person, when reached, was asked the sampled questions. The census schedule had been revised to be one of *continuous lines*, rather than one based upon family units. A "continous line" schedule has no break or interruption for the end of one family or a single individual and the beginning of another. It continues listing people uninterruptedly despite any relation or lack of relation that they may have to one another. A "family schedule," of course, shows a discontinuity between every family unit of whatever size. This was done to prevent bias in the sample, so that the person selected would not *tend* to be the father but that everyone would have an equal probability of being selected in the sample.

Since 1940 every census has included items that were sampled in samples of various sizes. The use of sampling is likely to expand continuously. The Constitution decrees that each person be directly enumerated, but characteristics of the population can be learned by sampling. There àre many reasons why its use will increase, but these are among the more important ones:

1. The scientific basis of sampling is now solidly established. "Errors" that result from the sampling process can be kept as low as desired and calculated with precision.

2. A sample is easier to process than a complete count; the results can be made available sooner.

3. The cost of the decennial census grows with the economy and the population. It has passed the $100,000,000 mark.

Congressional reluctance to appropriate such sums is a permanent consideration. A sample is cheaper.

4. The number of enumerators needed also grows with the population. Since census taking, a short-term occupation, has never been the road to wealth, enumerators are harder to find. In a time of prosperity, the quality of the enumerators declines. A sample requires fewer enumerators.

The economic depression left its mark upon the census in several ways. The bitter arguments that raged during the 1930's about how many people were unemployed drove home the point that such statistics were important to the economy of a country. The dangers in making such measurements only at ten-year intervals had now been made clear. The census count of employed and unemployed, it was believed, should serve only as a *benchmark*— a point of reference by which other measurements are judged.

From this thinking came the idea of the *labor force*. This is the part of the population that is at least fourteen years old and has a job or is seeking a job. The actual definition is more technical, but this is, basically, the group that the Bureau of the Census has been measuring. It now does so, on a sample basis, each month.

The census of 1940 also introduced new techniques for the enumeration of two very elusive groups of people—transients and infants. Transients do not "stay put" in any one place for a reasonable period of time. They may include traveling salesmen, actors and musicians "on the road," as well as the drifters who are not likely to call any place "home"; escaped prisoners are certainly "transient." Such groups have always tended to give conservative census planners severe headaches.

In the sixteenth census, April 8, 1940, was set aside as "transient day." On that day, an army of enumerators swooped down upon all places where such people were likely to be. Their aim was merely to count them, not to convert them to a more sober way of life.

Infants have always resisted accurate enumeration for the many reasons, including superstition, discussed earlier. This has been as true in the United States, although to a lesser degree, as it has been elsewhere in the world. A special attempt was made in 1940 to determine the *extent* of their underenumeration. Enumerators filled out special "infant cards" for about 700,000 children under four months of age. The cards were later matched against birth registration records. This was intended to serve the double purpose of measuring the underenumeration as well as the comprehensiveness of birth registration.

An unexpected lesson was learned from this experiment. People who did not register the births of their newborn children are the very ones least likely to report them in a census.

In 1906, Dr. Walter Laidlaw of New York City developed the concept of the *census tract*. The tract is a small area containing from 3,000 to 6,000 people who share many common characteristics. Most of them may belong to a similar economic group whose incomes do not vary too much from member to member and who may occupy the same type of housing. The census tract lies within a well-defined geographic place that is not likely to change from one census to another. The idea of the tract is uniformity of the parts and stability of the shape.

At Dr. Laidlaw's request, from data collected in the census of 1910, some tables were prepared for census tracts in eight large cities, including New York. This procedure was repeated after the next census. In 1930, the program was expanded to include eighteen cities; it was still experimental, however. The decisive change to the census tract as a basic census unit was made in 1940 when information was available for sixty-one cities. Today tract information is available for every city with a population of 50,000 or more in an ever-expanding program.

The idea of the census tract was inspired by a private citizen; the subject continues to be a meeting ground for the citizen and the Bureau. Local committees of private citizens promote the use of tract data and check upon the continued uniformity of the population residing there.

The two qualities—uniformity and stability—make the census tract useful for business, government agency, and scientific group. A national magazine may use tract data to plan a subscription campaign aimed at homeowners with annual incomes between $10,000 and $15,000. A maker of air conditioners, also on the basis of tract data, may decide whether to advertise in that magazine. The government uses it to plan a poverty program, to decide whether to build a health center in a community, expand public housing, or intensify a narcotics control program. A scientist can measure the effects of a water fluoridation program or free cancer control examinations. For him, it is a living laboratory with controlled units.

The census of 1940 proved something that the first census takers may have suspected—that people do not report their ages accurately. This census was the first since passage of the Social Security Act of 1935, which provided retirement benefits for workers who reached the age of sixty-five. As any expert could have predicted, large numbers of people adjusted their ages to fit the terms of the Social Security Act. Many who, on the basis of past records for the age groups, should have been in "60 to 64 years" group, moved up a notch to the "65 to 69 years" group. It is not important whether their leap to advanced age was inspired by the hope for earlier Social Security benefits or whether they suddenly repented of trying to hold on to younger years too long. Then or now, they had not reported their age correctly. The census of 1940 provided a rare laboratory to test what had long been suspected.

The decades of decline in the "nonwhite" population as a proportion of the total ended in 1940. The census showed them to be 10.2 percent of the total population, exactly the same as in the census of 1930. By the census of 1950, the first increase in more than a century was recorded for this group. "Nonwhites" represented 10.5 percent of all Americans. More significantly, the "nonwhite" population had increased more than the "white," the former by 17.1 percent, the latter by 14.1 percent. This pattern would continue into 1960 and 1970.

At the heart of this changed relationship was the decline in white immigration. Even as late as the decade from 1920 to 1930, immigrants represented more than 22 percent of the country's increased population. But from 1930 to 1940, they fell to less than 6 percent. And, from 1940 to 1950, only about 5 percent of the 19,000,000 increase in population in the United States was due to the arrival of immigrants.

In these years there also began the sharp decline in Negro mortality. As the flow of immigrants slowed to a trickle and the growth of the American population was due almost entirely to natural increase, the "nonwhite," mainly Negro, increase exceeded the white. As expected, its proportion of the total population increased.

Since the introduction of sampling in 1940, the number of *sampled* questions increased with each census. This came as no surprise to those who were aware of how the "simple six" of 1790 had grown to many more questions as census followed census. However, in the middle of the twentieth century, a new tool became available for analyzing census data, which made more questions possible. In 1951, UNIVAC I, the first true computer, was delivered to the Bureau of the Census to help tabulate the data from the census of 1950. It was the first in a long series. From that time, the bureau became not only one of the most extensive users of computers but also a pioneer in its adaptation to huge masses of data.

A historical note: In 1963, only twelve years after its baptism at the Bureau of the Census, UNIVAC I was retired. It was sent to the Smithsonian Institution in Washington, D.C., to rest beside the Wright Brothers' airplane.

After the 1950 census, $1,000,000, 1 percent of the total cost of $100,000,000, was spent in checking errors—the kind, their size and origin. This was a tribute to the passion for accuracy of the staff of the bureau. But it also reflected the tremendous advances in statistical technique and theory since World War II. Such measurements could now be made with a degree of precision that would have been impossible until then.

The census of 1950 will be remembered for one other remarkable change. The enumerator's pay was no longer based on the number of names he collected. He was paid a flat daily sum.

The eighteenth census of the United States in 1960 was one of the outstanding episodes in the long history of man counting his kind. Almost 180 million people were counted in little more than three months; ten years earlier, more than 150 million had been counted. Thus, within a decade, about one-third of a billion people were counted, compared, and analyzed and the results presented to the world in more than 200,000 printed pages.

In 1911 the Registrar General of England and Wales stated that the United States "produces a more elaborate census probably than any other country." The census of 1960 emphasized the fact that the degree of difference between the American census and those of the rest of the world had widened.

The statistics of the effort involved are staggering. More than 1,000,000 manhours, the unit that expresses the work done by one man for one hour, were spent in planning the census. This is as if about 600 people spent an entire working *year* doing nothing but the work of planning.

On the single day of April 17, 1960, there were about 160,000 men and women dispersed throughout the land carrying out the task of enumeration. Each had in his kit, among other things, an extremely detailed local map of his enumeration district that had been prepared by experts at the bureau. Over the years, these maps had become as well known and useful as those of the United States Geologic Survey.

In the year 1960 alone, Congress appropriated $86,500,000 for census purposes. After all the bills were paid, the census had cost more than $130,000,000.

The plans for this census called for many people to enumerate themselves on questionnaires delivered to them by the Post Office. Such an undertaking requires a great measure of cooperation. Since the cooperation could not be taken for granted, a tremendous propaganda barrage got under way well before April 1, 1960, "target day" of the census. Articles about the coming enumeration appeared in such national magazines as *Reader's Digest, Saturday Evening Post, National Geographic Magazine,* and many, many others. Every newspaper, radio and television station carried some message about the census. Movies were shown in the schools and before civic groups. Comedians in nightclubs and on television made jokes about the census. This was to be the first census taken at a time of widespread ownership of TV sets. When the din died down, it would have seemed that only cave dwellers without transistor radios could have avoided hearing about the coming enumeration of the population.

The entire population was to be asked only these seven quesions:

1. Name
2. Address
3. Relationship to the head of the household
4. Sex
5. Color or race
6. Month and year of birth
7. Marital status

Many more questions were to be asked of every fourth person who became part of the 25 percent sample. Among these were place of birth, amount of schooling, industry, occupation, income.

For ten days, beginning on March 21, 1960, the postmen of the country straggered under a much heavier load than usual. To *every occupied housing unit* in the United States they delivered two documents. The first was a short questionnaire called the *Advance Census Report;* the second was a statement asking the person to fill it out and hold it for the enumerator when he came to call. People who had not received the forms were urged to obtain them at their Post Office.

Every step, from the wording of the questions and the instructions, to the use of the postman, to the ultimate use of computers had been tested for three years. There had been miniature and model censuses in Yonkers and Philadelphia in the east, Memphis and Lynchburg, Martinsburg and Indianapolis, Dallas, and elsewhere in the country. For the census experts who went through these trials, the actual enumeration probably had few surprises.

On April 1, everywhere but in Alaska, where melting snow and ice make travel impossible at that time enumerators fanned out. The census of Alaska was taken in January, when the ice is firm. At the end of the first week, one-third of the country had been counted! At the end of the second week, the census had embraced almost three out of four people. By April 21, 90 percent had been enumerated. On July 7, less than a hundred days after the "target day," the Bureau of the Census reported the preliminary results of the count of the American people!

It was later announced that an estimated three out of five housing units had filled out the *Advance Census Report* before the arrival of the enumerator. This was a remarkable display of cooperation.

The speed with which the public report appeared was made possible by the use of the most advanced computers in the world to process the vast sea of information. The particular computer process used went by the friendly name of FOSDIC. As with all such names in this era, its origin was in the sequence of words that describe its function. It is also known as:

> Film
> Optical
> Sensing
> Device for
> Input to
> Computers

If a householder had completed the *Advance Census Report,* the enumerator merely copied the information onto a FOSDIC schedule; if not, he made the entries as they were given to him. Everything on the FOSDIC schedule was in code, based upon its positioning on the form. The enumerator merely darkened a circle for the appropriate answer. This is how a small section of a FOSDIC schedule appeared:

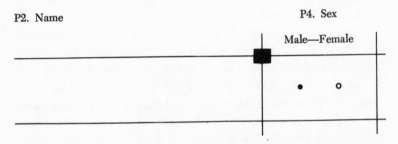

P2. Name

P4. Sex

Male—Female

The completed schedule was first photographed by a microfilm camera. The developed negative was then fed through a FOSDIC scanner. The small block square, called an *index mark,* directed the scanner to the answer area—in the above case, a male. The scanner, after reading the darkened circle, interpreted it to mean "male" and fed the information directly to computer tape.

In addition to the advantage of speed, which is self-evident, this method eliminates errors that arise from manual copying, coding, and key-punching.

Within eight months from April 1, as required by law for the reapportionment of the House, the Bureau of the Census delivered to the President the count of the population of each of the fifty states.

Even before the beginning of the twentieth century, there were people, including some members of the House of Representatives itself, who claimed that the House was becoming too large to be effective. In 1890, there were 357 members. A House of 300 members was regarded by many as ideal.

The members of the House who gave the problem serious thought came to believe for several reasons that a more sensible scheme of apportionment could be worked out if it were done by someone *outside* the House itself. In the first place, the large and small states were still looking for advantages. Secondly, the House was extremely reluctant to reduce its own size. Finally, there was an equal reluctance to reduce the size of any state's delegation, even when a census showed a shift of population.

After the census of 1900, the House membership had grown to 391. The House was then persuaded to call upon Walter F. Willcox, at that time with the Bureau of the Census, later professor at Cornell University and president of the American Statistical Association. From that summons, Professor Willcox's involvement with reapportionment spanned about half a century of American history.

Based on Willcox's calculations, the House was to have fixed its membership at 386 at the beginning of the twentieth century. Then, a new controversy broke out to disturb a short period of peace. Two schools of thought were involved. The first said that apportionment of the House was to be regarded as nothing more than a mathematical problem. Once a formula was worked out that took into account all provisions of Article I, Section 2, the problem would cease to exist. After each census the formula would be taken out, applied to the new census results, and a House free from controversy as to its composition would appear.

The second view, supported by Willcox, said that the issue was a matter of constitutional law. The mathematician could only present to the House the results of different methods of calculation. The choice lay with Congress itself.

Surprisingly, the final solution was, in a way, a compromise between the two views. It occurred to some authorities that one provision of Article I, Section 2, had never been properly considered. This provision said, "Each State shall have at least one Representative," which everyone had always taken for granted. After all, no state, no matter how small, had ever been denied its seat in the House.

In the end, it was realized by Professor Willcox and others that there were really *two* kinds of seats in the House. The first was a set of 48 seats—now 50—one for each state. These were guaranteed; they were "unapportionable." The difference between these 50 and the size of the House, 435 members, as set by Congress in 1912 were the "apportionable" seats.

This idea was finally accepted. Today the Bureau of the Census, to whom—in 1929—the House transferred the power to make the required calculations, starts its computations, based upon the most recent census, from a House with a minimum membership of 50.

When Alaska and Hawaii were admitted to statehood, each was granted a seat in the House, as required by the Constitution. The House then had 437 members until the census of 1960 after which it returned to 435. The calculations are made on the basis of what is called *the method of equal proportions.* The method became law on November 15, 1941; minor amendments were made in 1964. Its aim is to have the smallest possible difference in the average number of people whom each member of the House represents. For the mathematically minded, the method involves the calculation of geometric means as averages. It is a complicated method for hand calculation but not at all for a computer.

On the next page are calculations made by the bureau after the census of 1960. The sections shown are for a House of minimum size and the *priority list,* or order of distribution of seats, if the House should ever decide to increase its membership to more than 435.

The method seems to have worked to everyone's satisfaction. Today, there is no movement to change it, nor does anyone want to diminish or enlarge the House of Representatives.

After much controversy, the long-run drama called Article I, Section 2 of the Constitution may be said to have had a happy ending.

Method of "Equal Proportions" Used to Determine Representation by States in House of Representatives

(Unpublished calculations from United States Bureau of the Census based on census of 1960)

Size of House of Representatives		Population: Census of 1960		Multiplier (decimal not shown) to determine state's claim to given size	"Priority value": Product of multiplication of two columns to left
Code for method of "equal proportions"		State / Size of state delegation at given size of House			
3	421	Texas	23	9579677	4445542	425869
3	422	Iowa	7	2757537	15430335	425497
3	423	Oklahoma	6	2328284	18257419	425085
3	424	New York	40	16782304	2531848	424902
3	425	Michigan	19	7823194	5407381	423030
3	426	Tennessee	9	3567089	11785113	420385
3	427	California	38	15717204	2666904	419163
3	428	New Jersey	15	6066782	6900656	418648
3	429	Virginia	10	3966949	10540926	418153
3	430	Wisconsin	10	3951777	10540926	416554
3	431	West Virginia	5	1860421	22360680	416003
3	432	Georgia	10	3943116	10540926	415641
3	433	New York	41	16782304	2469324	414409
3	434	Maryland	8	3100689	13363062	414347
3	435	Ohio	24	9706397	4256283	413132
3	436	Massachusetts	13	5148578	8006408	412216
3	437	Missouri	11	4319813	9534626	411878
3	438	Pennsylvania	28	11319366	3636965	411681
3	439	Illinois	25	10081158	4082483	411562
3	440	California	39	15717204	2597622	408274
3	441	Texas	24	9579677	4256283	407738
3	442	Nebraska	4	1411330	28867513	407416
3	443	Kentucky	8	3038156	13363062	405991
3	444	Indiana	12	4662498	8703883	405818
3	445	New York	42	16782304	2409813	404422
3	446	Minnesota	9	3413864	11785113	402328
3	447	Michigan	20	7823194	5129892	401321
3	448	Arkansas	5	1786272	22360680	399423
3	449	California	40	15717204	2531848	397936
3	450	Kansas	6	2178611	18257419	397758
3	451	Mississippi	6	2178141	18257419	397672
3	452	Pennsylvania	29	11319366	3509312	397232
3	453	North Carolina	12	4556155	8703883	396562
3	454	Florida	13	4951560	8006408	396442
3	455	Ohio	25	9706397	4082483	396262
3	456	Maine	3	969265	40824829	395701
3	457	Oregon	5	1768587	22360680	395490
3	458	Illinois	26	10081158	3922323	395416
3	459	New York	43	16782304	2353104	394905
3	460	Colorado	5	1753947	22360680	392194

NOTE: If the size of the House had been increased to 436 after the 1960 census, Massachusetts would have had first claim to an additional seat since, on the basis of calculations, it had the highest "priority value."

U.S. Bureau of the Census

Chapter 6

1970: CENSUS OF CONTROVERSY

The nineteenth census of the United States, when it gets under way on April 1, 1970, will be a veteran of many storms. The census questions are no longer the source of controversy, nor is the proposed method of counting. Both are in the census tradition, even though they contain new elements. Nonetheless, the enumeration is being called a "Census of Controversy." The controversies may reflect the changing nature of the country and many people's uneasiness about the change.

The census of 1970 will be the most colossal ever carried out in man's history. More than one-fifth of a billion people will be enumerated. China and India may actually count more. The Soviet Union may also do so in the same year. But no nation's census can equal the wealth of detail that is accumulated about the people, their characteristics, and their way of life.

Like an old professional who has perfected his style, the Bureau of the Census has proposed an enumeration that includes very few surprises. As in 1960, the basic questions will be asked of everyone. Other questions will be sampled in different ratios. Some will be asked only of every twentieth person; others, of every fourth person.

One important new question, to be asked of every fourth person, will be aimed at finding out what people were doing five years before, in 1965. It will state:

In April 1965, was this person—

YES NO

- Working at a job or business (full or part time)
- In armed forces
- Attending school or college
- Doing something else (own housework, retired, etc.)

Of those who report that they were working, a sample will be asked at which occupation and in which industry.

The aim of the question is to try to determine the nature of *movement* in American life. How many people went from school to work? From the Armed Forces into college? In and out of a job? It may also help to locate those people who have been out of work for a long time, the "hard core" unemployed.

If the question is successful, it may also show movement toward greater responsibility *within* a kind of work. For example, a man who is *presently*, on April 1, 1970, a supervisor of office workers may *five years earlier* have been an office worker. Further analysis could then show how such changes are related to age, education, color, sex, and any other characteristic recorded by the census.

A sample of the population will be asked whether they have ever been enrolled in a vocational training program. A tremendous amount of money has been spent on such courses. The census question will be designed to try to determine whether the money has been well spent. Does   person with such training find a job more easily? Is it in the field for which he was trained? Is it at a higher level of skill than for persons without such training? Does he earn more money? Does he do as well as the person with only academic training? The answers will help to chart the future direction of such programs.

Another question that will be asked also stems from vast expenditures by all branches of government as well as private agencies. This question is designed to find out how widespread disabilities are and how long a disabled person has suffered from his. The object is to be able to distribute funds more effectively.

Such types of questions are not new to a census inquiry.

The method of collecting the data in 1970 will be a combination of "something old, something new." As never before, the census will make use of the Post Office in distributing and collecting census schedules. It is already referred to as the "mail out, mail back" census.

Copies of the *Advance Census Report* delivered by the postman in 1960 were to be held by the people until the arrival of the enumerator. The aim in 1970 is self-enumeration, with the completed schedule mailed back to a local census field office.

Self-enumeration schedules will be delivered by postmen in every part of the country that has city delivery postal service. This includes about 140 million people, or households that include about 65 percent of the entire population.

The Bureau of the Census and the Post Office have been working together since 1964 to perfect a mailing system to handle such an enormous load in so short a time. The aim was to develop a code to be preprinted on each schedule, or copy of the census, that would include *every house on every block;* that would define *exactly* where that house is located. This code, called the *Advance Coding Guide,* will show *between* which streets an address falls and on which *side* of the street.

The *Advance Coding Guide* will make possible the tabulation of census data for very small geographic units. The most frequent demand upon the Bureau of the Census by local government agencies and business has been not for more information but for greater geographic detail. With this code, it will be possible to answer questions such as these: How many children under ten years of age live on the north side of Madison Street between Cedar and Laurel Avenues? If the proposed expressway eliminates the east side of 18th Street from Avenue C to Avenue H, how many people will have to be relocated?

The *Guide*, which contains no confidential information, will be on sale to private users. Any agency or business that makes a survey of its own can relate its findings to the census.

For people living outside the areas of city delivery postal service and for those who do not mail back completed census schedules, there will be the traditional visit by the enumerator.

The tremendous amount of work that went into the development of the Address Register was not undertaken merely to meet the needs of the users of census data. In 1960 it became clear that radical new methods would have to be sought to guarantee the success of the next census. Then, about 160,000 enumerators were used. In 1970, using traditional techniques and with a normal increase in population, at least 200,000 would be needed. And if a greater effort were to be made to improve the enumeration of minorities, the need for enumerators would soar much higher.

It has been stated earlier that the more prosperous the economy, the lower the level of the average enumerator. To enlist almost one-quarter of a million enumerators with the required qualifications for a short-term job at modest pay in 1970 might well have become an impossible undertaking. It is hoped that the use of "mail out, mail back" schedules will cut the expected task force in half.

Mounting census costs have also been a concern to many, especially in Congress. The aim at mid-decade was to keep the cost of the next enumeration below $180,000,000. However, it is likely that before all the bills are paid for the census of 1970, it will have cost more than $200,000,000, or about one dollar to count each man, woman, and child in the United States.

Variations of "mail out, mail back" schedules have been used in several European countries with success. However, the countries are smaller, the people more alike, the customs different, and the schedules much simpler. In some countries, the people carry identity cards and report their movements to government offices.

The people of the United States are the most mobile in the world. With a high proportion always "on the go," part of the population will certainly not be at the address to which the census questionnaire will be addressed.

As in the past, there will have been many field tests before the "target date" of the census, April 1, 1970. Not only the "mail out, mail back" technique will be tested; every proposed question on the schedule will have been carefully checked for its wording, its positioning, even for the size of the type used in its printing.

To Fort Smith, Arkansas, fell the distinction in 1961 of serving as the first testing ground for the nineteenth census. Since then, experiments have been made in all or part of such widely scattered communities as Huntington, Long Island; New Haven, Connecticut; Louisville, Kentucky; Cleveland, Ohio; Yonkers, New York; St. Louis Park, Minnesota; Trenton, New Jersey; counties in North Carolina and Wisconsin; and a notable one, in 1968, in North Philadelphia, Pennsylvania.

In most communities, completed schedules were mailed back by an average of four out of five people. Such a rate of response would assure the success of the mailing procedure. In North Philadelphia, however, a community with a very high proportion of black people, as few as 30 percent of the schedules were mailed back.

The failure in North Philadelphia came in spite of a heavy publicity campaign before the mailing. Posters urging cooperation were put up in neighborhood bars, restaurants, supermarkets, shops, and in public places in the area. There was even a slogan coined for the test that read: *You are important. Don't be a missing person.*

The lack of response in the black communities will be the subject of conferences between the Bureau of the Census and the leaders of the Negro people until the day of the census.

Another source of noncooperation is likely to be the so-called "hippie" community, by whatever name it is known in 1970, across the United States. It is not likely that they will be much concerned with the success or failure of the enumeration.

Even though these problems are real, if they are the only ones, why is the next enumeration being called a "Census of Controversy"?

A proposal was made that a question asking about each person's religious affiliation be included in the census of 1970. The Bureau of the Census accepted the proposal for consideration. Immediately, a storm of protest followed. Since failure to answer a census question is punishable under the law, it was claimed that a compulsory question about an individual's religion was a violation of the constitutional guarantee of freedom of religion.

Canada and several European countries in which religious freedom is as deeply rooted as in the United States ask such questions of their people. In some colonial censuses such questions were not unusual. But such a question has never been asked in an American census. Instead, there have been censuses of religious bodies, or organized religious groups, made by the bureau until the late 1940's and then discontinued mainly because of inaccuracies.

The first census of religious organizations was made in 1850. Later ones were also conducted along with the decennial censuses until 1900. Then, starting with 1906, they were made in years ending with six. The last such census was begun in 1946 but never completed.

These were among the questions asked:

1. Denomination
2. Number of members
3. Change in membership in 10 prior years
4. Attendance at services
5. Income and expenditures
6. Value of property
7. Seating capacity of the church

The censuses were discontinued because the most important item—the number of members—could never be accurately determined. Each church defined a member in its own way. In some, it was the newly baptized child. In other churches a member was one who regularly attended services. Elsewhere, only those who went through a regular enrollment procedure were members. Some never counted but reported the same number of members from one census to the next. Very few had trained people who could keep a membership roster up to date, adjusting for new members, those who moved away, those who died, and so on. There were important denominations that refused to supply a count of members to the Bureau of the Census.

Since the end of World War II, there have been some basic changes in types of religious organizations. In some large cities, there have sprung up many so-called "store front" churches. Most are unaffiliated. Often they are based upon a dynamic or inspiring minister. They move frequently depending upon the rent and the growth of membership. They would be difficult to locate and include in any census of religious organizations.

There has even arisen a question as to what a religion is. The most notable example is that of the Black Muslims. In a celebrated case in 1968, Muhammad Ali, the heavyweight champion of the world formerly known as Cassius Clay, sued for exemption from the draft, claiming that he was a minister of that faith. The decision on the question will probably have to be made by the United States Supreme Court.

As information about the religious affiliations of the American people became almost nonexistent, the awareness of the need for such data grew. It was stated, for example, that a community's educational requirements may be affected by its religious composition. Even the research staffs of the major churches felt that there was a gap.

Public hearings on the issue were scheduled in August, 1966, by the House Committee on Post Office and Civil Service, the Congressional committee responsible for census matters. One of the first witnesses was Dr. A. Ross Eckler, Director of the Bureau of the Census.

Dr. Eckler told the Committee that questions are included in the census only after extensive public discussion. Each question must be in response to a need of the government and must receive wide support from important segments of the public. He stated that with regard to a question on religion, "We are . . . not advocating questions but we are sifting, reviewing the representations that have been made to us . . . we are trying to find out what would be the most useful selection for final composition of the schedule."

In testimony before the House committee, the research organizations of some churches favored a question on religion. But no spokesman for a religious body, or any private group identified with a specific religious organization, supported the proposal. Those who did not oppose it directly suggested that answers to this question be voluntary. On such a basis, it is difficult to see how useful information could be obtained.

There will be no question on religion in the census of 1970. The census may be controversial, but it will not be due to any religious issue.

In 1964, the United States Supreme Court, in the case of Wesberry vs. Sanders, declared: "As nearly as is practicable one man's vote in a Congressional election is to be worth as much as another's."

As a result of this statement of principle that came to be known as "One man, one vote," the census of 1970 was almost continuously in the news during the second half of 1967. The census became a political football between rival Congressional groups. The Bureau of the Census had to stand by helplessly, witness to a controversy it did not make and could not join.

The controversy had its roots in the change of America from a rural to an urban society. As the population of the country shifted to the cities, political power in most states remained rural. In some, a Congressman from a rural area may have represented 50,000 people, while ten times as many people in a city are represented by only one Congressman. Each succeeding census pointed up the growing inequality.

The Supreme Court ruled that equality had to be established. It laid down two conditions for Congressional districts within a state. First, the districts had to be approximately equal in population. Second, they could not be gerrymandered or drawn in such a distorted geographical manner as to favor one political party over another.

Powerful forces in Congress opposed the Supreme Court's decision. Their strategy was to delay any change in the districts until after the census of 1970. The main provision of a bill that received the support of House and Senate members stated, "No state shall be required to redistrict prior to the 19th Federal decennial census unless the results of a special Federal census" were available for use by the states. Since a state would not only have to *request* a special census but would also have to *pay* for it, "No state would be required to redistrict before the election of 1972," as Congressman John Conyers of Michigan pointed out.

The bill passed the House by a vote of 241–105. In November, 1967, it was defeated in the Senate, 55–22, after a bitter fight. As the *New York Times* declared the day after the vote, "Seldom has a bill had such a stormy legislative history."

Even without the bill, the first House of Representatives to be apportioned on the basis of the census of 1970 will undergo major changes in its composition. The most historic change will be that for the first time since 1810, the State of New York will no longer have the largest delegation in the House. That distinction will pass to California.

On the basis of computer estimates, the following changes will probably take place, assuming that the House retains its present size of 435 members.

Changes in representation

| | *Increases* | | *Decreases* | |
STATE	Number of additional seats	STATE	Number of lost seats	
California	6 (from 38 to 44)	Pennsylvania	2	
Florida	2	Illinois	1	
Arizona	1	Iowa	1	
New Jersey	1	Michigan	1	
Texas	1	New York	1	(from 41 to 40)
		North Dakota	1	
		Ohio	1	(may lose 2)
		Oklahoma	1	
		West Virginia	1	
		Wisconsin	1	

The Bureau of the Census was an innocent bystander in the "One man, one vote" controversy. It claimed to be neutral in the dispute over the inclusion of a question on religion in the census. But it did take sides in what may have been the beginning of one of the most significant controversies in the history of the American census. This controversy will continue, and on its outcome may depend the fate of the census as it has developed over the decades —as a national inventory.

The conflict started innocently enough with a proposal to include the Social Security number of every respondent in the census of 1970. On August 23, 1966, Dr. A. Ross Eckler told a Congressional hearing, "Inclusion of Social Security numbers would make it possible to use information from other records to supplement the census records." This was part of a proposal to create an enormous file, stored on computer tapes, of all the information available in government files about the people of the country. In a popular phrase it came to be called a "data bank."

In the process of reaching maturity, the average American will have answered many census questions; filed an annual income tax return with the Internal Revenue Service; applied to the Social Security Administration for a Social Security card; registered for the draft and served in the Armed Forces; filed an application for a home mortgage with the Federal Housing Administration (FHA); collected Unemployment Insurance; applied for a passport to the State Department in order to travel abroad; sought to qualify for Medicare payments. The list could easily be extended for many.

It has been estimated that the files of federal agencies contain 2.8 billion individual listings for Americans.

The heart of the proposal was to use computers to link all these records by a common thread—the individual's Social Security number. Those who favored the proposal called it a "data bank"; its opponents called it an "intelligence center." Soon, another label was pinned upon it. It was called "an invasion of privacy."

A linking of records of the kind proposed would open up wide opportunities for research. The advantages to governmental planning would be very great. But the proposal aroused very deep fears. The Joint Congressional Subcommittee on Economic Statistics, which strongly supported the idea of a data bank, tried to take both views into account. In a statement on August 22, 1967, it said that the data bank "would provide ready access to information needed for the Government's economic and social planning." But safeguards must be provided, it added, "to prevent Federal officials from having a pushbutton dossier on millions of Americans."

The data bank would be the responsibility of the Bureau of the Budget. This is an Executive agency, which means that it is responsible to the President. Since the proposal was first made, this agency has engaged in research to find some way of guaranteeing that all information fed into the bank would remain confidential. However, critics have pointed out that assuring *present* confidentiality is not a *permanent* guarantee.

It has been pointed out that not all the information in governmental files is simple fact—such as a person's age. In the *New York Times* of January 7, 1968, Professor Alan F. Westin of Columbia University claimed that the FHA used private investigators to find out whether people applying for home mortgages were happily married. The agency did not deny this. It explained that "one of the leading causes of foreclosures [of home mortgages] is divorce."

Whether the FHA is justified in making such investigations is not the point. A judgment as to whether a person is happily married is an *opinion*. Should opinions be part of everyone's personal file?

Professor Westin is an opponent of the data bank. According to his views, "The trend toward greatly increased collection of personal data, exchanges of information among collectors and consolidation of such personal information into central data banks represents by far the most serious threat to privacy in the coming decade."

One of the direct results of the proposal for a data bank has been the introduction of bills in Congress to limit the scope of the 1970 census. At one time, there were fifteen different bills with this aim in mind. Finally, a bill introduced by Congressman Jackson E. Betts of Ohio gained the most support. Under its terms, the census of 1970 would be limited to the following required questions:

1. Name   2. Address   3. Sex   4. Date of birth
5. Race   6. Marital status   7. Visitors in the home at
                                    census time

Answers to any other questions on the census schedule would be voluntary.

Statisticians, economists, and many others engaged in research tend to favor the data bank as an unequaled source of information. But their ranks are by no means unanimous. The magazine *Science*, a publication of the American Association for the Advancement of Science, said in an editorial on April 5, 1968, that it opposed Congressman Betts's bill to limit the census of 1970. It went on to say, "However, the origins of the legislation are in the national fear of large-scale statistical collections, computerized data banks, and infringement of individual privacy, and it should be noted that these concerns are growing."

Reflecting the views of many economists, Professor Harry Malisoff of City University of New York stated in an article in the October, 1967, issue of *New York Statistician*, "The potential [of the computer for good or evil] expresses itself in a voracious demand for data on persons with scant regard for the impact on the freedom of the individual in American society. The presumption that we can safely handle billions of microfilm frames of personal data at this stage of social development is both adventurous and perilous."

One of the most significant attacks upon the data bank was made in 1968 in the same publication. It was made by its editor, Dr. Abram J. Jaffe, a frequent consultant to the Bureau of the Census and one of the country's leading demographers. In an article entitled "Who Needs a 1970 Census?", Dr. Jaffe declared: "To say that such a computer dossier can be kept confidential is meaningless. If it is really to be kept confidential, no one may have access to it. In that case why compile it? If even one person has access to it, then there is no safeguard against possible tyranny, except to erase the [computer] tape. If the choice must be made between more and better statistics together with a computer tape dossier, versus fewer statistics and no dossier, then I vote for fewer statistics."

There is another consideration that has not yet been tested. Is it legal to assemble *all* information that a person gave *separately* to many agencies *without the person's consent?* Can it be assumed that, if requested, he would have given one agency *all* the information? Even if it were required by law, he might have made the choice of refusing and accepting a court test of his refusal.

A government agency pledges to keep confidential all information supplied to it by individuals. Some agencies have defended this procedure in court even against other government agencies. May it now volunteer such information given to it in confidence, even if the recipient is another agency's computer? These are questions that will be debated for some time to come.

The data collected by the Bureau of the Census is the key to a national data bank. It is the only agency that collects information for *every* American, from the just born to the most elderly. It is the only source of *regular* information. The national census is closest to a national register. It would be the foundation rock upon which any data bank would be constructed.

There will be no question asking one's Social Security number in the census of 1970.

In March, 1968, after Congressional hearings, it was announced that the proposal to create a data bank would no longer be considered at this session of Congress. However, it is safe to say that it will arise again and be hotly debated.

The Bureau of the Census has sought to be a neutral, nonpolitical, noncontroversial agency. There is no legislation that requires it to "advocate" or "promote" anything. It is merely supposed to gather data as a constitutional requirement and to analyze and present it in the national interest. One is led to wonder whether, from a long-range point of view, the bureau was correct in associating itself with the proposal for a national data bank.

Chapter 7

THE NEGRO IN THE
AMERICAN CENSUS

Never in American history, from colonial days to the present, has there been an accurate enumeration of the Negro people. The earliest records indicate that in 1620 there were 20 black men in colonial Virginia in a population of 2,200. Ten years later there were 50 Negroes living among the 2,500 colonists living there. In the same year, it is said that there were 10 blacks among 350 people living in colonial New York.

The round numbers—20, 50, 10—indicate that they were estimates or guesses rather than exact counts. As the black segment of the population grew with the years, the estimates of its size departed farther and farther from reality.

A census, by its nature, can never be an exact count of a nation. This is especially true of the United States. The presence of hostile Indians for so many years, the vast spaces, people always on the move toward geographic or economic frontiers, enormous additions of people by immigration—these have always made enumerations difficult. Thus, an error of 1 or 2 percent in the count of the total population is to be expected; professionally, it is regarded as an "acceptable" error.

However, the undercount of the Negro people throughout history has far exceeded these limits. The error in counting the black population of the country has often exceeded that of the white by as much as ten times! In the *details* of the census—for example, Negro men from 25 to 34 years of age—the differences in the size of the error between black and white become even more extreme.

Since the American census and the people who plan it are among the most highly regarded in the world, the question arises: Why has the Negro been consistently and seriously undercounted in the census of the United States?

The first blacks came to the American colonies as commercial property or slaves. The records of their coming and their presence are no better or worse than those for other goods. One authority stated, "In the middle colonies the first Negroes were probably brought to New York from Spanish or Dutch prizes in 1625 or 1626. Dutch records are meager but show a consignment of 5 in 1660 and another of 300 in 1664."

The colonial people imported slaves not only from "regular" sources such as the Royal African Company but from pirates as well. Most sources of supply were not the kind to keep records.

Once slaves arrived, they were subject to sale, barter, resale, or export. The traders in Virginia exported slaves to other colonies and even to Great Britain itself. Slaves who were not smuggled in were subject to duty. Some colonies, such as Pennsylvania, discouraged the slave trade by setting high import duties. In others, the duty was a source of revenue. As with other commodities, if a slave died within a certain time of arrival, it was possible to recover the duty paid for him. If he was being held for re-export, no duty had to be paid.

Had the records of slave shipments to colonial America been models of accuracy, it would still not be possible to estimate the black population from them. Yet, *any* estimates must come from the commercial records. Some are based upon the records of the settlement of differences between the Royal African Company and the local slave traders. Sometimes, these are supported by the earliest colonial counts of their population. Stella H. Sutherland, an authority on the black colonial population, has said, "The figures for Negroes for the 17th century, which are doubtlessly too low, are largely estimates based upon references to purchase and sale, to laws governing slavery, and occasionally to reports of more or less exact numbers."

By the end of the seventeenth century, the growth of the black population was due as much to natural increase as to continuing imports of slaves. As in the earlier years, many estimates are based upon observation rather than written record. Births and deaths of blacks were almost never registered. Such events even in white families seldom became a matter of public record. Many parts of the population record are simply observations such as the one reported by a writer, "Governor James Glen of South Carolina stated in 1749 that the number of Negroes in his colony increased rather than diminished during the nine years when prohibitive taxes and war 'prevented any from being imported.'"

Whatever the ratio may have been between natural increase and imports, the slave population mounted steadily throughout the colonial period. Although white settlers arrived in a steady stream, the rise in the black population far exceeded the white.

The table on the next page represents currently accepted estimates of the white and black populations in colonial America. The numbers are, of course, combinations of estimates for individual colonies from different sources. As discussed earlier, some colonies carried out fair and frequent enumerations; others merely estimated their populations for the most part. In some colonies, there never was a census during the entire colonial period.

In all but two decades, the rate of growth of the black population far exceeded the white. From 1650 to 1780, the white population increased about 45 times. In the same period, the Negro population multiplied itself a phenomenal 360 times! In 1650, about 3.2 percent of the colonial population was black. By 1780, better than one out of every five people in the land was a Negro. It seems almost superfluous to add that the black population, far more than the white, was understated.

The growth was very unevenly distributed among the colonies. In a "middle colony" such as New York, the white population grew a little more rapidly than the black. In the 100 years from 1680 to 1780 the white people increased 22 times; the black about

17.5 times. By 1780, every tenth person in New York was a Negro, most likely a slave.

The White and Negro Colonial Populations of America and Percent Increase from Decade to Decade, 1630–1780

Year	Total population	White		Negro	
		Number	Percent increase during decade[a]	Number	Percent increase during decade[a]
1630	4,646	4,586	—	60	—
1640	26,634	26,037	—	597	—
1650	50,368	48,768	—	1,600	—
1660	75,058	72,138	47.9	2,920	82.5
1670	111,935	107,400	48.9	4,535	55.3
1680	151,507	144,536	34.6	6,971	53.7
1690	210,372	193,643	34.0	16,729	140.0
1700	250,881	223,071	15.2	27,817	66.3
1710	331,711	286,845	28.6	44,866	61.3
1720	466,185	397,346	38.5	68,839	53.4
1730	629,445	538,424	35.5	91,021	32.2
1740	905,563	755,539	40.3	150,024	64.8
1750	1,170,760	934,340	23.7	236,420	57.6
1760	1,593,625	1,267,819	35.7	325,806	37.8
1770	2,148,076	1,688,254	33.2	459,822	41.1
1780	2,780,369	2,204,949	30.6	575,420	25.1

[a] All increases shown here, as well as in the narrative, are measured from the time when there were about 1,000 Negroes. To measure from a smaller number would produce meaningless results.

Virginia was by far the largest colony, with the greatest number of slaves. From 1660 to 1780, while the whites increased a little more than 12 times, there were 232 times as many blacks in the later year as there had been in the earlier. For three white people, there were about two Negroes.

The population records for South Carolina are quite poor. But it was a colony with a high density of blacks, with probably more blacks than whites. Here, the Negro population multiplied 65 times from 1690 to 1780; the white population grew about 35 times.

The adoption of the Constitution and the first census that followed in 1790 meant very little to the Negro in any real sense. However, it did have very great significance. From a mere commodity, Article I, Section 2 converted him to being three-fifths of a person. This section reads:

"Representatives and direct taxes shall be apportioned among the several states which may be included within this Union, according to their respective numbers, which shall be determined by adding to the whole number of free persons, including those bound to service for a term of years and excluding Indians not taxed, three-fifths of all other persons."

The last clause was included in the Constitution to encourage the Southern states to ratify it. In census history, however, it was a guarantee that the Negro would be counted regularly. Had the clause not been included, there is a strong likelihood that the black man like the Indian would not have been enumerated at all before the Civil War.

The first census of the United States revealed the extent to which slavery had spread over the land. In a population of about 3,929,000, about 757,000 were black. Of the blacks, about 700,000, or better than nine out of ten were slaves.

With independence from England, the white population began to increase more rapidly than the black. This trend was not to change until 1940. The reasons for the change in the rate of increase were the sharp rise in white immigration after independence and the banning of imports of slaves in 1808. In addition, the white death rate began a steady decline, while significant changes in the black death rate did not occur until the twentieth century.

The census of 1790 showed that one out of six families in the country, 17.2 percent, owned slaves. The average slave-owning family had slightly more than seven slaves. The slaves were distributed very unevenly throughout the states and territories of the new country, as the table on the next page shows.

More than 90 percent of the slaves were in the five Southern states.

Number of Slaves in the United States, 1790

State or territory	Number of slaves	Percent of total
Total	697,624	100.0
Virginia	292,627	42.0
South Carolina	107,094	15.4
Maryland	103,036	14.8
North Carolina	100,783	14.4
Georgia	29,264	4.2
New York	21,193	3.0
Kentucky	12,430	1.8
New Jersey	11,423	1.6
Delaware	8,887	1.3
Pennsylvania	3,707	0.5
Southwest Territory	3,417	0.5
Connecticut	2,648	0.4
Rhode Island	958	0.1
New Hampshire	157	a
Maine, Massachusetts, Vermont	0	

a Less than .01 percent.

The earliest censuses established precedents whose effects may not yet have entirely disappeared. As the chart on page 268 shows, for a long time the black and white populations were enumerated differently. The first census made a distinction between white men and women; white men were enumerated in two age groups. But all Negroes were counted without distinction as to either sex or age.

The second and third censuses separated white men and women and enumerated them in five age groupings. Again, the Negroes were merely counted.

In 1820, for the fourth census, a basic change was made. There were six age groupings for white men, five for white women. For the first time, age was a factor in counting the black population. Four age categories were established for them. These were fewer than for the whites, but it represented for the Negro a recognition of a fundamental distinction within a human population.

1790			1800 and 1810		1820			1830 and 1840	
Free whites		Slaves and free colored: Male and female	Free whites: Male and female	Slaves and free colored: Male and female	Free whites		Slaves and free colored: Male and female	Free whites: Male and female	Slaves and free colored: Male and female
Male	Female				Male	Female			
Under 16	None	None	Under 10	None	Under 10	Under 10	Under 14	Under 5	Under 10
16 and older			10 and under 16		10 and under 16	10 and under 16		5 and under 10	
			16 and under 26		16 and under 18	16 and under 26	14 and under 26	10 and under 15	10 and under 2⋅
			26 and under 45		16 and under 26			15 and under 20	
			45 and older		26 and under 45	26 and under 45	26 and under 45	20 and under 30	24 and under 3⋅
					45 and older	45 and older	45 and older	30 and under 40	
								40 and under 50	36 and under 5⋅
								50 and under 60	
								60 and under 70	
								70 and under 80	55 and under 10⋅
								80 and under 90	
								90 and under 100	
								100 and older	100 and older

[a] Beginning with the census of 1850, the entire population was enumerated by exact age.

The white population was divided into thirteen age classes for the fifth and sixth censuses. Negro classifications were increased to six.

In the census of 1850, everyone in the country had an individual line with his exact age entered on it. Since, in 1850, slavery was still a fact of American life, this showed that the earlier discrimination was not due simply to the fact that the blacks were slaves. It is more likely that *two different censuses were being taken simultaneously.*

There was an even more important difference between white and black in early census taking. Until after the Civil War and the elimination of slavery, a black person was listed on the census schedule as a *number,* never as a *name.*

The position of the Negro as slave made it a certainty that he would be undercounted. The slave owner, not the slave, was the source of information for the enumerator. By 1850, slavery was highly concentrated in the Southern states. About 350,000 families owned an average of about nine slaves each. Over 1,700 families owned more than 100 slaves each. On a sizable plantation, the overseer, or manager, was most familiar with the slaves. It was to him that an assistant marshal was likely to direct his questions about the slaves.

The overseer might or might not include newborn black infants in his counts. He might or might not include old and sick slaves who he thought would soon die. If his slaves were the basis for a property tax, it was certainly in his interest to understate them. There was no Southern assistant marshal who would be likely to question an overseer's report and seek to check it independently.

The enumeration of the Negro people during the years of slavery was not without incident. By far the most notable one involved the census of 1840. It stirred a controversy within the country and was hotly debated in the House and Senate. At first, it was a blow to the many whites who were fighting for black liberation. It delighted the spokesmen for slavery. Before the controversy ended, it was the subject of an international incident.

Twelve years after it was taken, the central character in the controversy still found battles to wage involving the census.

The whole affair began innocently enough. For the sixth census, a new question had been added. Its aim was to determine "the number of insane and idiots who were, respectively, at public or private charge." The term "idiot" at that time was used for anyone who was mentally retarded in any way.

The census of 1840 revealed a total population of about 17,000,-000, of whom about 14,000,000 were white and slightly less than 3,000,000 black. The results of the enumeration of the "insane and idiots" were as follows:

Total number of "insane and idiots"	17,456
White	14,521
Black	2,935
Living in Southern slave states	1,744
Living in the North	1,191

The published results of the census had the mysterious notation, "corrected at the State Department." The latter was still responsible for the census in 1840.

It was a matter of simple arithmetic to calculate the following ratios:

White "insane and idiots"	Black "insane and idiots"
North: 1 out of 995	North: 1 out of 145
South: 1 out of 945	South: 1 out of 1,558

The difference was small for whites. The Northern environment seemed to be slightly better for mental health.

For the blacks, however, the North seemed to be more than ten times as destructive of their mental health as the South. The results were much worse for some Northern states. The rugged land of Maine, for example, drove 1 out of 14 Negroes "insane or idiotic"; in Michigan, 1 out of 27 suffered the same fate; in New Hampshire, 1 out of 28.

In contrast, in the South, only 1 Negro out of 4,310 in Louisiana had any mental problem. In Georgia, there was 1 such unfortunate black out of 2,117.

The supporters of slavery were delighted with the census results. Their attitude was best expressed by Senator John C. Calhoun of South Carolina. He was at that time the leading spokesman for the South and was soon to become Secretary of State under President Tyler. Calhoun asserted, "Here is proof of the necessity of slavery. The African is incapable of self-care and sinks into lunacy under the burden of freedom. It is a mercy to him to give him the guardianship and protection from mental death."

He added that the abolition of slavery would prove to be "a curse rather than a blessing."

The census results came at a time when most people, in the North as well as in the South, believed that the Negro was biologically inferior. A wide variety of "scientific" publications were available that "proved" it. At this time the census was regarded as a *scientific* as well as constitutional activity. It was respected everywhere for its accuracy and impartiality. Thus, in 1840, the spokesmen for slavery found support for their views from a source that everyone held in high regard.

The shock felt in antislavery circles was very severe. How could anyone challenge the findings of the esteemed United States census? Where did one begin?

Dr. Edward Jarvis of Massachusetts was an eminent physician who specialized in mental illness. A few years before the census, he had been a founding member of the American Statistical Association and later became its president. He had a strong interest in vital statistics. More important, Dr. Jarvis had an inquiring mind and a deep sense of justice.

Dr. Jarvis began studying the published results of the sixth census. Since he was a specialist in the field, he carefully studied the findings of the first census of the "insane and idiotic." The more carefully he looked, the more he found what seemed to him "extraordinary contradictions and improbabilities."

He began an intensive investigation of the census of 1840, even examining the original census tally sheets. Soon, his early suspicions began to be confirmed. He found that in many towns in the North where "insane" Negroes had been reported, there were no Negroes at all! The census tabulation had shown six "insane" blacks in Scarsboro, Maine. The town had no Negro inhabitants. Dresden, Maine, with a population of three Negroes, was reported to shelter six "insane" ones. Worcester, Massachusetts, was really a collection station for the Negro "insane" with 133 reported. By coincidence, the state asylum had exactly that number of white *patients!*

However, even more disturbing, Dr. Jarvis found that the tally sheets of the assistant marshals had been tampered with. Albert Deutsch, who later analyzed the census of the insane for the *Bulletin of the History of Medicine,* stated, "He [Dr. Jarvis] examined the original census sheets; he showed how, in case after case, the local tallies differed substantially from the final tables drawn up in Washington. He showed how four different printings of the census of 1840 contradicted one another in important respects."

Dr. Jarvis published his findings in the January, 1844, issue of the *American Journal of the Medical Sciences* in an article entitled "Insanity Among the Coloured Population of the Free States." He thoroughly demolished the first census of "insane and idiots." But, in a sense, this was only the first shot in the battle.

The American Statistical Association, after studying Dr. Jarvis's findings, passed a resolution stating that "the most glaring errors are found in the statements respecting the prevalence of insanity, blindness, deafness, and dumbness." It found that "in many towns all the coloured population are stated to be insane; in very many others, two-thirds, one-third, one-fourth, or one-tenth of this ill-starred race are reported to be thus afflicted."

In conclusion, the association asked Congress to scrap the sixth census "as the good of the country shall require and as justice and humanity shall demand."

As Dr. Jarvis's findings became known, there were widespread demands that the census results be officially condemned. Such demands were heard on the floor of the Senate. Former President John Quincy Adams, now a member of the House of Representatives, asked the Secretary of State to reply to the charges against the census.

The Secretary of State at this time was none other than John C. Calhoun of South Carolina, serving President John Tyler, a Virginian. Calhoun appointed William C. Weaver, a Southern naval officer now employed in the State Department, to investigate charges against the census. But Weaver had acted as Superintendent of the Census of 1840! He was appointed to investigate his own work. Need it be said that he could find no fault with the census?

Congress never officially denounced the census of 1840. However, in 1845, a Senate committee went on record that it was "convinced of the general correctness of the statements and criticisms of the memorialists, in respect to the returns of the Sixth Census."

This tragic census would not die. A few years later, the British Ambassador sent a private memorandum to the Secretary of State saying that his government would like to see slavery abolished in Texas and in the rest of the world. Calhoun, in answer, justified slavery, pointing to the results of the sixth census.

As late as 1851, an article in the *American Journal of Insanity* cited as proof the findings of the 1840 census. When the article came to the attention of Dr. Jarvis, he wrote a letter explaining that the census had been discredited.

The investigations of Dr. Jarvis had been limited to the North. How, then, did one explain the findings in the South? Was there actually only one "insane or idiotic" Negro among 4,310 in Louisiana? Was it true that in the South one white man out of 945 was "insane" but only one black out of 1,558 was afflicted in the same way?

The decision as to who was "insane or idiotic" was made by the enumerator, the assistant marshal. It was simple enough to count those in mental institutions—*but blacks were almost never admitted to mental hospitals in the South.* In 1856, a report from Jackson, Mississippi, stated, "There is no provision under existing laws for the reception of slaves or free persons of color into the asylum."

Only his owner could commit a slave to an asylum anywhere in the South. However, if he did this, he would then have to pay for the slave's maintenance. The common practice was that the harmless insane slaves were ignored; the troublesome ones were sent to jail. Thus, an officially "insane" slave during slavery was a rarity.

After the Civil War, during the Reconstruction Period, when blacks were admitted to asylums, the number of Negro insane "rose." Later, when they were again closed to them, the number of insane "declined."

Senator Choate, of the Senate committee that had conducted the hearings on the sixth census, wrote that "in view of the . . . errors of the late census, the committee feel bound to suggest to the Senate the necessity of some legislation with a view to prevent similar errors and inaccuracies in the census to be taken in 1850."

The census of 1850 was the first to be carried out under the responsibility of the Secretary of the Interior. It was the first enumeration of *individuals* rather than one related to the household. Schedule No. 2 was designed for the slave population and asked the following questions:

> The name of the slave owner
> The number of his slaves
> The exact age of the individual slave
> The sex
> The color
> How many slaves were fugitives from the state
> How many slaves had been manumitted [set free]
> The number of deaf and dumb, blind, insane, or idiotic

Although each slave had a personal line on the schedule, the instructions to the assistant marshals stated, "In the case of slaves, numbers are to be substituted for names." And, since the date of birth of a slave was seldom more than a matter of someone's memory, the marshal was told, "If the exact age can not be ascertained, insert a number which shall be the nearest approximation to it."

The census of 1860 was the last under slavery. In most respects it was identical to the previous census. However, the final tabulations, for the first time in American history, contained information about another minority people, the American Indian.

As a dreadful human condition was about to come to an end, there were almost 4.5 million black people in the United States.

They represented 14.1 percent of the entire population, about one person out of seven. About nine out of ten blacks, 89 percent, were slaves. There were about 500,000, little more than 10 percent of the Negroes, who were free. No progress had been made in this respect, since in 1800 the proportion of slaves to free colored people had been exactly the same.

As the American census reflects the country's history, it contains the record of slavery; it both reflects and is part of the segregation and *apartness* that have been the core of the black man's heritage. There will be people responding to the 1970 census whose parents, and certainly grandparents, may have been only three-fifths of a person, who were numbers rather than names in the census record.

The first enumerations after the Civil War were not notable successes. In 1870, the conditions in the country, described earlier, made a precise enumeration impossible. The census totals, especially for Negroes, were too low and were revised in later years by the Bureau of the Census. There were, however, attempts made to understand the new free man of color. The general instructions to the enumerators in 1870 contained the following:

"Color.—It must not be assumed that, where nothing is written in this column, 'White' is to be understood. This column is always to be filled. Be particularly careful in reporting the class *Mulatto*. The word is here generic, and includes quadroons, octoroons, and all other persons having any perceptible trace of African blood. Important scientific results depend upon the correct determination of this class in schedule 1 and 2."

The same instructions were given to the enumerators in 1880. The "important scientific results" were never announced to the world.

In 1890, enumerators were asked to identify Negroes according to these descriptions:

"Black—   those persons who have three-fourths or more black blood;

"Mulatto—   those persons who have three-eighths to five-eighths black blood;

"Quadroon—those persons who have one-quarter black blood;

"Octoroon— those persons who have one-eighth or any trace of black blood;"

In the light of demands for such "exactness," it must be understood that determinations about "race" were made by the enumerator solely on the basis of his observations. No question was to be asked of the respondent as to his "race." The "findings" based on these color refinements were worthless.

As a direct consequence of the Civil War, in July, 1868, the Fourteenth Amendment to the Constitution was ratified. Section 2, entitled "Apportionment of Representatives in Congress," contains these words: "But when the right to vote at any election . . . is denied to any male inhabitant of such state . . . or in any way abridged . . . the basis of representation therein shall be reduced in the proportion which the number of such male citizens shall bear to the whole number of male citizens twenty-one years of age in such state."

Stated simply, Section 2 means that if black adult males were one-fifth of all the adult males in a state and the blacks were denied the right to vote, the number of representatives in the House from that state would be reduced by one-fifth.

The only practical way of finding out whether the right to vote had been denied on a broad scale was in connection with a national enumeration. Such attempts were made but never really

analyzed for this purpose. As a result, since the Civil War, no state
has had its representation in Congress reduced for denying Negroes the right to vote.

The arrival of the twentieth century and the establishment of
the permanent Bureau of the Census brought a higher level of
professionalism to American census taking. But it did not eliminate or even diminish the problems of enumerating the Negro.
However, more highly trained experts in universities and elsewhere, with knowledge of statistics and demography, now studied
the census findings. Their criticism had to be answered by census
authorities with equal ability.

The first census of the new century to come under serious criticism was the fourteenth census, in 1920. In an article in the *Scientific Monthly* of February, 1922, entitled "Enumeration Errors in
the Negro Population," Dr. Kelly Miller of Howard University
stated, "Various enumerations of the Negro population by the
Census office since 1860 have not been very flattering to the scientific reputation of the Bureau. These enumerations have been not
only inherently erroneous, but so conflicting and inconsistent as to
demand calculated corrections."

Dr. Miller pointed out that, since 1860, any increase in the
Negro population could only have been the result of natural increase. It should then follow a pattern similar to that for other
human populations. Instead, these were the results shown by census enumerations from 1860 to 1920:

Census year	Enumerated number of Negroes	Increase, census to census	
		Number	Percent
1860	4,441,830	—	—
1870	4,880,009	438,179	9.9
1880	6,580,793	1,700,784	34.9
1890	7,488,676	907,883	13.8
1900	8,833,994	1,345,318	18.0
1910	9,827,763	993,769	11.2
1920	10,463,013	635,250	6.5

As Dr. Miller said of these results, "Such variability has perhaps never been experienced by any human population."

In reply, the Bureau of the Census admitted some underenumeration of the black people in 1890. But, in an article in the same publication later in the year, a spokesman for the bureau denied that the Negro had been underenumerated in 1920. Then, Dr. Miller, in answer, said, "As this Bureau has admittedly committed grave errors in enumeration of the Negro population in two preceding censuses, it is but reasonable that the obvious discrepancy can be most reasonably accounted for by an error in the present count."

Then the ghosts of Dr. Jarvis and the notorious census of 1840 seemed to rise as Dr. Miller went on to state: "It is a source of surprise to note that the American mind seems to expect that any fact which affects the Negro will deviate from the normal course of human values. It is prone to accept with satisfaction wild assertions and unsupported theories, without subjecting them to the test of logic and reason. The calamity philosophers have already dipped their pens in ink to damn the Negro race to degeneration and death by reason of the latest census figures."

The census of 1920 did not stir debate in Congress. But, like Dr. Jarvis eighty years earlier, Dr. Miller later received support for his charges. Dr. Hugh H. Wolfenden, one of the world's most distinguished demographers, reporting on a survey in Washington, D.C., *in connection with the census of 1920,* gave this description in his book, *Population Statistics and Their Compilation:*

"Separate records [birth and death] were kept for white and Negro children, and the percent of children whose names were missing from the census schedules, but who were actually living in the District on January 1, 1920, were found to be much greater among Negroes than among whites. The constant percent of infants whose names were missing was taken as 9 for whites and 25 for Negroes. . . . They were assumed to be equally applicable in all other sections of the United States."

The final verdict on Dr. Miller's charges came in the highly regarded *Statistical History of the United States,* prepared under the direction of the Bureau of the Census itself. Early in the text, the statement is made, "These studies do suggest an appreciable under-enumeration of males in appropriate age groups, particularly among Negroes, in the Censuses of 1920 and 1940."

The census of 1920 had been the first since the end of World War I. During the war years, from 1914 to 1918, the previously steady flow of white emigrants from Europe to the United States came to a halt. The new opportunities for jobs in Northern industry was a powerful magnet attracting Southern blacks. Also, at the war's end, many black soldiers from Southern homes, returning from overseas duty, remained in the North. Although in 1910 about 89 percent of American Negroes had lived in the South, ten years later only about 85 percent made their home in that section of the country. This was a sharper decline in only ten years than had taken place in the fifty years from 1860 to 1910.

This was the real beginning of the growth of a new person on the census scene—the urban Negro. In the decades to come, the most serious problems of enumeration would center around him.

The four enumerations that followed—1930 through 1960—have been the objects of analysis by some of the world's outstanding demographers. Every analyst concluded that there had been serious underenumeration of the black population. Where the errors for whites had been 1 or 2 percent, or slightly higher, Negroes had been undercounted by as much as 15 percent. Those who examined the enumeration of classes within the Negro population, for example, men from 25 to 34 years of age, reported probable underenumerations as high as 25 percent.

Professor Daniel O. Price of the University of North Carolina compared the results of the census of 1940 with Selective Service registrations during World War II. His conclusions were that the white population had been undercounted by 2.8 percent; the black, by 13 percent. Other authorities estimated that the latter percent was even higher.

Professor Ansley J. Coale of Princeton University made a classic analysis of the census of 1950. He stated as his opinion, "The white population was apparently subject to an undercount of nearly 2.5 percent and the nonwhite population to an undercount between 12 and 13 percent."

The most thorough analysis of the census of 1960 was made by the Bureau of the Census itself. The two men most directly responsible for it were Drs. Jacob S. Siegel and Melvin Zelnick, the latter now a professor at Johns Hopkins University. In many ways, they followed the path charted by Professor Coale. Their analysis showed that blacks had been underenumerated by 10.5 percent. Among Negro men aged 15 to 44 years, about every fifth one may have been omitted from the census.

Upon completion of their study, Drs. Siegel and Zelnick stated in the *Journal of the American Statistical Association*, "There are important geographic variations in the completeness of enumeration. Coverage is probably poorer in the central cities of our metropolitan areas than in the suburban counties and probably poorer in the South than in the rest of the United States. Coverage is probably poorest in the slum areas of our big cities, but we do not have evidence from interview or other studies to support this conclusion. In conclusion, we know little in a formal manner regarding the reasons for underenumeration or the geographic variations in coverage errors."

These points are worth further exploration. They will be examined soon.

At the time of the nineteenth census of the United States in 1970, there will probably be just under 25,000,000 Negroes in the country. On a world basis, this segment of the population would rank among the thirty largest nations. Only slightly more than half the black people will still be living in a Southern state. About two out of five will be living in the North, the remainder in the West. The state with the highest number of black residents will be New York.

There will be more Negroes in New York than in Mississippi

numerically. But in Mississippi they will be one-third of the population; in New York, about one-tenth. The Southern states will
continue to have a higher *proportion* of Negroes in their population.

In recent decades, the Negro birth rate has been higher than
the white. Since white immigration has been at a very low level,
the black population has become a larger percent of the total. It
also means that it has become a *younger* population than the
white. In 1960, half the white population was under 30.3 years of
age. But, half the Negro population was under 23.5 years. Three
out of ten white people were under 15 years of age. But, 37 percent of Negroes were that young. These statistics have great importance in planning, especially in the matter of educational
policy.

These trends have been in the making for many years. The census of 1970 will only confirm them.

What kind of census will *this* one be for the Negro population?

The census of 1970, it was said earlier, has been developing in a
climate of controversy. There is every likelihood that the controversy will continue to the target date of the census. And much of
it will have its origin in the task of counting of the black population.

The relationship between white and Negro has been deteriorat-
ing steadily throughout the 1960's. In such an atmosphere, an accurate count becomes unlikely. In several test censuses, the poorest response to the "mail out, mail back" feature of the 1970
census has been in Negro neighborhoods. In such a community, in
North Philadelphia, Pennsylvania, despite heavy local publicity,
the mail response was only 30 percent. This was far lower than it
had been in any other tested community. Such a response, or non-
response, in black urban communities throughout the United
States would make it certain that the enumeration of the Negro in
1970 would be the poorest in census history.

A greater effort than ever before is planned by the Bureau of
the Census in 1970 to overcome this problem. If carried out, it

may result in major changes in census-taking methods. In June, 1968, in a speech to a convention of statisticians and economists, Dr. Herman P. Miller, chief of the Population Division of the bureau, described some of these plans:

"The Census Bureau has embarked on a major population coverage improvement program for the 1970 Census. . . . Some . . . were used recently in a test census in Philadelphia. These changes include the following:

"1. Census takers were recruited through a local community action agency first and then through the employment service where necessary.

"2. Preference was given to persons who lived in or near the area in which the test census was being conducted. Those who were employed tended to be persons who were active in community affairs. Some of the usual requirements that census takers be high-school graduates, that they work an eight-hour day, and that they pass an academic test were dropped.

"3. . . . test questions were more about the work itself than about general education and information. The staff was trained longer, and it was better supervised in smaller groups, and when work started in the blocks which were considered difficult and dangerous, census takers went out in teams rather than separately."

The Bureau of the Census also plans to set up special census offices in ghetto areas during the 1970 census. But this program will need a special appropriation of $10,000,000 from Congress.

With these measures, in view of the deep differences between black and white likely to exist in 1970, it is still doubtful that the undercount will be reduced. In his speech, Dr. Miller said, "We found that large numbers of the inhabitants in the ghetto area are suspicious of the census interviewers as they are of all officials and they are unwilling or afraid to report all of their household members to census interviewers."

Officials of the Bureau of the Census and leaders of Negro organizations met in 1968 to discuss problems of enumeration. The black leaders could see no advantage in a complete census. They were not impressed with promises of increased federal funds or increased Negro representation that could follow a higher official population. They told Dr. Miller rather that "if the count of young Negro males on a given city block increased suddenly, the Welfare Department would soon send investigators around to see if they were violating the welfare laws and the draft board would send investigators to try to find draft dodgers."

Almost on the eve of the 1970 census, Dr. Miller was not very optimistic. He told the audience that "no one can say whether any or all of these efforts will reduce the undercount of Negroes. I, myself, doubt that they will."

An enumeration is a cooperative activity between the counters and the counted. When minority peoples are involved, the success of an enumeration depends upon the general answer to the question, "Who are people?" It is important to examine the nature of the answers to this question throughout American history.

The census of 1970 will be the nineteenth in American history. During the first eight of these, the black man was mainly a slave. Whether or not he was counted was a matter of utter meaninglessness to him. He was only important to his *owner's* representation in Congress.

But the heritage of slavery is significant in census affairs as it is in other aspects of American life. During slavery, the Negro's sex, age, name, the characteristics that make one a *distinct person* were always of less importance than the white man's. The census takers did not create the difference, but history associates them with it.

The Negro's first experiences with the census as a free man were not very promising. In 1870, in the ninth census, he was undercounted on a vast scale. But, more importantly, the first censuses were early links in a chain of broken promises. The Fourteenth Amendment to the Constitution had promised the black man that if the Southern states denied him the right to vote, their representation in Congress would be reduced. People looked to the census to measure the extent to which this right had been denied. But, as stated earlier, no state, North or South, ever suffered any penalty for failure to grant the Negro equal voting rights.

Again, although the Bureau of the Census did not make the policy or excuse the penalties, it is historically associated with them.

In 1970, connection with the census of the issue of voting rights was again the subject of much heated discussion. The Civil Rights Act of 1964, Section 801, states: "The Secretary of Commerce shall promptly conduct a survey to compile registration and voting statistics in such geographic areas as may be recommended by the Commission on Civil Rights." The Bureau of the Census, in the Department of Commerce would, of course, be the agency that would be expected to "conduct a survey."

Before seeking action from Congress, J. Francis Pohlhaus, counsel for the NAACP, went to court to compel the Bureau of the Census to include a question on voting rights in the census of 1970. He produced as an expert witness for the NAACP, Dr. Abram J. Jaffe of Columbia University. Dr. Jaffe was one of the country's leading authorities on the census, having often, in the past, acted as a consultant to the Bureau of the Census. He told the court that by means of the census, it was possible to find out how many people "did not register or vote . . . for specific reasons, including denial . . . of the right to vote by the States."

The court denied the petition, and Congress took no action on this matter. There will be no question such as this on the 1970 census schedule.

The census is a specialized record of the history of the country. But, as an important event, it is also part of that history. A census is planned and administered by men drawn from the people of the country, as are the enumerators themselves. The attitudes, biases, and prejudices that exist in a population will find their expression in the census. This may be true, in some way, from the lowliest enumerator to the highest rank of census officials.

James D. B. DeBow of Louisiana was Superintendent of the Census in the 1850's. According to Dr. Kelly Miller, Mr. DeBow, "relying upon the low rate of increase in the Negro population, revealed by the census of 1870, proved to the entire satisfaction of those who were satisfied with this type of proof that the Negro could not withstand the competition of freedom and would, forthwith, fall out of the equation as an affected factor." There were other high census officials who, when immigrants were coming into this country in great numbers, expressed concern about their effect upon the future American population.

It was not an accident that in the census of 1930, persons of Mexican birth or ancestry were classified as "nonwhite." This was a *policy* decision, not a mistake of enumeration. In later years, it was corrected.

Aside from the separation of the population into male and female, the most fundamental census division is into "white" and "nonwhite." The latter group includes Negroes, American Indians, Japanese, Chinese, Filipinos, Koreans, Asian Indians, Malayans, and a few others. Throughout American history, the black population made up more than 90 percent of the "nonwhite." In the 1960 census, there were almost 19,000,000 Negroes and somewhat more than 1,500,000 other people of "color."

There have been demands that the Negro be given independence from the classification "nonwhite," that a distinct category be created for him. In this way, every tabulation that is made from the census material for whites would be made for blacks. Such a step has received the support of Professor Otis Dudley Duncan of the University of Michigan, as well as many others. The three basic divisions would then be "white," "black," and "other people."

From a statistical point of view, it is justifiable to place less than 2,000,000 people of many backgrounds from a population that may be 205,000,000 in 1970 into a class called "other people." But it is impossible to justify placing the 25,000,000 Negroes into an anonymous group. Such a step might have the additional advantage of removing the suspicion of the census held by many black people. It could serve as an indication of good intention.

Another possible source of antagonism toward the census on the part of the Negro people is the increasing frequency with which the blame for being undercounted is placed upon the Negro himself. More and more often there are references to his "life style" as the source of the difficulty. In March, 1967, an important official in the Bureau of the Census, trying to explain earlier underenumeration, said, "The nonwhites eluded census takers because of unstable home lives, illegal living arrangements, and the lack of fixed residences—sometimes living in missions, flop houses, and even all-night movie houses." In 1970, on the basis of past experience, more than 3,000,000 Negroes may be omitted from the census.

At a convention of statisticians in 1966, a delegate from the Social Security Administration made the following statement: "Problems of census-taking and survey operations in slum area have been identified . . . as of a much higher order than in many other situations. Would that the properly motivated local people presently pressing for national recognition of the need for improvement in the lot of the poor could be effectively challenged to understand the need for and to help work toward improved data on coverage and content in their local areas."

This is an extremely wordy and involved way of saying that Negro leaders who seek funds for programs should urge their brothers to let themselves be counted.

Experts from the Bureau of the Census have advised governments in almost every part of the world. They have developed enumeration plans for almost every conceivable way of life, including the nomadic. It is *their* responsibility to develop methods of enumeration for a people whose "life styles" are as varied as the American.

The question "Who are people?" is answered at the most fundamental level by the actual enumerator. If the customs and attitudes of a people allow an enumerator, consciously or unconsciously, to say, "What difference does one Negro more or less make?" or one Indian, or one Ibo, or one Moslem, or one Untouchable, then there *cannot* be a complete enumeration.

Who, then, are the enumerators in the American census and what effect do they have?

The effect of the enumerator has usually been to lower the quality of a census. In 1966, William T. Fay and Robert L. Hagan of the Bureau of the Census, in describing the 1970 census plans to statisticians, said, "We want to improve the quality of census data by diminishing the influence enumerators may have on the answers we receive. Scientific studies have demonstrated that enumerators influence answers to census questions in various ways."

The bureau, in discussing experiences during the 1960 census, said, "For some of the sample questions . . . improvement in the accuracy of the results was expected because earlier research . . . indicated that some enumerators tended to introduce consistent errors in the answers they recorded."

The following description by the Bureau of the Census indicates how enumerators obtain their appointment.

"By tradition, decennial census recruitment is carried out under referral system, with the national Administration designating the referral sources. District supervisors in 1960 were in most instances recommended by Senators and Representatives in Congress. Other District office personnel were recommended by local persons designated by the national referral authorities."

The district supervisors selected the enumerators in the largest cities. Elsewhere, appointments were made by crew leaders.

The appointments are political. The following exchange of conversation took place in August, 1966. The two men involved were Dr. A. Ross Eckler, Director of the Bureau of the Census and Congressman H. R. Gross of Iowa. The occasion was a Congressional hearing on the 1970 census.

CONGRESSMAN
GROSS: Just one other question. How will the 125,000
                        enumerators be selected that you may use?
                        Will it be on the basis of political patronage
                        or will they be selected on the basis of some
                        qualification?

DR. ECKLER: They will be selected in accordance with rec-
                        ommendations made but all of them will have
                        qualifications in the sense that they will be
                        given tests which show their ability to carry
                        on this kind of work. This has been true in
                        the last two or three censuses and we expect
                        it to continue, the system of asking for rec-
                        ommendations and then seeing the candidates
                        are given tests; those who are not able to pass
                        are not taken on.

CONGRESSMAN
GROSS: I wish the day would come in this country
                        when we could select enumerators . . . on
                        something other than a political basis. . . . I
                        hope the day will come when people perform-
                        ing these services will be free from politics,
                        Dr. Eckler.

The appointment of people to jobs of short duration at very
modest pay on a political basis is often unavoidable. This system,
by itself, is not at the root of the problem. The critical point here
is not being "free from politics"; *it is being free from prejudice.*

In areas where prejudice is common and political leaders control the selection process, the chances are very great that the enumerators will share the prejudice. It is also a selection process
that, in wide areas of the country, leads to the exclusion of the
Negro as an enumerator.

In recent years most of the enumerators have been retired

people and housewives. The country owes them a debt of gratitude for performing a difficult job with little reward. However,
such people by the routine of their daily lives are usually more
withdrawn from the give and take of American life than students,
workers, or professional people. They, more than others, are more
likely to be withdrawn from the main currents by their "life style."
They are more likely than others to be frightened by the ghetto
way of life.

At a conference at the Massachusetts Institute of Technology in
1968, Leon Pritzker and N. D. Rothwell of the Bureau of the Census were discussing feelings of hostility in relation to census work.
They cited this report from an enumerator in Washington, D.C.
"No one interfered with us, but peoples' appearance and behavior
would frighten a timid interviewer working alone."

Negro leaders are aware of these facts and are beginning to
demand that changes be made. State Senator Basil A. Paterson of
Harlem, as reported in the *New York Times* in 1967, said that "the
inaccurate count [in New York City] was due partly to timid and
inefficient census takers who failed to record ghetto residents out
of fear or indifference." The report added that Senator Paterson
would demand that "Negroes be used as census enumerators in
slum areas."

"In the current state of feeling in the ghetto," he said, "I just
don't think the Census Bureau would get much information if
whites are used. In any case, I'm convinced that the use of white
enumerators is a fundamental reason for the inaccuracy of earlier
censuses."

The Bureau of the Census is today a professional organization
in the best sense of the term. Everyone familiar with the men who
administer it or the work they produce has only the highest regard
for them. As a matter of personal and professional pride, they
would like to achieve an enumeration in which the only omissions
are due to chance. Their efforts, however, are subject to controls
from outside the bureau. These controls range from Executive

policy expressed by the Secretary of Commerce as a member of the President's cabinet to those exercised by Congress that is the source of the bureau's funds.

Whatever effects these may have, they are less important in attaining a complete enumeration of all Americans than the lack of equality for black people. As long as inequality exists in life, there will be inequality in the thoroughness of the enumeration of the white and black population. In the United States as elsewhere in the world, when the answer to "Who are people?" is truly "Everybody!", the problem of enumerating the Negro people will be much closer to a solution.

Chapter 8

THE AMERICAN INDIAN
AND THE CENSUS

At the Constitutional Convention, there was a great deal of discussion about the counting of the Negro, slave or free, in the decennial census. The agreement to consider him as three-fifths of a person was a compromise between interests that had been fully expressed. But there was almost no discussion about the Indian. The clause "excluding Indians not taxed" from the census was made part of the Constitution without objection. It was as if all delegates shared a common understanding. Even the origin of the clause is not known.

To the question "Who are people?", the unanimous answer of the Convention was, "Certainly not the Indian." He was more of a nonperson than the black man.

Until 1890, no one knew how many Indians there were in North America. The first serious attempt to estimate their early numbers was made by James Mooney, an ethnologist with the Smithsonian Institution, in the twentieth century. He estimated that in the area of the United States, there were about 849,000 Indians *at the time of their first contact with the white man.* This meant that he estimated the Cherokee population for one year, the Navajo for another. The estimates of other authorities range from about 750,000 to under 1,000,000.

From this early peak, the number of Indians declined by about one-fifth by the year 1800. Then followed decades of devastation and death. The Indians died from smallpox and tuberculosis; from the crippling effects of the whisky sold to him by the white man; from hardship and starvation that followed his forced removal from traditional homes; from war and massacre. In California alone, nine-tenths of the 250,000 Indians in the state were wiped out during the years of the rush for gold. By 1850 or so, it is estimated that there were only about 250,000 Indians left in the United States. There was little change in the Indian population for the next seventy years.

Early in American history, a phrase that became very popular was used to describe the Indian. He was called "the vanishing American." It was widely believed that the Indian was doomed to die out.

The position of the Indian in American life at that time was obvious to foreigners. Alexis de Tocqueville, a Frenchman who traveled widely throughout the United States, is regarded as one of the sharpest observers of American life. In 1831, writing about the Indians, he stated, "They were isolated in their own country, and their race only constituted a little colony of troublesome strangers in the midst of a numerous and dominant people."

Until recently, the opinion of the Indian was never sought on any legislation that affected him. Under various allotment acts, most of his land was taken away from him. Behind all this was the firmly held belief that he would not survive.

If the Indian was a doomed man, what was the point of counting him?

The Indian could not be completely ignored, however. The Constitution excluded only "Indians not taxed." And, according to the instructions to the enumerators in 1880, this clause "meant Indians living on reservations under the care of Government agents, or roaming individually, or in bands, over unsettled tracts of country." Those living among the white population, "engaged

as servants or laborers," or otherwise, had to be counted for purposes of apportionment. "Indians taxed" was interpreted to mean
Indians *liable* to taxes not those who actually paid them.

Until 1860 there was no reference to the Indian in any census.
The few who were counted were probably included among the
"free colored." The report of the 1850 census includes an estimate
of the number of Indians in various parts of the country. But these
are the estimates of one man, not the result of any enumeration.
Later scholars dismissed the estimates as having little or no foundation.

For the first time in census history, the report of the enumeration of 1860 showed the number of "Indians taxed" who had been
included. The same was true after the censuses of 1870 and 1880.
The following table shows the number of Indians included.

Census	"Indians taxed" included in the census				Total population (in millions)	Enumerated Indians as percent of total population
	Total	Percent change	Men	Women		
1860	44,021	—	23,924	20,097	31.4	0.14
1870	25,731	− 41.5	12,534	13,197	39.8	0.06
1880	66,407	+ 158.1	33,985	32,422	50.2	0.13

One does not have to be an expert to sense that these numbers
do not describe real people. From 1860 to 1870, the population is
almost cut in half. In the next ten years, it increases more than one-
and-one-half times. In 1860 and 1880 there were more men than
women; in 1870, the reverse was true. Since "Indians taxed" lived
among the white population, they were less subject to violent
changes in number. Therefore, the changes are the result of different techniques and emphasis rather than being real changes in the
number of "Indians taxed."

In 1890, one hundred years after the first census, it was decided
that all Indians in the country would be enumerated. "Indians not

taxed" and "Indians taxed" were to be counted separately in keeping with the constitutional provision. They were to be enumerated according to their tribe for which special information was to be collected. It was a landmark year in census history.

The decision was not made at a time when harmony existed between white man and Indian. Geronimo had surrendered only four years earlier. And the Battle of Wounded Knee was fought in South Dakota in 1890, resulting in a massacre of the Indians.

Before the actual enumeration, a decision had to be made as to who was an Indian. This has never been a simple matter. As late as 1953, a Congressional committee investigating the Bureau of Indian Affairs (BIA) declared, "There has been no standard definition of 'Indian' suitable for all purposes." And the bureau itself stated in 1968 that in planning to enumerate Indians, "The root of the difficulty is thought to lie in the determination of who is an Indian."

There are several accepted standards upon which to base a definition. The principal one is biological. A person with one-fourth or more of "Indian blood" is everywhere accepted as an Indian, but as Indians live more and more among the general population, this becomes more difficult to determine. Before the self-enumeration of 1960, an enumerator could only decide any such question on the basis of observation. Except in areas of high concentration of Indians, the degree of blood became an unworkable standard for deciding who was an Indian.

Another basis for decision is legal. Only those persons who are listed on official Indian registers would be regarded as Indian. Such registers, or rolls, are maintained by the Bureau of Indian Affairs. Supposedly, they are adjusted for births and deaths. If they were complete records, no census would be necessary, but in most cases they are incomplete. They also include Indians with the merest trace of "Indian blood." In some areas they include people who are not Indians at all. In the Southwest, for example, poor Mexicans try to enroll on Indian registers. They hope to share in the distribution of land or other benefits granted to the Indians.

Indian tribes maintain their own registers. But they can change the standards for admission whenever they wish. Some have been known to include white people who married or lived among Indians.

A third basis for deciding who is an Indian is called a cultural approach. This decision is based upon the way of life of a person. Does he live among Indians? Does he have an Indian name? Does he speak an Indian language? When did he last participate in an Indian ceremony? Does he regard himself as an Indian? Professor J. Nixon Hadley, an authority on the Indian, in using the term, says that "it will include all persons normally considering themselves a part of the Indian community, including both members of tribes not federally recognized and some persons not included in Census tallies."

The Bureau of the Census adopted the following definition: "In addition to full-blooded American Indians, persons of mixed white and Indian blood are included in this category if they are enrolled on an Indian tribal or agency roll or if they are regarded as Indians in their community. A common requirement for such enrollment at present is that the proportion of Indian blood should be at least one-fourth."

It is possible to find elements of all three standards in the census definition.

An enumeration of the Indians could not be planned in the same way as that of the general population. Most Indians lived on reservations. Only they and the Indian agents knew the land. Roads were few and poor. In many cases, the locations of Indian dwellings were not related to any road at all. Other barriers were language, widespread illiteracy, strange customs, and distrust of whites.

The Census Act of 1890 allowed the hiring of special agents to enumerate the Indians on reservations. In most cases they were people from the Bureau of Indian Affairs. At that time they were not responsible to regular census supervisors.

The problems of counting the Indian population are best seen in the enumeration of the Navajo Indians.

The Navajo are the largest tribe in the United States. In 1968, there were estimated to be about 115,000 Navajo in a total Indian population of about 600,000. Roughly, every fifth Indian in the United States is a Navajo. They live on a reservation area of about 24,000 square miles, about the size of the state of West Virginia. Their reservation sprawls over Arizona, New Mexico, and Utah. This territory was largely acquired by the United States after the war with Mexico in 1848.

The Navajo have always been one of the most Indian of Indian tribes. They have the highest proportion of full-blooded members. About four out of five do not speak English. Although a few have left the reservation to settle in Chicago in the east or Los Angeles in the west, most Navajo mix very little with whites.

From the time that they came under American rule, the Navajo were never regarded as friendly. During the Civil War, the government had to withdraw troops from the New Mexican territory for use at the front. The Navajo, seeing an opportunity, increased their attacks upon the white man. The United States could not retaliate by sending in more soldiers to fight the Navajo. Instead, it sent in Colonel Kit Carson with some of his men with orders to destroy the Navajo food supply. Carson, who knew the area well, roamed the Indian territory with his men, destroying crops and livestock.

Carson's raids exceeded all expectations. Before long, the Navajo were near starvation. Rather than die, they went to Fort Defiance, on their reservation, to surrender. The year was 1863.

There followed one of the most memorable events in Navajo history. Forced to evacuate their homes, the Navajo began their historic "long walk" to Fort Sumner, New Mexico, three hundred miles away.

No one knows how many Navajo there were before Carson's raids. Many died from the hardships that followed them. Others died on the way to Fort Sumner. Some hid in the remote parts of the reservation, others in the area around it. At Fort Sumner, during their captivity, the first count of the Navajo was made.

Brigadier General J. H. Carleton, in charge of Fort Sumner, counted 8,000 Navajo. Kit Carson estimated that less than half had been rounded up. In 1864, another count showed 8,354. A year later, the number fell to 7,169. In May, 1867, when a census was taken in connection with the distribution of ration tickets, there were 7,406 Navajo.

The "ration ticket" census was meant to be foolproof. To receive a ration ticket, each Indian had to walk through a gate to an enclosed area that was known as the "Navajo corral." As he passed through, he received a ration ticket for himself and tickets for members of his household who were sick or had duties elsewhere. No Navajo was allowed to leave until everyone had entered the "corral."

According to Dr. Denis Foster Johnston, an authority on the Navajo, they had learned to claim imaginary dependents and to forge ration tickets. But, at best, the count could only have included the ones who came to Fort Sumner. "In summary," says Dr. Johnston, "it can be concluded that even under conditions of captivity the Navaho population was not satisfactorily enumerated by the authorities in charge."

The Navajo returned home in 1868. To keep them from starvation, the government distributed rations and sheep.

For the next two decades, the estimates of numbers were extremely casual. In 1869, a special agent of the Bureau of Indian Affairs reported 8,181 Navajo. In 1875, the number grew to 11,768. Two years later, another agent added 50 men and 50 women. Then, round numbers came into favor. The estimate was 12,000 in 1880. Two years later, it was 16,000. The following year, 1,000 were added.

The first Navajo tribal roll was drawn up in 1885. Only those living on the reservation were entered on it. Upon completion, the recording clerk counted 13,003 names. It was also estimated that 8,000 additional Navajo were not living on reservation land.

When the tribal roll was analyzed, however, it was almost a farce. It showed a complete lack of understanding of the people enrolled. Navajo family names, for example, stem from the mother, not the father, as is customary in Western countries. But the roll was drawn up according to the father's name. Thus, when children were born, they could not be related to older members of the family. If deaths were reported, names could not be matched. The rolls could not be kept up to date.

Worse than this, Navajo names were often "translated" into English, with the spelling left to the individual clerk. Sometimes, Navajo were "given" names that clerks made up for them.

Navajo marriage customs allowed a man to keep more than one wife. But clerks recorded only one marriage on the roll.

The Indians reported their children by *sex*, with girls most often first. Clerks assumed that the children were being reported by age, with the oldest first; this is how they were entered.

Dr. Johnston wrote that "the 1885 roll must remain an outstanding example of the fictitious results to be obtained when the members of a given culture are enumerated according to procedures appropriate to a different culture."

This was the situation among the Navajo just before the census of 1890.

The responsibility for enumerating the Navajo on their reservation was given to an Indian agent named D. L. Shipley. The records are not clear, but it is assumed that Mr. Shipley hired about four or five assistants. The enumeration was completed in August, 1891, more than a year after it had started. It showed that there were 17,204 Navajo Indians of whom 16,102 lived on the reservation.

Modern authorities believe that the Navajo, especially those living off the reservation, were undercounted. The instructions given to the enumerators were such that an undercount was unavoidable. All Indians not living in tribal relations were to have been counted by the regular enumerators. But if an Indian stated that he was away from the reservation *temporarily,* the regular enumerator was told to omit him; the special agent on the reservation would include him. Regular enumerators knew little of Indian life. Since it took more time to enumerate an Indian and the enumerators were then paid on the basis of how many people they counted, it is likely that regular enumerators ignored many Indians in their areas.

There were additional problems in counting the Navajo. The reservation is huge, and they often do not live in communities. Many of them, living in tribal relations and under the Indian agency, still live away from the flexible boundaries of the reservation. The extent of any underenumeration is subject to speculation, considering the state of Indian records.

The problems were summarized by Dr. Roland B. Dixon, one of the men responsible for processing the Indian records of the census of 1910, and his conclusions are quoted by Dr. Johnston.

"The enumeration of the Navaho is . . . somewhat uncertain, owing to the local conditions. The tribe is a nomadic one, roaming over a very large extent of country, so that an absolutely accurate enumeration would be an extremely difficult, if not impossible task. Comparison with returns of even greater uncertainty (since founded almost wholly on estimate) made in the reports of the Commissioner of Indian Affairs are of little real value. . . . The discrepancy between this figure of about 28,000, which has been returned . . . with little variation since 1905, and that of 22,455 obtained by the present census, is large. That 28,000 is . . . too large and the enumeration . . . too small seems probable. An exact enumeration, however, is . . . practically impossible."

The Bureau of Indian Affairs estimates the Indians living on or near reservations. Its count includes "any Indians residing in the area during a year, or even longer." It estimates the population it serves. Since its budget depends, in part, upon the size of this population, it is not likely that its estimates would be low.

The problems in enumerating the Navajo had their equal with

other Indian tribes, But, good or bad, complete or incomplete, in 1890 the American Indian was counted and became, officially, a person.

The Indian was enumerated in every subsequent census, with the results shown in the table below.

The Total Indian Population in the United States, 1890–1960

Census year	Indians included in the census				Total population (in millions)	Indian as percent of total population
	Total	Percent change	Men	Women		
1890	248,253	—	125,719	122,534	62.9	0.39
1900	237,196	− 4.5	119,484	117,712	76.0	0.31
1910	265,683	+ 12.0	135,133	130,550	92.0	0.29
1920	244,437	− 8.0	125,068	119,369	105.7	0.23
1930	332,397	+ 36.0	170,350	162,047	122.8	0.27
1940	333,969	+ 0.5	171,427	162,542	131.7	0.25
1950	343,410	+ 2.8	178,824	164,586	150.7	0.23
1960	523,491	+ 52.4	263,269	260,222	179.3	0.29

The changes in the Indian population from one census to another are very erratic, but the explanation for them is simple. In 1890, 1910, and 1930, special efforts were made to enumerate all Indians and to show their tribal membership. These were the census years of increase. In 1900, 1920, and 1940, the enumerations were routine; no tribal information was sought. The enumerated Indian population showed little change or actually decreased. In 1950, there were special efforts only in most reservation areas; again, no tribal information was obtained. In 1960, by means of the *Advance Census Report,* the Indian off the reservation could identify *himself* as an Indian. The result was a tremendous increase in the recorded population.

In several censuses attempts were made to determine the extent to which the American Indian kept to his way of life. Some had questions on the number of wives an Indian man had. There were frequently questions about his amount of schooling. An attempt was made to find out how many Indians wore "citizen's dress" in 1890. He was asked, in 1910, "Whether he was living in a 'civilized' or an 'aboriginal' dwelling." The schedule in 1950 asked him whether "In 1949, did he attend or participate in any native Indian ceremonies?"

In 1930, after forty years of experience in enumerating the Indians, the population schedule was the same for Indian and white, except for one item. Where white people were asked the birthplace of their mother and father, the Indian was asked his tribal affiliation and the degree of his Indian blood.

Responsibility for Indian Affairs had been transferred in 1849 from the War Department to the Bureau of Indian Affairs in the Department of the Interior. From then until 1930, the bureau's agents had acted as the enumerators of the Indian. In 1930, the Bureau of the Census assumed the full responsibility. The advantages were in the use of a greater number of enumerators and the elimination of divided authority. But the cooperation of the Indian agents continued to be an important factor, as will be seen.

In Navajo country, enumerators received these special instructions: "In New Mexico, Arizona, and California, enumerators should take special care to differentiate between Mexican laborers and Indians. Some Mexican laborers may endeavor to pass themselves as Indians. Persons residing in the region should have no difficulty in differentiating between the two types."

The general opinion was that the 1930 census of Indians was excellent. Writing in 1965, Dr. Johnston said, "The 1930 census produced more reliable statistics on the population of the Navaho than any enumeration conducted before or since that time."

In 1950, some intensive efforts were made to enumerate the Indians on reservations, where about 72 percent lived. Otherwise, the three censuses after 1930 were undistinguished. However, the use of the *Advance Census Report* in 1960, a mailed questionnaire that permitted the urban population to enumerate itself, resulted in a great increase in the number of Indians.

The striking result of the 1960 census is the great increase in the number of Indians reported in states that did *not* have large numbers of Indians. Arizona, New Mexico, Oklahoma, and South Dakota account for about 52 percent of the Indian population in the United States. They were the only states in 1950 that had 20,000 or more Indians living in them. From 1950 to 1960, their combined Indian population increased 24.5 percent. In that same time, in all other states, the number of Indians increased about 70 percent!

The Bureau of Indian Affairs has often been criticized for its policies. Whatever the merits of the criticism, its assistance is still necessary in any enumeration on Indian reservations. Its agents know the area and the location of homes. The many agents who are themselves Indians help overcome any language difficulties. Among the Navajo, for example, about 80 percent do not speak English. The bureau states, "There apparently is a tradition of keeping information from outsiders among some Indian groups, which leads the BIA to prepare the ground in advance of an inquiry." Today, there is no other agency that can perform this function.

In January, 1960, the Commissioner of Indian Affairs sent a memorandum to Indian administrators throughout the country. He instructed them to cooperate with the census in every way. The following were among the specific instructions:

"The Census representative will request assistance . . . in obtaining qualified personnel to act as enumerators and crew leaders . . . it is very important that persons selected for these positions be thoroughly familiar with the reservation and particularly with the customs, the language, and the areas in which they will work . . . [they] must be able to obtain the confidence of the Indian population. . . .

"The Agency Superintendent should also recommend . . . qualified Indians who may be available for Census work.

"It is of the utmost importance that we obtain the complete cooperation and confidence of the Indian population. . . . The Agency Superintendent should stress that the Census is not being taken in order to obtain information which will be used to deprive the Indians of their rights or their property . . . that the information may not be used for purposes of investigation, regulation, or taxation."

On a contemporary note, the memorandum also states that if enumerators "are authorized . . . to use horses," they will be reimbursed at reasonable rates.

The census of 1970 has raised great expectations for the modernization of information about the Indians. For the first time since 1930, tribal affiliation may be asked. Outside the reservation, the "mail out, mail back" feature will allow urban Indians to identify themselves. This should result in a maximum count. The Bureau of Indian Affairs said in 1968 that "there is the possibility of a follow-up by mail, or perhaps by interview, of persons identified as Indians in the 1970 census." This is a step that has been recommended by many authorities toward improving the accuracy of the count of Indians.

Dr. Denis Foster Johnston, in discussing their high birth rate and how little is known about it, says that the Navajo "may be said to typify the populations of the underdeveloped regions of the world." This is true in other ways. Their illiteracy rate is as high as that of many developing nations. Their average income is almost as low. In 1968, the United States sent VISTA volunteers, the domestic equivalent of the Peace Corps, into Navajo country.

The fact that in 1960 the Indians had to be reassured that a census would not be used for taxation brings the census story almost full cycle.

More Indians are leaving the reservations. However, rather than losing their identity, there seems to be a growing consciousness of their Indianness among them. As with the blacks, they are becoming more active in seeking equality. It is probably no accident that the Civil Rights Act of April, 1968, linked America's two great minorities, the Negroes and the Indians. As have the blacks, the Indians may begin to look more carefully at the census to see how it can serve them.

Chapter 9

HISTORY, PROJECTIONS,
AND OTHER MATTERS

The decennial census is the "diary" of America. In its youth, the nation's "diary" was simple. As the country matured, the content became more complex. If, now and then, an important event such as the Great Depression is missing, the same is often true of personal diaries.

What does not appear in the tabulations often appears elsewhere in the census record. One common place is the record of Congressional hearings on census matters. The great controversy about the data bank can be found reported here. Future historians, reading about it, may sense that there had already occurred some loss of privacy in American life. They may also interpret it to mean that there was great fear, expressed only indirectly, of one of mankind's truly historic inventions, the electronic computer.

The westward expansion of the country is one of the great demographic movements of history. It is deeply etched into the census record. The story will reach a climax of sorts in 1970 when the population of California officially passes that of New York.

The bitterness that surrounded the controversy over the census of 1840 clearly foreshadowed the coming struggle over slavery. In the same way, the payment of the Southern enumerators after the

Civil War for their work in the census of 1860 may have been a clue to the softening of postwar attitudes.

The often stormy movement for women's equality, called by many the suffragette or feminist movement, is in the record of Congressional hearings on the census. In January, 1878, Mary F. Eastman, a leader of the movement, demanded that the tenth census enumerate women who were employed as "laborers and producers." In the same month, the Association for the Advancement of Women placed in the record a request that the census tabulate women's earnings and that women be employed "to collect vital statistics concerning women and children."

Sometimes petty "family affairs" break into the national "diary." In July, 1892, the North Carolina State Dental Association sent a resolution to Congress "protesting against the action of the census bureau in classifying dentists as manufacturers." They threatened to refuse to complete census schedules unless a change were made.

The relationship between the white and black people of the country, shifting in form from the earliest days, is there to be read and interpreted. On the other hand, the absence of any entry at all from 1790 to 1850 says more about the relationship between the white man and the Indian than would one hundred tables.

Where else can one find the story of the dramatic change of America from an agricultural to a mighty industrial nation? Or of the unequaled shift of its people from a rural to an urban way of life? Or of the growth of surburban populations after World War II? Or of the movement of the Negro from the Southern farm to the Northern city?

The demographer and statistician can find much more in the record. The better one understands the "language" of the census, the more one can learn about the people whose history it keeps. From the changes in the age distribution of a people, a demographer may know when they fought their wars. He may even be able to distinguish between the times of plenty and the times of depression.

A statistician can make meaning from the rate at which auto mechanics replaced blacksmiths. The appearance of television repairmen in the lists of occupations signals the birth of an industry. The disappearance of elevator operators indicates a change in the nature of mechanization since the elevator itself has not disappeared; elevator constructors are still installing them. The growth of the electronic age is fully reflected in the great increase in the number of computer programmers.

What the rocks tell the geologist about the history of the earth, the census tells a demographer about the history of a people.

At the New York World's Fair of 1964–1965, a population "clock" was on exhibit. As the seconds ticked away, one human being after another was added to the population of the United States. The addition was as regular as a healthy heartbeat. A mathematically minded person who timed the "beat" could say, "In five minutes the population will be 189,437,503." Most people probably assumed that the number was as accurate as their watches.

On November 20, 1967, at 11:03 A.M., the same "clock" in the lobby of the building in Washington, D.C., that houses the Department of Commerce and the Bureau of the Census, showed that the population of the United States was exactly 200 million.

Most experts knew that this was fiction. They also knew that the longer the "clock" kept ticking *at the same rate*, the farther away it would be from the true population. The ticking of the "clock" was based upon a *projection*, or forecast, of the population.

Projections may be short-range, as in the above example, or long-range. But, in either case, they are based upon the assumption that the future will not be too different from the past. They assume that a population trend with roots in the past, continuing in the present, will extend into the future.

This is the only way that projections can be made. Any other approach relies too heavily upon personal opinion and soon becomes guesswork.

Short-range population estimates made between census years are called *intercensal* estimates. They are calculated by means of the following simple formula:

Population
at time of + Births − Deaths + Immigration − Emigration = future
census   population

Estimated

Births and deaths are linked as *natural increase*. Immigration and emigration result in *net migration*.

At the end of 1967, the Bureau of the Census announced that the population of the country was 200,271,231. Based upon a sample, the bureau estimated the population at the beginning of 1967 as 198,106,231. It added to this 3,572,000 births and subtracted 1,852,000 deaths. The final adjustment was to add a net immigration of 444,000.

The *rate* of population increase was 1.093 percent. A simple method of predicting the population at the end of 1968, or even 1970, would be to add 1.093 percent for each year to the population at the end of 1967. The prediction for the end of 1968 would probably be fairly accurate. If important changes in the rate of increase were in the making, they would probably not be too significant in a period as short as one year.

Over a longer period, this method conceals many traps. It is known that births and deaths are underreported—but not equally. The statistics of immigration and emigration have serious gaps— but they, too, are not equal. Thus, when a census is taken, even after a very stable period, it always shows a population that differs from the best estimates.

Long-range forecasts are more complicated. An advanced mathematical technique has been developed for calculating them. People who make such projections usually begin with a distribution of the population by sex and age. The probabilities of survival in each group are known. The person making the projection would also take into account such factors as the age at which women tend to have their first child; trends in family size; changes in the death rate and in infant mortality; and other factors. In the

United States, a distribution of the population by color would be important. Many factors, such as birth rate, for example, are different for the black and white population.

After all the careful calculations, the projections will probably be wrong!

It is usually embarrassing to a demographer to bring up his past projections. In 1940, experts at the Bureau of the Census predicted a population in 1980 of between 135 and 158 million. Long before the census of 1970, the American population was beyond 200 million.

The president of the American Economic Association forecast, for a recent decade, an increase in population of 5,000,000 to 6,000,000. The actual increase was four times as great.

Professor Frank Notestein, president of the Population Council, is the dean of American demographers. In September, 1950, writing in the *Journal of the American Statistical Association,* he said, "Personally, I think it likely that during the next fifty years the growth of this type of population [United States and most other industrialized nations] will average less than half of one percent per year." For the next fifteen years, the actual growth of the population of the United States was almost four times the size of the prediction.

These examples are cited only to illustrate the perils in projecting populations. Professor John Hajnal of the University of Manchester said, "However much we improve our tools to take care of all that happened in the past, something will sooner or later crop up for which we are unprepared."

No demographer could have predicted the dimensions of the increase in the birth rate in the United States after World War II. And if he had used *this* increase to predict future growth, his prediction would have been made meaningless by the fact that by 1967 the birth rate fell to the lowest level in American history!

As the 1970 census approached, there was considerable disagreement as to how long the low birth rate would continue. The astonishing fact was that it came at a time of great prosperity.

Usually low birth rates are associated with hard times. Who would risk a projection from this level?

Whatever the risks to personal reputations, forecasts will continue to be made. In an advanced society, the future population must be estimated so that plans can be made to meet its needs. The results of the 1970 census will be used, for example, to plan the educational and recreational needs of the people of the twenty-first century. On the basis of the census results, many projections will be made.

To avoid the appearance of acting as prophets and to minimize the embarrassment of estimates that, in looking back, appear to be ridiculous, those who must make projections now use a new approach. Forecasts are now usually made within a minimum and maximum range. This method is best illustrated by a recent example from the Bureau of the Census.

In August, 1966, during hearings before the House Committee on Post Office and Civil Service, Dr. A. Ross Eckler was asked the following question: "Dr. Eckler, how many people do you estimate we will have at the 5-year intervals in the United States between now and the year 2000?"

In answer, Dr. Eckler submitted the table shown on the next page, which appeared in *The Congressional Record, 1968*.

The projections shown in the table are at four levels. At the earliest date, in 1970, the difference between the lowest and highest estimate is 3.7 million people. Ten years later, the difference has grown to 22.8 million. And, by the year 2000, thirty-five years after the making of the projection, the maximum estimate exceeds the minimum by 78.8 million. It is about 28 percent higher than the minimum.

Even with so wide a range, and barring any great catastrophe, it is still possible that, as the century ends, there may be more or less Americans. The people will decide.

Men make projections because they must. Psychologists might add another reason. There are very few human activities as tempting as predicting the future.

Estimates and Projections of the Population of the United States,
by Series: 1965–2000

(In thousands, Includes Armed Forces overseas.)

Year	Series			
	A	B	C	D
1965 [a]	194,583	194,583	194,583	194,583
1970	208,615	207,326	206,039	204,923
1975	227,929	223,785	219,366	215,367
1980	250,489	243,291	235,212	227,665
1985	274,748	264,607	252,871	241,731
1990	300,131	286,501	270,770	255,967
1995	328,536	309,830	288,763	269,485
2000	361,424	335,977	307,803	282,642

[a] Estimate of July 1, 1966.

NOTE: All projections assume slight decline in death rates.
All projections assume net annual immigration of 400,000.
The only difference is in the projection of births, based upon levels in different years:

A 1953
B 1949
C Average of 1945 and 1946
D Average of 1941 and 1942

When the census "clock" showed a population of 200 million, most authorities knew that the actual population of the country was probably closer to 206 million. Every census has errors. And unless the count has been deliberately falsified, the errors are in the direction of an undercount of the population.

The American census is planned by a staff of professionals of great talent. It is liberally financed and well administered. And yet Professor Ansley J. Coale, one of the outstanding authorities on the census, said, "It is clear to all who consider the question that data from the United States decennial censuses of population are less than perfect. Persons who should be included are omitted, others are counted twice, and characteristics of the persons included are sometimes misreported."

The errors that occur are not anyone's "fault." Morris H. Hansen, formerly an assistant director in the Bureau of Census, stated, "No matter how much skill, money, and time are invested in developing statistical inquiries, errors are bound to occur."

In the early censuses, errors occurred because a small population was spread over a vast territory, transportation was primitive, Indians were hostile, many people were illiterate, the marshals were untrained and underpaid, and a host of other reasons. Not one of the above stated reasons was any longer true, but the censuses of 1940, 1950, and 1960 still contained errors of various dimensions.

After every census, the bureau's own staff calculates estimates of the size of the errors. But despite absolute honesty and the best intentions, it is difficult for anyone to make an objective estimate of his own errors. It is important even to the bureau itself that independent estimates be made. Men such as Professor Coale, who devote their great talents to analyzing the census data, perform a public service.

There are some standards that can be used as measures of the completeness of an enumeration or the accuracy of classification It is known, for example, that male births everywhere exceed female births by 3 to 6 percent. However, the mortality rate for male infants is higher, and there is, therefore, an approach to equality in numbers. With maturity, since men fight wars, drive more cars, smoke more, and do more dangerous work, their death rate is higher. Thus, in industrialized countries such as the United States, there are more women than men in the total population.

Facts such as these, expressed as numbers, can be used to check the completeness of an enumeration.

Another check is to follow a *cohort* from census to census. A *cohort* is, in a sense, a group that marches through life together. The men who will be between 40–44 years of age in the 1970 census were 30–34 in 1960; 20–24 in 1950, and so on. The survivors of those 5–9 years old in 1970 will be 15–19 in 1980 and 35–39 in the year 2000. The size of a cohort is changed only by death and net migration. Since the effect of both factors are fairly well known, a cohort can be traced from census to census.

A departure from any of these standards can be recognized by an expert. It would lead to question about the adequacy of an enumeration.

Sometimes an unrelated event makes it possible to check census results. The compulsory registration of the country's young men under the Selective Service Act of World War II made a comparison with census results possible. Under the law that created Medicare, all people of age sixty-five and over had to register by July 1, 1966, to be eligible for its benefits. Again, there was an opportunity to compare census results with an outside set of data.

Such comparisons, however, have only a limited value, not only because they include only a part of the population. Registration totals lack definiteness; they do not have the accuracy of census counts. Where there is a reason to evade registration, some people will evade it. Sometimes, as with Medicare, despite wide publicity, people are unaware of a requirement or an advantage. However, *serious* census errors would be detected in the process of comparison.

In 1968, the Bureau of the Census admitted that in the previous census there had been an underenumeration of 3 percent. In a country as large as the United States, it means that almost 6,000,-000 people were not counted.

It is important to realize that the error of 3 percent is not distributed uniformly throughout the population. There may have been practically no error in the enumeration of women 60–64 years old. But the black population may have been undercounted by more than 10 percent. And black men in the ages from 25–29 years may have been miscounted by as much as 20 percent. The *total error* of a census is a kind of *weighted error* of all undercounts.

The most common error in any census is in the reporting of people's ages. When a 30-year old person gives his or her age as "29," he or she becomes a "missing person" in the 30–34 years age group. It is often difficult to determine whether the person was not counted at all or is concealed in another age group.

It may come as a surprise that among a people with such a high level of literacy, so many do not know how old they are, much less the *exact* date of their birth. It was estimated that about 19,000,-000 people, 65 years of age or older, were eligible for Medicare benefits. The Social Security Administration was willing to accept almost any proof of age from them. In one case, the *New York Times* reported, officials accepted a tattooed date on a former sailor's chest as proof. Yet, at least 2,000,000 people had absolutely no proof at all!

The enumeration records of the Bureau of the Census turned out to be one of the best sources for proof of age. For people lacking other proof, at a small fee, the bureau searched its old records. The accuracy of *these* was also doubtful. A study was made of 130,000 individual, original enumeration records from the census of 1900. The objective was to see how reported *ages* matched reported *dates of birth*. There was no match in 12,526, or almost 10 percent, of the records.

When one considers that in the years from 1890 to 1920 about 45 percent of births in the United States were not officially registered, the people's haziness about their age is not surprising.

The actual enumeration of the population is only one step in the taking of a census. Before FOSDIC, the data had to be coded, keypunched, tabulated, printed. Although each step is carefully checked, errors survive. And each step contains a potential for error.

The census "detectives," Professors Ansley J. Coale and Frederick F. Stephan of Princeton University, scanned the census results in detail for "clues." Based on the census of 1950, they reported one of the strangest cases on record. They called it "The Case of the Indians and the Teen-Age Widows." It was described in June, 1962, in that famous "True Detective" magazine, the *Journal of the American Statistical Association.*

Here is the table they found in one of the more obscure sections of the census tabulations.

Number of Widowed Teen-age Males

Age, in years	Number of widowers
14	1,670
15	1,475
16	1,175
17	810
18	905
19	630

It seemed strange that so many fourteen-year-old "husbands" should have lost their "wives." But it was even stranger that as the ages went *up*, the number of widowers went *down*.

They also discovered that there had been 565 fourteen-year-old "widows." And that 215 "women" of fourteen years had been divorced in time for the census.

And, at age 14, there were 1,320 divorced "men." By age 17, the number of such men had fallen to only 575.

As in many mystery stories, the first corpse is only the beginning. While still struggling to solve these mysteries, they were stunned to uncover another. They called this one "White Children of Household Heads Become Young Indians." They might have called it "Indians are Made, not Born." The "clues" are in the table below.

Male Indians of the Northeast

Age group	Number
5–9 years	757
10–14 years	1,379
15–19 years	668
20–24 years	1,297
25–29 years	596

The up-and-down "drunken stagger" of the numbers indicated that something was seriously wrong. Then another "clue" turned up. The number of widowed and divorced Indian men 14–24 years of age was more than twice as high as in the larger and likelier age group of 25–44 years.

Paying their own fare, the two professors went to the Bureau of the Census, presented their evidence, and said, in effect, "How come?"

After a thorough investigation, it was found that certain errors in key-punching had passed through uncorrected. It is standard practice to assign each column of an 80-column key-punch card a specific code. Thus, column 24 may contain the code for "Sex" of an enumerated person, with "1" representing "Male" and "2" representing "Female"; column 25 may contain the code for "Race," with "1" standing for "White," "2" for "Negro," "3" for "American Indian," and so on. If the code in column 24 is punched into column 25, it is easy to see that an entire sequence may be thrown into confusion. This is what had happened.

As Professors Coale and Stephan later explained their artificial Indians, ". . . a white person when relationship to the head [of the household] was *child* would be coded as a male Indian, while a Negro child of the household head would be coded as a female Indian. If the white child were male, he would appear as an Indian in his teens; if female, as an Indian in his twenties."

This kind of key-punching error is known as "off-punching." When it passes uncorrected, it is guaranteed to bring nightmares to any statistician.

During the "One man, one vote" controversy in 1967, many Congressmen urged that no change be made in Congressional districts until after the census of 1970. They claimed that the data from the previous census no longer described the American people. Whatever their motives, their claim had a real basis.

In January of that year, in a speech not related to the controversy, Dr. A. Ross Eckler, director of the Bureau of the Census, said, "The very detailed statistical description of our population which is produced by our decennial censuses . . . has a major drawback. It grows obsolete quite readily in areas undergoing rapid growth or social and economic change. . . . It is estimated that about 20,000,000 people enumerated in the 1960 Census now live in a different State and more than half the 1960 population is now living in a different dwelling."

To eliminate the "major drawback" in the ten-year interval between censuses, it has been proposed that an enumeration be made every five years.

The campaign for a five-year census is actually about a hundred years old. The first request for legislation to authorize it was made by President Grant. In 1872, while reporting to Congress on the progress of the ninth census, he proposed a five-year census. One year later, he asked Congress to act in time to permit an enumeration in 1875.

President Grant had taken these steps at the suggestion of General Francis A. Walker, then Superintendent of the Census and later president of the American Statistical Association. In 1874, Walker himself issued a statement on behalf of a five-year census. Later that year, he was supported by Columbus Delano, Secretary of the Interior, the department responsible for the census.

Since this concentrated campaign, the issue has never really died. If nothing else, the American Statistical Association kept it alive by regularly passing resolutions in favor of it and sending them to Congress.

In 1965, the years of agitation finally resulted in legislative action. A bill was introduced in Congress that would have authorized a special census in 1966. Its aim was to obtain more up-to-date population data in connection with the "One man, one vote" debate. But Chairman Harley O. Staggers of the House Subcommittee that handles census matters made it clear that the objective was *a permanent mid-decade census.*

At the public hearings on the bill, more than fifty witnesses appeared to testify, almost all in favor of the bill. The supporters included senators and representatives, governors, mayors of large cities, and spokesmen for large companies. One of the most impressive witnesses was the supervising statistician for the Bell Telephone System. He testified that his company had to plan the spending of $3,000,000,000 in construction funds that year. The expenditure would be based upon the distribution of population shown by the 1960 Census that the company knew to be out of date. The absence of a mid-decade census, for his company, meant a partly misdirected use of funds.

Other witnesses testified that any governmental agency that allocated any funds on the basis of population was faced with the same problem. Dr. Philip M. Hauser, formerly acting director of the Bureau of the Census, summarized the reasons why a five-year census had become so urgent. He said:

"First, there never was a time in the history of the United States when we experienced as rapid and significant population changes as during the present decade.

"Second, there never was a time when there was a greater demand for basic economic and social intelligence in the form of statistics for programs not only of government, but of the important private sector . . . ranging from various types of businesses . . . to educational facilities, not to mention specifically . . . the Great Society program.

"And, third, localities are using census information on matters of vital concern to them and which may well affect the destiny of large populations in central cities and metropolitan areas throughout the country."

There was no action in Congress that year, but there was a general feeling that the issue would not die. In 1967, a bill specifically authorizing a five-year census was introduced. The issue could now be considered apart from the emotions aroused by the "One man, one vote" battle.

Again, prominent witnesses appeared to tesitfy. Congressman Morris K. Udall had been an early witness. He had pointed to the huge sums of money distributed by the federal government as grants to state and local governments. Most were based, at least to some extent, upon population. He now said:

"Counsel advises me that a preliminary estimate for the current fiscal year shows that $8 billion figure that I used for the fiscal year 1963 is over $13 billion now. So I think it emphasizes even further the importance of having up-to-date statistics in administering these various programs of Federal grants-in-aid and seeing they get where the people actually are now instead of where they were in 1960."

A somewhat different approach was taken by Senator Robert C. Byrd of West Virginia when he testified. He told the committee:

"Mr. President, the other day I had need to know the population of my State, West Virginia; so I called the Census Bureau. They told me West Virginia's population in 1960 was 1,860,421. But 1960 was seven years ago, and I was interested in the population today, or as close to today as possible. The Census Bureau people told me they estimate the population as of last July at 1,794,000.

"The best they could offer was an educated guess. It may be close to the actual population, but it is still an estimate. For Raleigh County or the town of Sophia, they do not even have any guesses. Nothing more recent than the figures from the 1960 Census.

"As a matter of curiosity, I inquired how many pigs there are in the State—and how often they are counted. I learned that the pigs were counted at the end of 1964 and at the end of 1959, just 5 years apart. The pig population in 1959 had been 148,238, and 5 years later it had dropped to 77,791.

"The Census Bureau counts pigs every 5 years—but counts people only once in 10 years. This is the time-table established—not by the Bureau of the Census, but by Congress. If it seems to represent a distorted sense of values—that pigs should be counted twice as often as people—let us not look elsewhere to point the finger of blame. The time-table is established here, in Congress."

On August 10, 1967, the House of Representatives finally voted on a five-year census bill. It approved it by a vote of 265–127. However, the Senate failed to take any action. But this was the closest the hundred-year old proposal had come to fulfillment.

Many people realize that the issue is not dead. The changes in the nature of American society will make it more and more urgent with each passing year. It took a long time to create a permanent census office. Today, it is hard to imagine how a growing and dynamic society ever did its business efficiently without it. Not too many years from now the feelings about a five-year census may be the same.

Part III

THE POPULATION OF THE EARTH

Chapter 1

HOW MANY BILLIONS ARE ENOUGH

Today, as never before in history, scientists from every field have become interested in the population of the earth. Their interest is not in the methods of counting people; it lies in the significance of the numbers revealed by the counting. It is exceptional when an issue of a general scientific magazine does not include some comment on the number of the earth's inhabitants.

The basic reason why Nobel Prize winners and the President's Science Advisory Committee have become involved with the problem of population is that *today* there are more than 3,500,-000,000 people in the world. Barring an atomic catastrophe that would make all counting meaningless, before the end of the century the earth is likely to be inhabited by 6,000,000,000 people. At that time, most readers of this book will still be raising their own contributions to this growth.

Each six days of the week, about one million people are added to the family of man. And unlike the biblical story of creation, there is no pause on the seventh day. On that day is added a "city" about the size of Nashville, Tennessee. To this phenomenal multiplication has been given the name "the population explosion."

There is probably more misunderstanding about the nature of the population explosion than about most problems that confront mankind. It is widely believed, for example, that the problem is one of food; how will the "poorer" people of the world escape starvation? Others believe that the problem is space; the planet is becoming too crowded. Still others believe that a continent-wide and wealthy country such as the United States has no problem, once it has met its obligation to offer food, money, and technical advice to those in need of them.

Each of these beliefs contains a tiny grain of truth, but they are only a few tiles from a complex mosaic. The "explosion" is as serious for the United States and other industrialized nations of the world as it is for Egypt or Costa Rica or India. The *nature* of the problem may be different, but it is no less serious.

Over the face of the earth there lives an average of 64 people per square mile. The area of Antarctica is not included in this calculation. Since the earth does not expand, this "average" is in a state of continual growth. The average includes the 2 people per square mile in Mongolia as well as the more than 8,600 people occupying the same amount of space in Singapore. The United States closely reflects the universal average with about 55 people. The Soviet Union, with more people but much more space, is only half as densely populated; only 27 people have to share this square mile. The rest of Europe must accommodate about 340 people in the same unit of space.

Australia and Canada, wealthy countries, have, respectively, only 4 and 5.5 people for each square mile of their enormous territories. China, almost always regarded as "crowded," averages about 225 Chinese. India, pictured as "teeming," has about 400 inhabitants per square mile. With each passing year, on every imaginary square mile of the earth's surface, room must be found for more and more people.

The people of the world cannot be redistributed. It isn't possible, for example, to send some of India's millions to the unpopulated regions of Canada, Australia, or Mongolia. The great migrations of the past, involving *significant* numbers of people, are not likely to occur again. Today, the population of a country must be considered within its space.

One-third of the earth's 30 billion acres is covered by glacier or desert. The remainder, after subtracting city, swamp, and jungle, is not necessarily available for cultivation. Only about two-and-a-half billion acres of the total land surface is used for growing man's food and other products. This area is not static. Man is constantly changing it. In some places he tries to reclaim the desert or to grow food where it has never grown before. Egypt's Aswan Dam will ultimately irrigate a vast area. In the Soviet Union, a link between the Ob and Yenisei Rivers will create an island about five-sixths the size of Italy; it will irrigate about 50 million acres of idle land in the steppe areas.

In the United States, on the other hand, rich, fertile soil is left unseeded so as not to create uneconomic surpluses. Also, each year about one million green acres are converted to concrete and asphalt for homes, highways, airports, and shopping centers. In other highly industrialized countries, the same process is under way. Thus, over the earth's surface, there is an unending tug-of-war for the use of the land.

About 10,000 years ago, each person on earth could have claimed as his share about ten square miles. An eminent demographer has estimated that by 8000 B.C. there were about 5,000,000 people on earth. His estimate is based upon an accumulation of archaeological evidence that indicates about how many settlements there were then and how densely they were inhabited.

At the beginning of the Christian era, the population of the earth may have increased to about 300 million. The evidence now consists of some primitive counting, biblical stories, the written records of travelers, and the Roman censuses. Although this estimate, as well as the earlier one, is subject to great error, it provides a reasonable working hypothesis. During this 8000-year interval, the population of the world had doubled six times. On the average, it had taken more than 1,000 years each time for the people to increase twofold. The time between doublings then fell to little more than 700 years.

The period from 1650–1815 is a notable one in the story of the population of the earth. It includes the first American and British censuses and the beginning throughout most of Europe of the registration of births and deaths. Generally, estimates of population became more reliable. During these 165 years, the population of the earth not only doubled but passed the one billion mark.

In the twentieth century, the rate at which mankind was multiplying itself increased significantly. By 1920, only 105 years later, the population had again doubled. Some informed people, aware of the trend, began to discuss whether there was an "optimum," or most desirable, size for the population of the earth. Sir George H. Knibbs, the great Australian statistician, said in 1911, "The limits of human expansion are much nearer than popular opinion imagines."

It is a virtual certainty that within a year or two from 1975, the population will not only have doubled again, after only 55 years, but will have passed the 4,000,000,000 mark. Since, as has been clear throughout the book, the author believes that all evidence points to universal underenumeration, this total will probably have been reached by 1970 or very shortly thereafter. It is the best estimate of demographers that in the mid-1980's there will be 5,000,000,000 people and that some time before the end of the century 6,000,000,000 people will be looking to the earth for food and shelter.

To forecast beyond this century, as in science fiction, one enters a region of wild speculation. Too much depends upon decisions that man will have to make. However, at a rate of natural increase of 1 percent a year, a population will double in about 70 years. The rate of natural increase is calculated by this simple formula:

$$\frac{\text{Number of births—Number of deaths}}{\text{Total population}} = \frac{\text{Rate of natural}}{\text{increase}}$$

At a rate of 2 percent, the doubling is achieved in little more than 35 years; at 2.5 percent, in about 28 years. When the rate reaches 3 percent, characteristic of some countries, twice as many people can be expected in little more than a generation, or 23 years.

Toward the end of the 1960's, the people of the earth were increasing at a rate between 1.8 to 2 percent, very unequally distributed throughout the world.

In considering the increase in the population of the earth, one

World Population Growth

Population (*In millions*)

6,000

5,500

5,000

4,500

4,000

3,500

3,000

2,500

2,000

1,500

1,000

500
300

B.C.–A.D.

Year (A.D.)

100 200 400 600 800 1000 1200 1400 1600 1800 1900 2000

6,000 [a] (Low projection)

4,000

1967 (U.N. estimate) 3,400
3,281

2,515

1,650

1,260
980

790

REMARKS

1. The population "explosion" is due to the *change in the rate* of population increase beginning in the 18th century.

2. Barring catastrophe, the year 2000 is too near at hand for important changes to take place.

3. Without planning on a widespread scale, it is as likely that the rate of population growth will *increase* as that it will *decrease*.

[a] U.N. estimates range from 5,500–7,000

does not have to be concerned about migration. Unless space habitation becomes a reality, there will be no other place for a living person to go.

In 1798, Reverend Thomas Robert Malthus, an English political economist, wrote his *Essay on the Principle of Population.* He maintained that poverty was unavoidable since population increased geometrically while the means of subsistence grew arithmetically. Every writer on population since his time has been haunted by the views of the Rev. Malthus. Today, as the gap between the number of people and the supply of food widens in the developing nations, it seems to many people that his ideas are being demonstrated on a mass scale.

However, although adequate food is the most immediate need in these countries, it is not the heart of the problem. There have also been other developments in the world that neither Malthus nor any other political economist of his time could have foreseen.

More than anywhere else, Malthus's hypothesis has been brought into question by developments in the United States. In the first place, from the 1950's the rate of population growth has been declining *despite unparalleled prosperity.* Then, the food supply has far outrun any increase in population, despite deliberate withholding of rich farmland from agricultural production. In the United States, less than 11 million people who dwell on farms produce enough not only to feed 200 million Americans but also surpluses that have helped avert famine in many parts of the world. The farm population continues to decline while production continues to rise, with upper limits still far in the distance.

But the fundamental fact about American farming, as in a few other highly industrialized countries, is that it is under *control.* On these highly mechanized farms, "the factories in the field," the output of food and other farm products is planned and can be forecast, as in a large industrial plant.

Such an agriculture was beyond the vision of any man of Malthus's time.

It is ironic that in making his analysis of population, Malthus used the results of the first American census of 1790!

The enormous increases in output in the United States and in other developed countries have not kept the world as a whole from becoming poorer and poorer. This is due to the changing proportions of people stemming from the two branches, rich and poor, of the family of man. In 1925, two out of three people, including Communist China, lived in the poorer countries; by 1975, the proportion will have grown to three out of four. Unless dramatic changes that are not now in sight occur, this disproportion will continue to grow.

World Agricultural Production

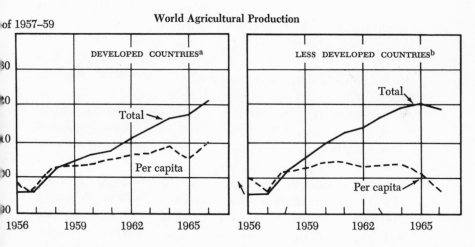

ᵃ North America, Europe, USSR, Japan, Republic of South Africa, Australia, and New Zealand.

ᵇ Latin America, Asia (except Japan and Communist Asia), Africa (except Republic of South Africa).

U.S. Department of Agriculture

The numbers on the left side of the graph (90–130) are called *Index Numbers*. They are relative to, or percentages of, the average agricultural production during the years 1957–1959. These were presumably "normal" years. In the developed countries, during the years when *total*, or all, agricultural production increased, the amount available to each person if it were evenly divided, called *per capita*, also increased.

In the less developed countries, even during years when *total* agricultural production increased, the amount available *per capita* often decreased. This was due to a birth rate that exceeded the increase in production. Thus, the *total* had to be divided among a greater population.

According to estimates by the United Nations, at the end of this century the population of the developing countries will have increased by 108 percent; that of the others, by 40 percent. At the climax of that growth, mankind may enter the twenty-first century with four out of five people living in today's poor, dependent nations.

The dramatic victories over disease and death after World War II are at the root of the growing disparity in population growth. In the 1930's, the death rate in the poorer countries had fallen by 6 percent. Throughout the 1950's, however, it fell by 20 percent and was still declining rapidly. This startling change in rate was, for the most part, the result of health measures initiated by teams of medical experts from the United Nations, the United States, and other advanced nations.

The attack was directed upon the major destroyers of life, with techniques and drugs developed during World War II. Probably the most successful campaign was against malaria, a disease that kills or leaves its victim in weakened condition for life. In 1950, on Taiwan, there were 1,200,000 victims of malaria, of whom 12,000 died. In little more than a decade, by 1961, there were fewer than 100 cases of malaria and not a single death!

As late as 1953, in India, there were annually 75,000,000 cases of malaria that resulted in about 1,000,000 deaths. Of all illness in the country, one out of nine people were ill with malaria. In only eight years, by 1961, there were fewer than 100,000 cases of malaria. So sweeping was the effect of the virtual eradication of this destroyer that, during this period, the life expectancy of the average Indian leaped from 27 to 40 years.

There were similar victories over malaria in other parts of the world. Mauritius is a small country in the Indian Ocean with fewer than 1,000,000 people. The average Mauritian could expect to live 33 years. Almost overnight, within an eight-year period, life expectancy soared to 51 years. Under conditions of more normal development, it had taken Sweden 130 years to bring about an 18-year increase in the life expectancy of its citizens.

In the underdeveloped part of the world, death had always been an expected visitor, almost a constant companion. People had many children in the hope that some, especially sons, would survive. Children represented a form of old-age insurance. But as the chances that children would survive increased, there was no decline in the birth rate. Rather, there was often an increase. A spiral of increasing population growth was set in motion that has shown no tendency to diminish. The upward trend continues as one stage is fed by an earlier one.

As health improved and life expectancy increased, more young men and women survived to marry and have children. Those already married could have more children over a longer span of married life. As the mother's health improved, more of her children were born alive; more also survived the hazards of infancy. As more children survived, the average age of the population was lower. This meant that a greater proportion of the population was always approaching the age of marriage and childbearing. While in the developed countries of Europe, 23 percent of the population is under 15 years of age, in Latin America, Africa, and Asia, 40 percent are that young.

This upward spiral of population continues because the age at marriage, the attitude toward having many children and other ancient customs that affect the size of the population have not changed since death became a less frequent visitor in the developing nations.

Since 1930, the population of the developing nations has grown about twice as fast as that of the developed nations. Today, the poorer countries have about 70 percent of the world's adults and 80 percent of its children. In many of these lands, the people are increasing at a rate of 3 percent or more each year, insuring that their populations will double in 23 years or less. In Central America, the rate of increase is 3.5 percent. In countries such as Costa Rica, Mexico, and Brazil, the rate is higher.

In the developed countries, the death rate has been fairly stable. Until such major causes of death as cancer and heart disease are conquered, there will be no significant declines. The rate at which their populations increase, however, has been dropping for many years. In the United States and the Soviet Union, this rate has been remarkably identical for a long time.

After World War II, there was a rapid increase in the rate of population growth in both countries. The decline began sometime about 1957. Today, both are increasing at a rate of about 1.1 percent a year, among the highest rates in the developed part of the world. The rate of growth is as low as 0.4 percent a year in Hungary; at this rate, the population will not double for 175 years.

The search for food is a constant accompaniment of existence in the developing parts of the world. Depending upon how it is defined, malnutrition affects from one-half to two-thirds of the population. Food not only lacks variety, but even for many who have enough to eat, it may also lack essentials. Shortages of protein affect more than the majority who simply do not have enough to eat.

As recently as the 1930's, the less industrialized countries exported food. By 1966, now having twice as many people, they imported 31,000,000 tons of food. Demand had increased from sheer weight of number, but food production had also fallen by 2 percent, according to estimates of the United Nations. Rising population and falling production combined to cause a decline of 5 percent per person in available food.

In Latin America, the race between population growth and food production is being lost. In 1965, according to the United Nations, there was no change in the level of food production. In 1966, it rose by about 1 percent; in 1967, very slightly higher. *At the same time the population was growing at a rate of 2.7 percent each year.*

Simply to catch up with any backlog since 1964, food production would have to increase by 7 percent each year. This is regarded as an impossible goal within the predictable future. The simple arithmetic of all this is that the average person in Latin America has less food, while others die of starvation.

In Chile, one of the more forward-looking countries of Latin America, food production over this period was increasing by 0.9 percent each year. The population, however, was increasing by 2.2 percent.

Brazil, the giant of Latin America, is potentially one of the richest countries in the world, but it is a giant in chains. Brazilians increase at a rate of about 3.6 percent each year. Barely twenty years go by before there are twice as many Brazilians searching for work and food. This is what it means to the country, according to Mr. Celso Furtado, former Minister of National Planning: "The 4.6 percent increase in agricultural production maintained over the past 15 years is a creditable figure and it has mounted to 4.8 percent in the past 5 years. Nevertheless, the gain has been largely offset by the growth of population. . . . Relatively speaking, the supply of agricultural goods has become smaller."

It may seem to be a contradiction that, with population increasing at a rate of 3.6 percent a year and agricultural production at 4.8 percent, the latter should be relatively more scarce. Aside from other factors to be discussed later, "agricultural production" may include coffee, as in Brazil, or cotton, as in Egypt. These are "cash crops" that may or may not result in more food.

This interrelationship between food and population is not significantly different in other areas of the developing world. In Africa, production of food in the late 1960's was still below the levels prior to World War II. In the Republic of the Sudan, when improved irrigation led to increased food production, an increase in population growth followed.

Food production in the Far East, excluding China, reached the levels of World War II in 1959. This peak was maintained for three years, after which production again fell to lower levels.

India is most often cited as an example of a land suffering from widespread poverty. The picture familiar to Westerners of the gaunt, hungry Indian is not a product of propaganda; it is a reflection of reality. In 1967, monsoon rains ended a terrible three-year drought. The number of Indians who died of starvation during this period will never be known. Only an endless relay of ships carrying food, mainly from the United States, but from other countries as well, kept the loss of life from soaring beyond all control.

Drought and famine are hardly strangers to India, but even in the "best" of years, harsh poverty is the condition of almost *all* Indians. Only a very tiny minority is free from concern about the bare necessities of life. According to Dr. Pitambar Pant, formerly a division chief of the Indian Planning Commission the poorest 10 percent of the population has as little as five cents a day to spend. And the richest 5 percent, except for the very tiny minority, spends only an average of fifty cents a day for all its needs.

If all of India's available food were doled out evenly, each person would have a daily supply of about 18 ounces. However, as with all averages, there are very many who have very much less. The extraordinary difficulty in easing this frightful poverty is described by Dr. Pant in the September, 1963, issue of *Scientific American:*

"To increase consumption of food grains by 2 ounces per head per day will require an annual increase of 9,000,000 tons. This means an increase of more than 10 percent in domestic production or an increase of import expenditures of ¾ billion dollars—more than half of India's export earnings. Similarly, to provide the 4 or 5 million workers who join the labor force every year with capital equipment of $200 each adds up to $1 billion per year—equal to all the aid India expects to receive during its third 5-year plan. Because of the high rate of population growth a good part of the investment is required merely to keep the average per capita income constant."

At India's present rate of population growth of about 2.5 percent, before the end of the century there will be 1,000,000,000 Indians where there are now 500,000,000. However, the rate of increase is likely to go beyond 2.5 percent unless measures to limit population growth are quickly successful. The Indian population is a young one with about half the people under 20 years of age. Many are, therefore, at or near the age of marriage and childbearing.

The immediate need in the developing world is for more food. But, if the number of mouths continues to grow as fast or faster than the available food, the only result is that more persons share the hunger. Unless this self-defeating cycle is stopped, the cry "more food" will be repeated endlessly.

The cycle can be stopped either by reducing the rate of population growth or by drastically increasing agricultural production. Before discussing the former, it is well to examine whether the latter is possible. This requires some analysis of the differences in agricultural production in the two worlds.

The daily diet of the average person in the developing countries is so meager that any increase in food output could be absorbed, even if population growth did not outrun it. As in India, huge increases make trivial differences in the daily diet. In the wealthy countries, increases in food production are stored or sold outside the country; in the poorer, they are eaten.

If a surplus is great enough to exceed immediate needs, it is still not likely to be stored for the future. Storage facilities are inadequate; transportation to central storage is usually primitive. The complicated network for storing surpluses in the highly industrialized countries—collection, storage, distribution; refrigerated trucks, trains, airplanes, warehouses; canneries, freezing plants, food-processing facilities—are almost entirely unknown in the developing countries.

When an excess exists in the poor countries, it is likely to be sold for foreign exchange with which to buy other needed goods. Sometimes it is sold merely to pay interest on outstanding foreign debts. In some developing countries, this may run as high as one-quarter of all export earnings.

To say that "agricultural production has increased 4.8 percent," as in Brazil, does not mean more food. It may mean more coffee in Brazil, more cocoa in Ghana, or more cotton in Egypt. If the world price for these commodities, not controlled by the producing countries, has fallen, more production will not mean more food.

A major difference between agriculture in the developing lands and in the industrialized is in the scale of things. In India, as elsewhere, the land has become fragmented over the centuries; it has been shared by sons and distributed as dowry among daughters. There are millions of farms of less than two acres. Small-scale agriculture cannot make use of any of the techniques for increasing production that are available to the "factories in the field" in the United States. The result is that input of labor is high and output of food is low.

In the United States, the Soviet Union, and in other industrialized countries, the large farms utilize the most advanced machinery. They can take advantage of research programs and make the kinds of investments that will yield long-range returns. It has been said that it is cheaper to pour diesel fuel into a tractor than oats into a horse. Also, when there are no horses or other work animals to be fed, there is more land on which to grow human food.

The typical peasant in the developing country sows his seed, then searches the sky for rain. A plague of insects can bring the reality of starvation overnight. A cold spell may cut his crop in half. He is entirely dependent upon the forces of nature; he has no *control* over his production.

The highly technical agriculture of the wealthy nations has substituted control for risk. Production can be planned and output predicted. Huge combines do the field work in little time. Irrigation networks, chemicals to enrich the soil and destroy the pests, strains of seed developed to resist hostile elements and yield maximum return—these have made a modern farmer's risks no greater than the threat of a strike to an industrial plant.

It is one of the ironies of our time that the richer the country, the less is the waste of food.

In the United States, 5.5 percent of the population lives on farms. This 1 person out of 18 feeds himself, the other 17, and a substantial part of the rest of the world. The output on American farms increases as planned and greatly exceeds the growth of the population.

In the developing countries, on the other hand, as much as 80 to 90 percent of the people live on farms. There is an unending struggle to keep the country from starvation.

Pakistan announced in 1968 that, with the use of high-yield seed developed by the Rockefeller Foundation, rice production was 14 percent higher than in 1967. Less than one week later, the United Nations warned that Asia's food supply was uncertain and was likely to worsen. The world organization said that by 1970 the need for rice and other grains would probably exceed the area's production by a wide margin.

A great deal of publicity has been given to the possible production of food from artificial sources. Some overenthusiastic people have even claimed that they would provide the solution to the food problems of the developing nations. Dr. Ivan L. Bennett, Jr., was chairman of the President's Science Advisory Committee on the World Food Supply. He expressed the committee's opinion when he said in the September, 1963, issue of *Scientific American* that publicity given to "the synthesis of food from petroleum, food from algae, and similar processes is raising false hopes and lessening public concern about the seriousness of the food supply in the developing nations."

It may be added that where artificial foods were introduced on a trial basis, there was almost no public acceptance. They went against long-established habits of taste, smell, custom, and religious principles.

The long-range answer to the population explosion in the developing countries cannot simply be "more food" to feed more mouths. This race is being lost. What is needed, ultimately, is a transformation of the economy. The methods of a modern agriculture must be introduced. But this will require large investment as well as a literate, technically trained population that can use the modern technology. It means, in a phrase that has been heard more and more often, breaking the cycle of poverty.

Until this occurs, and as a first step toward achieving it, the rate of growth of the population must be limited. In the past, in the advanced countries, the rate of growth declined as industrialization and urbanization increased. Whether a lower growth rate can be achieved without them is one of the great, unanswered questions of our time.

Throughout the Western world and later in the Soviet Union and Japan, it was found that the average size of families went down as industrialization developed. Much of the decline is due to the fact that the growth of industry means the growth of cities. Within the city, families find that they have less space than they had on a farm or in a rural area. Large apartments may be unavailable or too costly. The result is that parents tend to limit the size of their families.

Other factors tend to reduce the size of the family in an industrial-urban environment. Schools, especially at higher levels, are usually superior and more readily available. The emphasis upon, and the need for, advanced schooling is greater. But such schooling is costly. Parents, wanting their children to have the advantages of higher schooling, tend to limit their number.

People go to school for a longer time in an industrial-urban community. Educated women seek careers or work for some time after completion of their schooling. Since work opportunities are available and often attractive, many women work for some years after marriage. Thus, either marriage or family-building occurs later in life. The result is a smaller family size.

In most of the developed countries of the world, this movement toward lower average family size has occurred spontaneously. In the Communist countries and elsewhere, it has often taken place in spite of government programs that favored larger families. France and the Soviet Union, for example, provide generous allowances for large families, paid leave for pregnant women, and other inducements for the formation of large families. Yet, in both countries, the birth rate has been declining.

The Japanese government adopted a policy of encouraging smaller families to relieve the pressure upon its crowded islands.

Within twenty years, from 1946 to 1966, the birth rate was cut in half. Today, its population is increasing at a rate of slightly less than 1 percent. Many population experts maintain that the birth rate would have fallen without government encouragement since it happened during a period of great industrial expansion.

In an effort to limit their explosive growth, about thirty developing nations have introduced family planning programs. The hope was that this would enable the food supply to catch up with current needs; also, that any improvement in economic conditions would not be undone by the need to share it among a greater number. Almost all the programs were undertaken at the urging of the Western nations or by population control organizations in these countries. In 1967, the United States decided that it would lend official assistance to any country wanting to introduce or expand a program of population control.

These programs have been started in such diverse countries as India, Pakistan, Mexico, South Korea, Taiwan, Turkey, and Egypt. In each country, tremendous obstacles were encountered. In many, especially in Latin America, there has been strong religious opposition to family planning programs. But the greatest barrier everywhere is the set of traditional beliefs that encourage large families. In much of the underdeveloped world, children have been a form of insurance against the hazards of old age. This attitude often remains after a move from a farm to an urban environment.

Population control programs were first introduced into some countries about ten years ago. The results to date are not too encouraging. In many countries, the goals themselves are extremely modest. Even if completely achieved, the rate of population growth would still exceed increases in food production. Pakistan, for example, aimed to reduce its birth rate from 50 to 40 per 1,000 population by 1970. This is not likely to be accomplished. In other countries, the goals have been left vague.

In many of these countries, a large family is a more desirable objective than personal prosperity. Surveys have shown that most people want at least three or four children. Many of the women do not visit the family planning centers until *after* their family has reached this size.

Dr. S. Chandrasekhar, the Minister of Health in the Indian government, is one of the world's outstanding demographers. He is an enthusiastic supporter of population control. When the program started in India, its aim was to reduce births from a rate of about 40 to 25 per 1,000 people as soon as possible. It was hoped that a nationwide network of family planning centers would be established. A tremendous publicity campaign accompanied the program.

After ten years, there are about 8,000 village clinics. But in that vast country there are hundreds of thousands of villages. It would more than exhaust all the available medical and technical facilities to cover the country with family planning clinics. Thus, even if the enormous indifference, even hostility, of the people could be overcome, India's present resources would only permit a very modest effort. Meanwhile, the population continues to grow at an alarming rate.

In May, 1962, Egypt made its family planning program part of its National Charter. It thus became an official government undertaking. At the ceremonies, President Gamal Nasser said, "Population increase constitutes the most dangerous obstacle that faces the Egyptian people in their drive toward raising the standard of production. . . . Attempts at family planning deserve the most sincere efforts supported by modern scientific methods."

At a later date, President Nasser told an Egyptian audience, "Every one of you wants me to find work for his brothers and children, not only for the boys but also for the girls. How can I do this if each person has ten, twelve, eight, or seven children? Two, three, or four children are enough."

The family planning program did not really get under way until 1965. From a population of about 31,000,000, perhaps 400,000 women took part, at most. Many of these, as indicated earlier, already had families. Egypt's rate of population increase of about

3 percent a year, which exceeded increases in agricultural output, was not affected.

One of the first domestic casualties of the June, 1967, war with Israel was the population control program. Publicity to encourage women to participate in population control was either reduced or stopped entirely. No new clinics were opened. The budget was cut by more than half, from a high of about $2,000,000. The program director, who had left, was not replaced.

Some progress, however limited, has been made in Taiwan and South Korea. It is estimated that about 10 percent of the women have joined the programs in those countries. There are indications that the rate of population growth has been somewhat reduced. It is significant, however, that the United States exerts a strong influence upon both Taiwan and South Korea. It has made great investments in their economies and encouraged industrialization. Many demographers attribute the reduction in population growth as much to this as to the family planning programs.

Professor Kingsley Davis, the director of International Population and Urban Research, does not believe that family planning programs will result in important changes. At the end of 1967, having studied the results in various countries, he said, "The social structure and economy must be changed before a deliberate reduction in the birth rate can be achieved."

In view of the newness of the family planning programs and the tremendous obstacles to overcome, the question may still be unanswered.

There can be little doubt that their high rates of population increase are an obstacle to development in the poorer nations. Relatively, they fall farther and farther behind the industrialized nations. In the September, 1963, *Scientific American*, Professor Asa Briggs, dean of the School of Social Studies at the University of Sussex, England, said: "Even if the underdeveloped countries were to increase their average incomes ten times faster than the economically advanced countries, the gap [between the rich and poor nations] would still widen."

The tragic truth of our time is, however, that the wealthy nations have most of the industrial and agricultural growth; the poor nations have the population growth.

The science of *ecology* is concerned with the mutual relationship between man and his physical environment. Until about twenty years ago, it was a "quiet" science. It was little known, and ecologists were not much in the news. Suddenly, it assumed a dominating position. It became increasingly clear to many people that man, by his numbers and his acts, was affecting his environment in ways that threatened his very survival. The nature of the problem was stated by LaMont C. Cole, professor of ecology at Cornell University, in these words, "Man, in the process of seeking a 'better way of life' is destroying the natural environment that is essential to any kind of human life at all; during his time on earth, man has made giant strides in the direction of ruining the arable land upon which his food supply depends, fouling the air he must breathe and the water he must drink and upsetting the delicate chemical and climatic balances upon which his very existence depends."

For the most part, the acts that threaten man's survival arise in the developed nations of the world; the Sudan, for example, does not contaminate the air or make the atmosphere radioactive.

The effect of population growth in the industralized countries is not an inadequate food supply or increasing illiteracy. It is a much more complicated process. It speeds up certain actions that directly affect the physical environment.

The rate of population growth in the developed nations of the world is slightly higher than 1 percent a year. This is far below the rate in the developing nations but is still *higher* than the world rate in the first half of the twentieth century. At the present rate of growth, the people of the developed world will double in about fifty years.

There is no assurance that the rate will remain at this level. In several countries pressures are building up for sharply higher rates of growth. Complicated economic processes that were not foreseen are coming into play, forcing reconsideration of population policy. Economics and ecology are presenting rival claims.

The population of Japan, now 100 million, has increased at a rate of 1 percent or less per year for over ten years. It is most often cited as a country that has carried out a successful policy of population control. However, in 1968, reports began to appear about dissatisfaction with the low growth rate. The following report in the *New York Times* of February 23, 1968, is typical:

"Japanese demographers are worrying over harmful consequences becoming apparent as a result of their country's low population growth. A report issued by the Demographic Research Institute of the Welfare Ministry warns that a troublesome by-product of Japan's low rate of population growth will be an increasing labor shortage already evident in some fields. The institute also warns that if the present situation continues, the population will soon start to decline."

The Japanese economy lives by exports. A growing labor force is a necessity. When it does not expand, different industries compete for the limited labor supply. This has forced wages upward, and Japan fears the loss of a competitive advantage in world markets because of higher labor costs. Should this trend continue, the government may use all means at its disposal to encourage greater population growth.

France is another country that seeks increased population. President Charles de Gaulle has said that the average French family should have 3 children rather than the average of 2.2 that now prevails. To bring this about, the government has taken steps that are available to any government that seeks to pursue a policy of greater population growth.

Housing conditions have been improved, with more and larger apartments available. Educational opportunities for children have been broadened, schools improved and modernized. A system of generous family allowances is in force. Under it, a man earning $150 per month who had nine children attending schools below the college level would receive a family allowance of about $240 per month. A family with three or more children receives a variety of Social Security benefits, including free medical care. The family also receives discounts on public transportation and purchases in stores, as well as cheaper school lunches for the children.

A government that decides to sponsor a specific population policy, whether of growth or decline, has a tremendous arsenal of economic weapons available to it.

The Communist world, at least in theory, does not believe that overpopulation is a real problem. Karl Marx and Friedrich Engels, the nineteenth century "fathers" of Communist theory, attacked the Rev. Malthus for his ideas. In contemporary times, Nikita Khrushchev, former premier of the Soviet Union, in his usual, colorful language, expressed the Communist attitude in a speech in January, 1955. He told his audience, "Bourgeois ideology invented many cannibalistic theories, among them the theory of overpopulation. Their concern is to cut down the birth rate. . . . It is quite different with us, comrades. If about 100 million people were added to our 200 million, even that would not be enough. Under socialism the raising of the birth rate is regarded not only as a means of providing greater labor power. The Socialist State also looks at the matter from the viewpoint of the nation's future."

However, the facts of economic life spoke more forcefully than Premier Khrushchev. By 1959, as a result of the lower wartime birth rate, the number of people joining the working force each year had dropped to half that of three years earlier. This meant that everything had to be done to encourage women either to remain in or join the labor force. And it is almost always and everywhere true that a high proportion of women in the labor force and a high birth rate do not exist side by side.

There were other factors that caused the Soviet birth rate to decline to the level of the United States. Urbanization was growing steadily, and the cities lacked adequate housing; most apartment units were small. Also, a new generation of trained and educated women sought careers or work opportunities. Families were started later in life and remained small in size.

By 1968 there were public expressions of concern about the declining birth rate. Fifteen percent of all Soviet citizens were receiving pensions by then, and the proportion was rising. This meant that a shrinking work force would support a growing number who had completed their working years. The fear of Soviet economists was twofold: that the changing ratios would affect the rising standard of living and that the labor force itself would soon be inadequate for expanding industry.

It would not be too surprising if the Soviet Union began a strong campaign to raise its birth rate in the years ahead. By mid-1968, there were some indications that just such a program might well be under way.

The highly industrialized nations of the world have set in motion a chain of events whose end products may threaten man's survival. The more technologically advanced the society, the longer and more complicated does the chain become; also, the more unpredictable the final result.

Any rate of increase in an advanced nation is significant. One man buying one more automobile with which he will burn thousands of gallons of gasoline and for which he will need that much more paved road has a greater effect upon the environment than any number of Libyans. As a society becomes more wealthy and more numerous, the needs and demands of its members grow.

One of the effects of growth is more garbage. How this comes about can be illustrated by the transformation of the simple glass bottle. Not too many years ago most of them were returned and reused. Today, they have been replaced by the disposable bottle or the metal, plastic, or paper container. Thus, annually, billions and billions of containers have to be burned, buried, or sunk. A 150-pound man creates his weight in garbage in one month. By the year 2000, he is expected to double his garbage creation. A greater population will further increase the volume.

A self-defeating cycle has been created, as was illustrated in New York City in 1967. To reduce serious air pollution, the city ordered a halt to the burning of garbage in apartment-house incinerators. It found almost immediately that it lacked the men and equipment to handle the additional load.

In 1968, the garbage collectors of the city went on strike. The city began to smother in its undisposed garbage. Within ten days of the start of the strike, the mayor declared a health emergency. More and more cities face more and more garbage crises each year.

The carbon-oxygen cycle involved in photosynthesis in green plants is a sensitive relationship that allows man to exist on earth. To a greater and greater extent, modern man has been tampering with this process. How far his interference can extend without causing harm beyond repair cannot easily be foreseen. Some scientists have warned that critical levels are being approached.

A common example of such interference is seen in the expansion of suburban living, a characteristic of American life after World War II. Pressure outward from the city leads to the destruction of green land around it. As homes are built upon this land and the population grows, certain requirements follow the homes—schools, churches, shopping and community centers, drive-in movies, and a host of other services. Since suburban dwellers need access to central cities, more roads must be built. In this way, a family with a half-acre home attracts more than this amount of land to serve it. More green land is destroyed.

Suburban dwellers have a higher ratio of car ownership and drive more. They generate a disproportionate amount of air pollution. Also, a water table that may have been adequate for previous use often becomes dangerously low with use by a large population or develops a high salt content.

Every one of the above processes interferes to some degree with the carbon-oxygen cycle.

A paradox of our time is that the pressure of population that contributes to suburban growth also generates a demand for rural space as recreational areas. Thus, the growth of population creates built-in contradictions.

Many hazards accompany modern life. Professor Abel Wolman of Johns Hopkins University has estimated the contributions to air pollution from various sources. Motor vehicles, he estimates, are responsible for 60 percent; power plants, 14 percent; industry, 17 percent; heating and garbage disposal, 9 percent. These sources are part of modern life; all these activities involving combustion affect the process of photosynthesis. A greater population creates a greater volume.

The waters, too, have become polluted. Lake Erie, according to scientists who have studied it, has no life. It would take 500 years, if it could be done at all, to restore it to the condition it was in only 25 years ago. The process of pollution is underway on other unique bodies of water. Lake Tahoe in Nevada, one of the most beautiful in the world, is becoming polluted. The same process is under way in Lake Baikal in the Soviet Union, despite the protests of Soviet ecologists. This lake is the world's deepest and contains unique species of life.

The huge oil tanker *Torrey Canyon* ran aground off the coast of Cornwall, England, in 1967. After splitting in half, its thousands of gallons of oil drenched the beaches with disastrous effects upon life in the surrounding waters. A scientist has stated that if the tanker were carrying an agricultural pesticide, all plant life and, with it, photosynthesis would have been destroyed in the North Sea. The major portion of the earth's photosynthesis takes place in the plant life at sea.

The tanker *Torrey Canyon* was newly built to meet the growing needs of industrial populations.

In the area of Denver, Colorado, a huge pit, miles deep, was dug into the earth. It was to serve as a "sewer" for poisonous radioactive waste water. At its construction, it was hailed as a forward-looking safety measure. In 1967, earth tremors were felt in the city. In 1968 a more severe series followed, and it was feared that the first man-made earthquake would soon follow.

The problem seems to be without solution since no one has thought of how to dispose of the mass of poisoned water if it were pumped out.

Meteorological studies in La Porte, Indiana, going back to 1925 showed unusual rainfall, thunder and hail storms. Scientists finally traced it to heat, smoke, and haze created by the large industrial complex in the Chicago area about thirty-five miles away. La Porte was the receptacle for these unusual atmospheric conditions.

There was a proposed project several years ago, since abandoned, to clear huge areas of the Amazon River basin rain forest in South America. The aim was to clear land for agricultural development. In Colombia, some large tracts were actually cleared. A study started in 1942 showed a sharp drop in rainfall at two experimental measuring stations. When the scientists involved were asked whether there was a cause and effect relationship, they answered, "We don't know."

The chain of events is so complex in many of modern industrial man's projects that, in estimating the effects, the answer must usually be, "We don't know."

No one knew that poisoned waste water in the earth would, in some complex geological fashion, undermine the earth.

No one knew that pesticides used on an Iowa farm would show up years later in the blubber of seals taken off the coast of Scotland.

Man's ecological interference often takes a long time in showing its effects. But as Professor LaMont C. Cole said in 1968, "Man should try to know the consequences of his actions before he takes them."

Many scientists believe that a real threat exists to man's environment in the uncontrolled tampering with the earth's soil, air, and water. In 1968 this concern was expressed by a subcommittee of the House of Representatives. It supported an International Biological Program to investigate "just what man and technology are doing to life on earth." It stated that the program would be concerned with "one of the most crucial situations to face this or any other civilization—the immediate or near potential of man to damage, perhaps beyond repair, the ecological system of the planet on which all life depends."

The objective of the program is to study the mutual relationship between man's activities and his growing numbers. According to the committee's members, one of the major obstacles to overcome is the lack of public understanding of the forces at work and the nature of the danger.

Another indication of the importance that scientists assign to the problem is the revival of an old question. Again, men are asking, "Is there an optimum population for the earth?" According to Professor Cole, "It now becomes more urgent that social and natural scientists get together and try to decide what an optimum size for the human population of the earth would be."

Many scientists are pessimistic about the likelihood of solving the world population problem. In 1968, Professor Cole gave a talk before the American Association for the Advancement of Science. Its title was "Can the World Be Saved?" The answer was, in essence, that it depended upon man himself.

Professor Kingsley Davis believes that present family planning programs will not be effective. The world goal, he says, should be *zero* growth of population. In 1967 he said that "*any* growth rate, if continued, will eventually use up the earth." Governments should use every weapon at their disposal, he believes, to eliminate population growth.

Professor Arthur Kornberg of Stanford University, Nobel Prize winner in genetics, told a committee of the United States Senate in 1968 that population growth was the most important problem facing mankind today.

To say that a problem is "important" or "urgent" or "difficult" is not to say that it is impossible to solve. The family planning program has started in many countries. These are countries with low literacy rates, where centuries of traditional ways of thinking must be overcome. That the programs have not achieved the goals of their most enthusiastic supporters does not mean that they have failed.

In Latin America, the idea of family planning is contrary to the religious beliefs of most people. For the most part, the Catholic clergy opposes the program. Yet, in Puerto Rico a substantial segment of the population has accepted it. In 1967, official delegations from several countries attended a family planning conference. Such a step would have been unthinkable even ten years ago. The program may suffer local setbacks, as in Egypt. But it is a worldwide movement that can no longer be stopped.

The problem of feeding the growing population of the world is more complex. There will be advances in the production of food beyond even those achieved in this century. Milk may be produced from carrot tops and pea pods. An acre of land that yields 80 bushels of corn today will yield 500 before the end of the century. Cows that breed 10 calves in a lifetime today may multiply their breeding a hundredfold. These forecasts follow two years of research by the Ford Motor Company, one of the world's largest manufacturers of tractors.

But these "miracles" will be for the rich, industrialized, large-scale agricultural producers. Only the surpluses may be available to others.

However, agricultural research conducted by the Ford and Rockefeller Foundations has been directed at the needs of the developing nations. High-yield, fast-growing seed for rice, wheat, and corn have already been distributed and grown. The Philippines, Mexico, Pakistan, India, Tunisia, and Turkey have already benefited from this research.

It is important to note, however, that these programs, as well as the family planning program, originate in the developed nations of the world. The world will shortly face the question of whether the developing nations can remain for long in a state of dependency.

In the industrial nations, the problems related to population and ecology are more complex. Economics and ecology clash more and more frequently in many parts of the world. However, scientists and an informed public are becoming more conscious of their responsibilities. Population is no longer the exclusive concern of statisticians and demographers. All mankind has become involved. The best hope for a solution is in the recognition of the problem and the realization that it is a matter of universal concern.

Man continues to count his kind—more accurately, more frequently, and over wider areas of the earth. But for the first time in history, the growth of the population of Pakistan is of importance to the man in the United States. And the number of cars, the size of the factories, the amount of chemicals used on farms in the United States as the population grows will, in a way not yet clear to many, affect the life of the average Pakistani.

BIBLIOGRAPHY

It is impossible to include in a bibliography every piece of reading matter that went into the making of this book. To attempt to do so would not only be wasteful; it would be misleading. An author may read a book for background without ever consciously using one sentence from it. Or, he may use a sentence or two.

Very little is listed here from the wealth of material prepared by the United States Bureau of the Census. This agency prints a tremendous number of publications on plans, procedures, and results of trial censuses. It is *the* source of information on the census of 1970.

The same is true of the many census publications of the United Nations.

There are almost no citations from the *New York Times*, although articles on population appear frequently since, today, population is news.

The Journal of the American Statistical Association, as well as the reports from the annual proceedings of that organization, are little represented. The same is true of the magazine *Science*.

The *Congressional Record* is also not listed here, although it is a rich source of information about census plans and reflects the debate in the country about the mid-decade census, the invasion of privacy, and other census issues.

Of course, all sources were used when they were important to the story. An author uses *all* sources that he hopes will make his story more interesting, exciting, and illuminating.

The works listed below may bring additional insight into some aspect of census history.

THE WORLD SCENE

1. General

Beaujeu-Garnier, J. *Geography of Population*. New York: St. Martin's Press, 1966.

Knibbs, Sir George H. *The Census of the Commonwealth of Australia, 1911,* Vol. I. The Australian Commonwealth Printing Office.

Koren, John, ed. *The History of Statistics* for the 75th anniversary of the American Statistical Association. New York: The Macmillan Co., 1918. (Also contains articles on United States census history.)

Meitzen, August. "The History, Theory and Technique of Statistics." Supplement to *The Annals* of the American Academy of Political and Social Science, March, 1891.

Petersen, William. *The Politics of Population,* Garden City, N.Y.: Doubleday and Co., 1964.

United Nations. *Handbook of Population Census Methods,* Volumes I, II, and III. New York, 1958 and later.

Wickens, Charles H. "Methods of Ascertaining the Rates of Mortality," *Journal of the Institute of Actuaries,* London, January, 1909, pp. 23–84.

Wolfenden, Hugh H. *Population Statistics and Their Compilation.* Chicago: University of Chicago Press, 1954.

2. Ancient Censuses

Wolfe, A. B. "Population Censuses Before 1790," *Journal of the American Statistical Association,* December, 1932, pp. 1–14.

3. Developing Nations

Lauriat, Patience. "Field Experience in Estimating Population Growth." *Proceedings, American Statistical Association,* Social Statistics Section, 1966, pp. 250–265.

United Nations, Dept. of Economic and Social Affairs. *General Principles of Population Projections as Aids to Development Planning.* Population Studies No. 38, New York, 1965.

4. Africa, Other Than the Sudan

Barbour, K. M., and Prothero, R. M. *Essays on African Population.* New York: Fred. A. Praeger, 1962.

Federal Census Office. *A Note on the Population of Nigeria.* Federation of Nigeria, 1963.

Goldthorpe, J. E. "Attitudes to the Census and Vital Registration in East Africa." *Population Studies,* Vol. III, No. 2, November, 1952, pp. 163–171.

Nigerian Economic Society. "Patterns of Population Growth." *The Nigerian Journal of Economic and Social Studies,* Vol. 6, No. 1, March, 1964.

5. The Sudan

Krótki, Karol J. *The 1953 Pilot Population Census for the First Population Census in Sudan.* Khartoum: Sudanese Ministry for Social Affairs, Department of Statistics, 1955.

Krótki, Karol J. *21 Facts About the Sudanese,* Khartoum: Ministry for Social Affairs, Population Census Office, 1958.

Philosophical Society of the Sudan. *The Population of Sudan, Report on the 6th Annual Conference.* Khartoum: Ministry for Social Affairs, Population Census Office, 1958.

United Nations, Dept. of Economic and Social Affairs. *Population Growth and Manpower in the Sudan.* Population Studies No. 37, New York, 1964.

6. The Soviet Union

Holubnychy, Vsevolod. "Organization of Statistical Observation in the USSR." *The American Statistician,* June, 1958, pp. 13–17.

Lorimer, Frank. *The Population of the Soviet Union: History and Prospects.* League of Nations, Geneva, Switzerland, 1946.

Milbank Memorial Fund. "Population Trends in Eastern Europe, the USSR, and Mainland China." *Proceedings of Nov. 4–5, 1959,* New York, 1960.

Ullman, Morris B. "Content of the 1959 USSR Census of Population." *The American Statistician,* December, 1959, pp. 14–18.

7. China

Aird, John S. "Estimating China's Population." *The Annals* of the American Academy of Political and Social Science, January, 1967, pp. 61–72.

Chandrasekhar, S. *China's Population Census and Vital Statistics.* Hong Kong: Oxford University Press, 1960.

Chen, Nai-Ruenn. *Chinese Economic Statistics: A Handbook for Mainland China.* Chicago: Aldine Publishing Co., 1967.

Chen, Ta. "Population in Modern China." *The American Journal of Sociology,* Vol. 52, July 1946–May 1947.

Eastern Economist. "Details of China's First Census," December 10, 1954.

Ho, Ping-ti. *Studies in the Population of China, 1368–1953.* Cambridge: Harvard University Press, 1959.

Hsieh, Chiao-min. *China: Ageless Land and Countless People.* Princeton, N.J.: D. Van Nostrand Co., 1967.

Latourette, Kenneth Scott. *The Chinese: Their History and Culture*. New York: The Macmillan Co., 1964.

Shabad, Theodore. *Counting 600 Million Chinese*. Far Eastern Survey of the American Institute of Pacific Relations, April, 1956.

Willcox, Walter F. "A Westerner's Effort to Estimate the Population of China and Its Increase Since 1650." *Journal of the American Statistical Association*, September, 1930, pp. 255–269.

THE UNITED STATES

1. General

Bogue, Donald J. *The Population of the United States*. Glencoe, Ill.: The Free Press, 1959.

Bureau of the Census. *Procedural Report on the 1960 Census of Population and Housing: Working Paper No. 16*. Washington, D.C.: Govt. Printing Office, 1963.

Cummings, John. "The Permanent Census Bureau: A Decade of Work." *Journal of the American Statistical Association*, Vol. 13, December, 1913, pp. 605–638.

Rossiter, William S. *A Century of Population Growth*. Washington, D.C.: Bureau of the Census, 1909.

Wright, Carroll D., and Hunt, William C. *The History and Growth of the United States Census*. Washington, D.C.: Govt. Printing Office, 1900.

2. Early Census History

Bureau of the Census. *The Statistical History of the United States from Colonial Times to the Present*. Stamford, Conn.: Fairfield Publishers, 1965 (original prepared by the Bureau of the Census).

Farrand, Max. *The Framing of the Constitution of the United States*. New Haven, Conn.: Yale University Press, 1963.

Hamilton, Alexander, Jay, John, Madison, James. *The Federalist Papers*. Modern Library Edition, with Introduction by Edward M. Earle, 1937.

Robinson, James Harvey. "The Original and Derived Features of the Constitution." *The Annals* of the American Academy of Political and Social Science, Oct., 1890, pp. 203–243.

White, Leonard D. *The Jeffersonians: A Study in Administrative History*, 1801–1829. New York: The Macmillan Co., 1956.

Willcox, Walter F. "Method of Apportioning Seats in the House of Representatives." *Journal of the American Statistical Association*, December, 1954, pp. 685–695.

3. Counting the Black Population

Deutsch, Albert. "The First U.S. Census of the Insane (1840) and Its Use as Pro-Slavery Propaganda." *Bulletin of the History of Medicine,* May, 1944, pp. 469–482.

Jarvis, M. D. "Insanity among the Coloured Population of the Free States." *The American Journal of Insanity,* Vol. VIII, 1851–1852, pp. 268–282.

Miller, Herman P. "1970 Census Data Relating to Employment Problems in the City." *Proceedings of the North American Conference on Labor Statistics,* U.S. Bureau of Labor Statistics, June 20, 1968.

Miller, Dr. Kelly. "Enumeration Errors in the Negro Population." *The Scientific Monthly,* Vol. XIV, February, 1922, pp. 168–177.

Pettigrew, Thomas F. *A Profile of the Negro American.* Princeton, N.J.: D. Van Nostrand Co., 1964.

Pritzker, Leon, and Rothwell, N. D. *Procedural Difficulties in Taking Past Censuses in Predominantly Negro, Puerto Rican, and Mexican Areas.* Conference on Social Statistics and the City, Washington, sponsored by Joint Center for Urban Studies, Cambridge, Mass., June 22–23, 1967.

Valien, Preston. "General Demographic Characteristics of the Negro Population in the United States." *Journal of Negro Education,* Vol. 32, No. 4, Fall 1963, pp. 329–336.

4. The Indian Population

Hadley, J. Nixon. "The Demography of the American Indians." *The Annals* of the American Academy of Political and Social Science, May, 1957, pp. 23–29.

Johnston, Denis Foster. *An Analysis of Sources of Information on the Population of the Navaho.* Washington, D.C.: Smithsonian Institution, Bulletin 197, 1966.

5. Projections and Forecasts

Dorn, Harold F. "Pitfalls in Population Forecasts and Projections." *Journal of the American Statistical Association,* September, 1950, pp. 311–334.

Hajnal, John. "The Prospects for Population Forecasts." *Journal of the American Statistical Association,* June, 1955, pp. 309–322.

Notestein, Frank W. "The Population of the World in the Year 2000." *Journal of the American Statistical Association,* September, 1950, pp. 335–349.

6. Census Errors

Coale, Ansley J., and Stephan, Frederick F. "The Case of the Indians and the Teen-Age Widows." *Journal of the American Statistical Association,* June, 1962, pp. 338–347.

Coale, Ansley J. "The Population of the United States in 1950 Classified by Age, Sex, and Color: A Revision of Census Figures." *Journal of the American Statistical Association,* March, 1955, pp. 16–54.

Hanson, Robert H., and Marks, Eli S. "Influence of the Interviewer on the Accuracy of Survey Results." *Journal of the American Statistical Association,* September, 1958, pp. 635–655.

Zelnick, Melvin. "Errors in the 1960 Census Enumeration of Native Whites." *Journal of the American Statistical Association,* June, 1964, pp. 437–459.

7. Religion

Good, Dorothy. "Questions on Religion in the United States Census." *Population Index,* January, 1959, pp. 3–16.

WORLD POPULATION

Cole, LaMont C. "Can the World Be Saved?" *New York Times Magazine,* March 31, 1968, pp. 35, 95, 97, 100, 106, 108, 110.

Davis, Kingsley. "Population Policy: Will Current Programs Succeed?" *Science,* November 10, 1967, pp. 730–739.

Durand, John D. (special editor). "World Population." *The Annals* of the American Academy of Political and Social Science, January, 1967.

El-Badry, M. A. "Population Projections for the World, Developed and Developing Regions: 1965–2000." *The Annals* of the American Academy of Political and Social Science, January, 1967.

Scientific American, September, 1963 (special issue). See especially: Briggs, Asa, "Technology and Economic Development"; Davis, Kingsley, "Population"; Pant, Pitambar, "India"; Revelle, Roger, "Water"; Scrimshaw, Nevin S., "Food."

INDEX

Abbot, Charles, 41
Aboriginal populations, 67, 68, 124, 138, 143
Adams, John Quincy, 68, 217, 218, 229, 272
Address Register, 1970 census, 251
Advance Census Report, 242, 244, 250, 300, 302
American Indians, 300, 302
Advance Coding Guide, 250-251
Africa, 73-74, 77-78, 81-91
colonial censuses, 82-91
first census in the Sudan, 91-117
Age, distortions of, 75-76, 98, 104, 126-128, 131, 133, 135, 136, 155-157, 194, 212, 213, 220, 239, 306, 313, 314
Age grouping, 218, 220, 308
Age "heaping." *See* Age, distortions of
Aird, John S., 158-159
Alaska, 77, 228, 243, 246
Algeria, 88, 90
Allotment Acts, Indians, 68, 292
American Journal of the Medical Sciences, 272
American Philosophical Society, 217, 219, 221
American Statistical Association, 217, 219-220, 226, 230, 245, 272, 317
Apportionment, legislation for, U.S., 66, 91, 97, 116, 125, 167-168, 175-176, 181, 183-191, 196, 205-208, 214-217, 225, 233, 244-245, 256-257, 316
colonial period, 167-168, 175-176
debate, 181, 183-191
1870-1970, 225, 244, 245, 256, 257, 316

1790-1860, 196, 205-208, 214
within states, 233
Arabic (Sudan), 103, 107
Arabs, 93
Article 1, Section 2, 66, 177, 183, 187, 191-193, 195, 205-206, 214-217, 229, 232, 245-246, 266
Articles of Confederation, 181-183, 189
Asia, 74, 81, 119
Athens, 29-30
Augustus, Emperor, 31, 33-34
Australia, 26, 67-70

Babylonians, 12, 17-18, 20, 26
Baltimore, Md., 178
Bancroft, George, 170
Barbour, James, 68
Bari (Sudan), 102, 107
Beaujeu-Garnier, Mme. J., 67
Beloch, K. J., 51, 57
Benchmark, 237
Betts, Rep. Jackson E., 259
Biafra, 90
Birth rate
U.S., 308-312
world, 312
Births, registration of, 19, 32, 39, 46-49, 61, 79, 83, 89, 95, 98, 116, 136, 159, 219-221, 228, 238, 264, 294, 308, 314, 325
Black Americans. *See* Negroes in the census, U.S.
Bodin, Jean, 59, 60
Bolshevik Revolution, 121, 124
Boston, Mass., 165, 174, 178, 200, 219-220
Brazil, 333
Breslaw, tabulations of, 60

Van Buren, Martin, 217, 219
Venice, 37, 51-53
Vermont, 166, 177, 180, 195, 202
Virginia, 167-168, 179, 184, 186-187, 189, 203-204, 216
Vital statistics, 61, 63-64, 117, 123, 128-130, 133-135, 159, 219, 221, 228, 234, 308
Volkov, E. Z., 122, 125

Walker, Francis A., 317
War Department, U.S., 301
War of 1812, 163, 203
Washington, D.C., 202-203, 209, 222, 278, 289, 307
Washington, George, 178, 194, 198, 200, 204-207
Watson, Elkanah, 209-210
Weaver, William C., 273

Webster, Daniel, 206, 214-216
Westin, Alan F., 258-259
White, Leonard D., 68, 217-218
Willcox, Walter F., 139, 231, 245-246
William the Conqueror, 37, 39, 43
Wisconsin, 199
Wolfe, A. B., 33, 41
Wolfenden, Sir Hugh H., 26, 278
Women, equal rights for, 306
Women, reporting of, 25, 74-75, 101, 103
China, 138, 143-145
World population, estimated, 81

Yellow Registers (China), 143

Zanzibar, 85, 89
Zelnick, Melvin, 280